Louisiana Voices: Remembering World War II

Compiled and Edited by Janet Barnwell

Contributing Editor Stanley E. Hilton

Introduction by Stephen Ambrose

Selected from the Collections of the
T. Harry Williams Center for Oral History, LSU

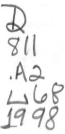

Cover design by Maradee Cryer
Text design by Pamela Dean

Dedicated to
Captain Peter Soderbergh USMC Ret.
1928-1998
Williams Center interviewer
teacher, advisor, friend

Cover photograph from the 1942 Gumbo

Louisiana Voices: Remembering World War II

Illustrations

Acknowledgments

Louisiana Voices: Remembering World War II brings you the unique, intensely personal recollections of thirty-two men and women who served in that conflict. The Williams Center did not set out to collect information on the war. Most of the material in this book is drawn from interviews conducted to document a career in the oil business, a life spent in pursuit of racial justice, a student's experience at LSU, or any number of other topics. We do not claim that they are either comprehensive or representative in their depiction of World War II. They are rather a selection of particularly vivid, moving, and illuminating snap shots, a sampling of our collection and of the range of experiences that Louisiana veterans recall about that epic era.

The T. Harry Williams Center for Oral History was established by LSU in 1991 to collect and preserve the history of Louisiana and her people through the use of tape-recorded interviews. By 1998 the Williams Center's collections included nearly 1,500 interviews. The thirty-two interviews in this volume were carefully selected from this larger body of work. To compensate for the intrinsically episodic nature of this collection, Stanley E. Hilton, professor of history at LSU, has written an introductory essay for each chapter. These essays provide a context for the individual experiences and perspectives of the interviewees and deepen and enrich our understanding and appreciation of our narrators' stories.

It is those stories that are the heart, soul, and purpose of this book, and it is to those men and women who served their country in World War II and generously shared their memories with us that we offer our deepest appreciation and gratitude.

Janet Barnwell, a Ph.D. candidate in English at LSU, selected and edited the interview excerpts. This editing was for clarity and continuity only. We have not changed the speakers' words or grammar, although we have deleted false starts, repetitions, and tangents not related to the immediate story. Added information appears in brackets.

In addition to the fine work of Janet Barnwell and Stanley Hilton, the Williams Center wishes to acknowledge the efforts of our interviewers: Janet Barnwell, Dr. Everett Besch, Melisse Campbell, John Capdeveille, Ruth Thompson Carville, Maxine Crump, Pamela Dean, Jack Fiser, Adele Foster, Mary Hebert, Julian Pleasants, Peter Soderbergh, and Tara Zachary. We also wish to thank Noah Rost, Marcia Willis, Laura Pattillo, Will Crain, and Ricky Breland of our staff , Merle Suhayda of the Imaging Lab at LSU's Hill Library, and James Murrill and Thomas Powell for help with the final stages of preparation of the manuscript.

Publication of this book was partially funded by a donation from the Cadets of the Ole War School and the contributors to the endowment of the Estelle Skolfield Williams Graduate Assistantship.

Pamela Dean, Director
T. Harry Williams Center for Oral History
September 1998

Introduction

This is a wonderful collection of the oral history memoirs of a representative group of the Louisiana men and women who fought World War II. It includes enlisted men and officers, nurses, doctors, blacks and whites, French and English speaking, the works. The individuals speak with their own voices, in their own words — the raw materials of history. They speak with an authenticity that no one who wasn't there can ever match. They say it better than the historians, the novelists, the screen-writers, or the journalists.

Many of the veterans have never before spoken about war. This is because they have felt no one could possibly understand, because their memories were too painful, because they feared no one cared, because they had their careers to make and didn't want to dwell on the past. But as they reached their seventies, their minds went back to their youth, and they began to realize — with help from interviewers from the T. Harry Williams Center for Oral History — that people did care, and wanted to know, and would try to understand. So they talked, and we are all richer because they did.

The voices of Louisiana blacks is a special feature of this volume. The U.S. Armed Forces in World War II were segregated. Black soldiers, sailors, and airmen were treated in the most degrading way imaginable. It was a national disgrace. Here we were fighting the world's worst racist with an army that treated African Americans as if they were dogs. German POWs who were in camps in Louisiana were shocked at the way the white people of Louisiana treated the black people of Louisiana. We have come a long way, thank God. As one evidence of how far we have come, read the oral histories of the African Americans in this volume, then reflect on the obvious truth that they could not possibly have been published in 1945 (not that anyone in 1945 would have thought to ask African Americans about their experiences).

I've been doing oral histories with the men and women of World War II for three decades. I estimate I've done over 2,000 such interviews. I learn something new from each one of them. Reading this collection, I could only wish that I'd had it available when I wrote *D-Day* and it's sequel, *Citizen Soldiers*, as there are so many stories here that would have fit right into my narrative.

And what a splendid set of story tellers! And how well they express themselves, and tell the truth about war. "Combat is not a thing that has any glory to it," according to Cyril Guidry. I've heard that from every combat veteran I've interviewed. Combat is the worst human experience. To begin with, you are trying to kill other young men, which is an unnatural act that is forbidden in the Bible, in the most direct injunction possible: "Thou shalt not kill." Other young men are trying to kill you. In combat, you live totally in the present — there is no past nor any future — it is "a day to day existence," as Guidry put it. You go weeks without changing clothes, months without a shower. Hot food rarely reaches the front line. Three hours of sleep a night is a lot. The tension is constant. The physical demands are unbearable, but they must be endured. These are just the beginning of the misery, the degradation, the exhaustion, the terror, the humiliation of combat. It can only be glimpsed through the words of the men who went through it and survived. That is the closest you can get to the experience. That is what we get from *Louisiana Voices: Remembering World War II.*

Harry Williams was my mentor. He was a path-breaking oral historian. He taught me what I know. He was especially keen on letting the characters speak for themselves. "They can always say it better than you can," he would tell his students. To see how he was right, read this volume. It is altogether a fitting tribute to a great man and a great historian.

Stephen Ambrose, 1998

Chapter One

Louisiana Voices

Dupuy Anderson

[Interviewed by Maxine Crump, 8 December 1993, Collection # 4700.0418]

Born in 1918, Dupuy Anderson studied to become a dentist at Meharry Medical School in Nashville, Tennessee, and Southern University in Baton Rouge. During the war, he was an officer and served as a dentist with the famed Tuskegee Airmen, an all-black unit, at its Alabama base. Originally, the Army assigned him to Ryan Army Airfield in Baton Rouge, but when the officers there saw that he was black, they turned him away. Incidents such as this led Anderson in the post-war years to get involved in the civil rights movement. He was vice-president of the Baton Rouge NAACP, a member of the mayor's Biracial Committee, and, in 1950 and 1965, a candidate for mayor himself. In 1964, on behalf of his daughter, Freya Anderson Rivers, he was party to the suit that brought about desegregation at LSU. Today, Dr. Anderson lives in Baton Rouge.

Robert Barrow

[Interviewed by Peter Soderbergh, 24 March 1992, Collection 4700.0097]

"I had a love affair with the Marine Corps from the outset," says Robert Barrow, who rose through its ranks from private to Commandant of the United States Marine Corps in a career that spanned five decades.

Barrow grew up in rural West Feliciana Parish, near St. Francisville, and attended LSU from 1939 to 1941. When Barrow went to San Diego for his basic training in 1942, it was the first time he had ever been out of Louisiana or Mississippi. Soon, he was even farther away from home, organizing and supplying small bands of guerrilla forces behind enemy lines in Japanese-occupied China.

Barrow served under the legendary Colonel Louis B. "Chesty" Puller in the Korean War and was a commander himself in the Vietnam War. In 1979, President Carter appointed Barrow Commandant of the Marine Corps and member of the Joint Chiefs of Staff. President Reagan later appointed Barrow to the Foreign Intelligence Advisory Board. Today, Barrow is retired and lives in St. Francisville with his wife, Patricia.

Thomas Blakeney

[Interviewed by Ruth Thompson Carville, 1 October 1992, Collection 4700.0181]

Inspired to attend LSU by his uncle, an assistant football coach at the university, Thomas Blakeney hitchhiked the 600 miles from his home in Stephenville, Texas, to Baton Rouge in 1935, arriving the same night Huey Long was shot. During his time at LSU, Blakeney worked as a trainer under legendary football coach Biff Jones and studied zoology. He went into the U.S. Army directly after graduation in 1939.

A veteran of the North African and Italian campaigns in World War II, Blakeney also served in Vietnam in the early 1960s. He returned to LSU in 1966 as Commandant of Cadets for the ROTC program, just as student protests against the war in Vietnam were heating up. Blakeney fought unsuccessfully to maintain compulsory status for ROTC at LSU and retired as a full colonel in 1969. He lives in Baton Rouge.

John J. Capdevielle

[Interviewed by Everett D. Besch, 10 September 1992, Collection 4700.0178]

Baton Rouge native John Capdevielle graduated from University High in 1938, LSU in 1942 and then joined the U.S. Army. During World War II, he took aerial surveillance photos, which he developed in a captured German van equipped with a darkroom. After the war, he returned to LSU where he took what he thought would be a temporary job as house manager for men's dormitories. He ended up staying thirty-eight years. Capdevielle retired in 1984 as Director of Men's Housing.

Steve A. Chappuis
[Interviewed by Mary Hebert, 30 November 1995, Collection 4700.0638]

During his thirty-one years in the U.S. Army, General Steve Chappuis says he saw the armed forces undergo an increase that was "so dramatic that it's really hard to describe. It was a quantum jump."

Joining the U.S. Army soon after graduation from LSU in 1936, Chappuis fought in the invasions of Normandy and the Netherlands, and in the Battle of the Bulge. During his career in the military, Chappuis worked in the Netherlands, at the Pentagon and at NATO Allied Forces Southern Europe Headquarters in Naples, Italy.

A native of Rayne, Louisiana, Chappuis now lives in Tacoma, Washington with his wife, Kay.

John A. Cox

[Interviewed by Jack Fiser, 19 July 1995 and 4 October 1995, Collection 4700.0746]

The most decorated LSU alumnus of World War II, John Cox earned the Legion of Valor, two Purple Hearts and two Silver Stars among many other medals.

Born in Peach, Texas, Cox moved to Louisiana as a child and graduated from LSU in 1938 with a B.S. in horticulture. He earned his M.S. in horticulture and plant pathology the following year, studying under LSU horticulturist Julian Miller.

Cox was drafted into the U.S. Army in 1942 and spent most of the next four years in the South Pacific. He was severely wounded during the invasion of the Philippines, ending his plan to make the army his career. Instead, he returned to horticulture and rose through the ranks of the Louisiana Cooperative Extension Service to become its director.

A lifelong LSU booster, Cox sometimes goes by the nickname "Tiger." He met his wife Frances at LSU when they were both young crack shots on the men's and women's rifle teams. All three of their children are LSU graduates, and Cox attributes his military success to LSU ROTC, calling it, "one of the reasons that this country won World War II. We're not speaking Japanese now because of that."

Joseph Dale

[Interviewed by Jack Fiser, 12 August 1995, Collection 4700.0731]

"I guess you might say my middle name is 'Volunteer' because I always felt like what I was doing was rather boring, and if you volunteered, you were bound to find something more exciting," says Colonel Joseph Dale, whose thirty-year career with the U.S. Army spanned World War II, the Korean War and the Cold War.

In World War II, Dale crossed the Elbe with the British Army and was among the first to meet up with the Russian Army on the other side. In the Korean War, he helped plan the breakout from the Pusan perimeter and the landing at Inchon. Later, he spent a year in pre-revolutionary Iran, keeping watch on the Russian border.

Dale finished out his service as Commandant of Cadets at LSU, taking over from his onetime schoolmate Thomas Blakeney. After retiring from active duty, Dale stayed on at LSU directing the campus safety department and administrating employee benefits.

John Doles, Jr.

[Interviewed by Estelle Williams, July 1998]

John Jones Doles, Jr., was born in Plain Dealing, Louisiana. His father owned the local bank and his mother ran an insurance agency. Doles attended LSU and in May, 1942, was inducted into the army as a corporal in the artillery ROTC. After he finishing the ROTC course at

LSU and attending OCS, Doles was commissioned a second lieutenant in September 1943. In 1944 he was sent to France where his division was assigned to the 7th Army under General Alexander Patch. He later served under General George S. Patton as well. Doles was wounded in Germany and received the Purple Heart and the Bronze Star.

After the war Doles returned to LSU, graduating in 1948 with a degree in engineering. He took over the family businesses and plantations in Plain Dealing and in 1951 married Mai Frances Lower, daughter of Mrs. T. Harry Williams. They have four daughters.

Doles remains an ardent fan of LSU sports, especially football, and a supporter of the University.

Mary Frey Eaton
[Interviewed by Pamela Dean, 5 August 1994, Collection 4700.0504]

Daughter of "Mr. LSU," Major Fred Frey, Mary Frey Eaton virtually grew up on the LSU campus. Eaton was educated in East Baton Rouge public schools and graduated with a B.A. from LSU in 1947 during her father's tenure as Dean of the University. She has remained a strong supporter of LSU ever since.

Currently, Eaton is serving as

president of the Metropolitan Council of East Baton Rouge Parish. Her impressive record of community service includes working with the Children's Coalition, Myriam's House, Baton Rouge Convention and Visitor's Bureau, United Way, and LSU Foundation to name only a few.

Eaton is the widow of L. W. Eaton, the mother of five, and the grandmother of three.

Celine Ganel
[Interviewed by Janet Barnwell, 14 May 1997, Collection 4700.0816]

Born to a French-speaking family in Donaldsonville, Louisiana, Ganel worked as a stenographer and court reporter before joining the Women's Army Corps (WAC) in 1944. She worked first in the Pentagon, then applied for an overseas position, which turned out to be in a hotel in newly-liberated Paris. "I couldn't have had a nicer assignment," she says.

After the war, Ganel went to LSU on the GI Bill, received a B.A. and an M.A. and then worked briefly as a junior researcher for the Department of State in Washington, D.C. For fifteen years, Ganel worked as a researcher, senior research associate and project director for Public Affairs Research Council (PAR) in Baton Rouge. She then returned to Donaldsonville to work for the Welfare Department and served for two years as Ascension Parish welfare director.

Jack Gremillion
[Interviewed by Mary Hebert, 26 April 1995, Collection 4700.0532]

Longtime Louisiana Attorney General Jack Gremillion went to LSU Law School but passed the bar in 1937 before he attained his degree.

Not long after, he worked as an attorney for the State Department of Revenue and married Doris McDonald.

When war broke out, Gremillion was drafted into the U.S. Army infantry and was sent to France where he was assigned to a group of replacements for dead or wounded officers. Severely wounded in the battle for St. Lô, he spent a year in a British hospital before being sent home.

After the war, Gremillion returned to Baton Rouge and grew increasingly interested in politics. He was elected attorney general on Governor Earl Long's ticket in 1954 and was reelected four times. Today, he lives in Baton Rouge.

Cyril Guidry
[Interviewed by Adele K. Foster, 28 March 1996, Collection 4700.0671]

"Combat is not a thing that has any glory to it," says Cyril Guidry. "It's just mud, sweat, moving slow and that is all. You live from a day to day existence."

Born on Union Plantation in Iberville Parish in 1915, Guidry was drafted into the military in July 1941 and fought in North Africa, the Mediterranean and Europe. In addition to receiving the Purple

Heart and other medals, Guidry was one of thirty-seven people in the First Army to receive the *croix de guerre* from the French government. Guidry returned to Louisiana and worked for many years with Solvey, which became Allied Chemical. Today, he lives in Plaquemine, Louisiana.

Murray H. Hawkins
[Interviewed by Jack Fiser, 10 July 1995, Collection 4700.0824]

Cincinatti native Murray "Buddy" Hawkins received a B.S. in physical chemistry from LSU in 1938 and stayed on to earn his M.S. in physics two years later. He spent many years as the head of the university's Department of Petroleum Engineering.

As a civilian contracted to work for the U.S. Navy, Hawkins was at Pearl Harbor on December 7, 1941, and had to seek shelter from the Japanese attack. He signed up with the navy soon after and spent the war years as a technical officer.

Hawkins now lives in Baton Rouge with his wife, Julia.

Wilbur Joffrion
[Interviewed by Mary Hebert, 27 November 1995, Collection 4700.0369]

A native of Alexandria, Louisiana, Will Joffrion, after attending LSU for one year, went to and graduated from the U.S. Military Academy at West Point and served more than eleven years on active duty in the U.S. Army. In 1958, he entered the property and casualty insurance business and transferred to the U.S. Army Reserve.

After a total of thirty-five years of active and reserve duty, culminating in his final command of the 377th Theater Army Air Command in New Orleans, Joffrion retired from the Army Reserve in 1981 as a Brigadier General. In December, 1989, he became the Louisiana state director of the Selective Service System and in August, 1990, was appointed a member of the Governor's Advisory Commission on Military Affairs.

Joffrion and his wife, Beebe, live in Baton Rouge and have four children as well as four grandchildren.

O.B. Johnson
Interviewed by Adele K. Foster, 23 May 1997, Collection 4700.0821]

"I was very fortunate in my whole career," says General O.B. Johnson. "I commanded all the way up from the squadron group, wing, division and air force, and I loved to be a commander; I loved to run things."

Born in 1920 in Natchitoches Parish, Johnson joined the U.S. Army Air Corps in 1941, he says, "primarily to get free flying lessons." He ended up staying for thirty-four years. In

World War II, he led a squadron flying P-61s, some of the first radar-equipped fighter planes, in night-flying missions. His squadron had the best night-flying record in the Air Corps.

Johnson participated in the Berlin Airlift and later served in Japan during the wars in Korea and Vietnam. Before retiring from the military in 1973, he commanded the Washington Defense System and the Fourteenth Aerospace Force, in charge of satellites. Today, he lives in Baton Rouge.

T. Earle Johnson
[Interviewed by Pamela Dean, 30 March 1992, Collection 4700.0100]

A pioneer in the field of speech communication, T. Earle Johnson spent forty-one years as an instructor and professor at the University of Alabama but earned his undergraduate degree from LSU where he taught for two years. Among his many accomplishments, Johnson founded the Speech and Hearing Center at the University of Alabama, co-founded the Southern Speech Association, and lobbied the U.S. government to make children with speech and hearing impairments eligible for federal aid.

The University of Alabama made him a Professor Emeritus of Speech in 1969, and, in 1990, named its music and speech building after Johnson and Professor Emeritus of Music Wilbur Rowland.

Johnnie Jones

[Interviewed by Mary Hebert, 4 September 1993, Collection 4700.0321]

Civil rights lawyer Johnnie Jones was a student at Southern University when he was drafted into World War II. Promoted to warrant officer, he participated in the D-Day landing at Omaha Beach and stayed under fire in Normandy for the next 150 days.

After the war, Jones attended Southern University Law School and grew increasingly involved in the NAACP and the civil rights movement. He served as lead attorney for the 1953 Baton Rouge bus boycott and for the students who held Baton Rouge's first sit-in, as well as attorney in the East Baton Rouge Parish school desegregation case. The Baton Rouge students' case, *Garner vs. Louisiana*, was the only sit-in case to be upheld by the Supreme Court. Jones also represented Reverend B. Elton Cox after Cox was arrested for demonstrating in front of Baton Rouge City Hall. That case also went to the Supreme Court, which upheld the right to hold peaceful demonstrations.

Jones ran for public office several times, beginning with a campaign for district attorney in the mid-1950s. In 1968, he was appointed assistant parish attorney and then was elected to the Louisiana House of Representatives, a position he held from 1972 to 1976. He was the first African-American from East Baton Rouge Parish to hold that post.

Robert LeBlanc

[Interviewed by Mary Hebert, 11 November 1995, Collection 4700.0567]

General Robert LeBlanc began his military training in Citizen's Military Training Corps, CMTC, summer camps and LSU ROTC. Upon his graduation in 1942, he was called to active duty in the U.S. Army and volunteered for the Office of Strategic Services. LeBlanc served in both France and China during World War II.

LeBlanc left active duty in 1945 but later joined the Louisiana National Guard and organized Company H in Abbeville, Louisiana. He was assigned director of the Guard's Emergency Operations and commanding general of the Louisiana Army National Guard Command in New Orleans.

Ellen Bryan Moore

[Interviewed by Mary Hebert, 26 September 1995, Collection 4700.0537]

The first woman elected to public office in Louisiana in her own right, and not appointed to fill out the term of a deceased male relative, Ellen Bryan Moore was also among the first women in the state to join the U.S. Army through the Women's Army Corps.

Growing up in the old Baton Rouge state prison complex, where her father was a warden, Moore joined the army in 1942 and soon set to work as a recruiter in Houston and Baton Rouge.

After the war, Moore went to LSU on the GI Bill and finished her M.A. in psychology. She also married Haywood Moore and had two daughters. She was elected Register of the State Land Office six times, beginning in 1952. Moore served on the State Democratic Committee and helped found Louisiana's Head Start program.

Anthony Palumbo

[Interviewed by Adele K. Foster, 18 March 1996, Collection 4700.0672]

Baton Rouge resident Anthony Palumbo was born to Italian immigrant parents in Rochester, New York, in 1914. After graduating high school during the depths of the Depression, he joined the Civilian Conservation Corps, CCC, with which he did forest control in Idaho and road work near Bear Mountain, New York. Called to active duty in the U.S. Army in 1942, he was assigned to lead a black company at Fort McClellan, Alabama.

He later spent a year in Casablanca, and fought in France and Germany. In 1945, he saw Buchenwald concentration camp. "That's something that's going to be ingrained in my memory forever," he says, "And hopefully, I'll never see it again."

Nina Nichols Pugh

[Interviewed by Melisse Campbell., 26 August 1993, Collection 4700.0333]

"My graduation was a dirge," says Nina Pugh, whose years at LSU, 1941-1945, were overwhelmed by the war and the loss of many of her fellow students. The daughter of an LSU math professor, she was valedictorian of her class and later taught Latin and Greek. A non-practicing lawyer, she did legal research for her late husband, Judge Thomas B. Pugh II, as well as LSU's Center of Civil Law Studies. She has also done legal work for such causes as the YWCA and the Alcoholism Council.

Today, she lives in Baton Rouge and still occasionally takes classes at LSU.

Grover Rees

[Interviewed by Pamela Dean, 7 October 1992, Collection 4700.0078]

Grover Rees was born in 1891 in Breaux Bridge, Louisiana, where, he says, "Nobody, including my parents, spoke English." A graduate of the LSU class of 1912, Grover Rees was a veteran of the First World War. He worked his way through Harvard Law School by selling aluminum cookware door-to-door, and was for many years legal counsel for Gulf Oil. Reese was 102 when interviewed and remembered his days at the Ole War Skule vividly. When Rees celebrated his 100th birthday, over fifty members of his immediate family, including five children, thirty-three grandchildren and twenty great grandchildren, joined him and his wife Consuelo Broussard Rees.

Louie Reinberg
[Interviewed by Mary Hebert, 8 February 1996, Collection 4700.0635]

Louie Reinberg left his home in Zachary, Louisiana, to attend LSU in 1931. He spent the next four years in ROTC, and then later, with a recommendation from Major (later General) Troy Middleton, he received a commission in the U.S. Marine Corps. During World War II, Reinberg fought in the South Pacific, and later served in the Korean War. He retired from the U.S. Marine Corps in 1959 as a brigadier general and returned to LSU, where he served as director of the LSU Foundation, 1962-1977.

Oscar Richard
[Interviewed by Everett Besch and Quinn Coco, 9 September 1993, Collection 4700.0359]

Oscar Richard grew up in Sunshine, Louisiana, where his father owned the Golden Gate Plantation and Syrup Manufacturing Company and a general store. A few months after his graduation from LSU in 1942, Richard went on active duty in the U.S. Army Air Corps and flew in B-17s as a bombardier.

In 1944, six months before the D-Day Invasion, Richard's B-17 was shot down over France and all but one member of the crew were captured. Richard spent the next sixteen months in Stalag Luft 1, a German POW camp near the Baltic Sea.

After the war, he served as LSU's public relations director and director of Information Services. He and his wife, Billie Ruth, have five children.

Raymond Rockhold

[Interviewed by Adele K. Foster, 1 July 1997, Collection 4700.0828]

Raymond Rockhold, the third of eight children, grew up in Jonesboro, Louisiana, in a house with no telephone or electricity built by his father. A young Rockhold joined the Citizen Conservation Corps, CCC, in 1933. His job, which paid thirty dollars a week, gave him the opportunity to work briefly at Camp Beauregard.

From 1934-38, prior to joining the Marine Corps, Rockhold attended LSU. He and twelve others invested in a lightweight "puddle jumper," or Piper Cub airplane, which allowed him to earn his pilot's license. Rockhold also owned and operated a boarding house near the LSU campus and was part-owner of a Baton Rouge nightclub.

During World War II, Rockhold loaded machine guns for planes flying over the Pacific. After the war, he worked in real estate and the restaurant business.

Wiltz Segura

[Interviewed by Mary Hebert and John J.Capdevielle, 25 January 1996, Collection 4700.0633]

New Iberia native Wiltz Segura decided to join the U.S. Army Air Corps one day in the early 1940s when he saw several P-40 fighter planes land in Lafayette. "A P-40 airplane in those days was as impressive to me as a space shuttle," he says. The pilots "wore riding britches and those boots, and they looked fantastic. And I said, 'I've got to figure a way to get into that outfit.'" Thirty years later, General Segura retired from the U.S. Air Force service with 10,000 hours of flight time behind him.

In World War II, Segura flew 102 combat missions in China. He was shot down twice but both times managed to parachute out of his damaged aircraft and escape capture. After the war, he was a test pilot and commanded fighters in Vietnam. He also served as wing commander at Homestead Air Force Base when a Cuban air force pilot suddenly landed a Mig fighter plane and defected to the United States. One of a few high-ranking Air Force officers at the time who could speak Spanish, Segura personally handled the situation and explained it to then President Nixon.

Today, Segura lives in New Iberia with his wife, Joy.

Ralph Sims

[Interviewed by Adele K. Foster, 3 July 1997, Collection 4700.0827]

At the time of the Japanese attack on Pearl Harbor, Ralph Sims was program director at Baton Rouge radio station WJBO. Reading accounts of the bombing over the airwaves helped convince him to sign up with the U.S. Army Air Corps. After the war, Sims first returned to the radio industry, then went into real estate, and retired as head of marketing at Fidelity National Bank. He was active for many years in United Givers, the Rotary Club and in other community activities.

Carlos Spaht

[Interviewed by Mary Hebert, 22 June 1993, Collection 4700.0292]

A graduate of LSU and LSU Law School, Carlos Spaht fought on the Burma Road during World War II. When he returned to Baton Rouge after the war, he established a reserve unit and served as its commander for fifteen years. He was appointed a district judge in 1946 and, at the suggestion of Earl Long, ran for governor in 1952. After hisdefeat in that election, he returned to private law practice but later served as executive counsel for Governor McKeithen. Spaht also served as chairman of the LSU Board of Supervisors and president of the LSU Alumni Federation.

Charles Titkemeyer

[Interviewed by Everett Besch, 18 June 1993, Collection 4700.0307]

Longtime professor and head of admissions of the Department of Veterinary Anatomy at LSU's School of Veterinary Medicine, Charles Titkemeyer joined the U.S. Army Air Corps in 1942. Stationed in North Africa, he served as navigator on B-24, heavyweight bombers that, he says, "looked like a bumblebee."

The day he was discharged from the military, he was admitted to veterinary school in Columbus, Ohio. He went on to get his M.S. and Ph.D. at Michigan State University. He stayed on as an instructor at Michigan for several years and through the Agency for International Development, taught in Indonesia and Nigeria. In 1969, he came to the LSU School of Veterinary Medicine as its third employee and stayed until his retirement eighteen years later.

Ida Turcan

[Interviewed by Adele K. Foster, 23 June 1997, Collection 4700.0829]

After graduating from nursing school in 1939, Mandeville native Ida Turcan joined the U.S. Army as a nurse in 1941. "My brothers were all in the army or navy by then, and I felt like Uncle Sam was calling me too," she says.

After the war, Turcan returned to Louisiana and worked at Touro Hospital, New Orleans, as a head nurse and supervisor. She received her degree in Nursing Education from LSU in 1956. During Hurricane Audrey in 1957, she was working for the American Red Cross. She ended her career as a nursing instructor at Our Lady of the Lake Hospital in Baton Rouge.

Aubrey Williams

[Interviewed by Julian Pleasants, 11 September 1997, 4700.0899]

Arriving at LSU in 1940, Williams soon grew deeply involved in journalism, first as a reporter, then as the managing editor, his junior year, of the LSU *Reveille*. He was also a weekend reporter for the Baton Rouge *Morning Advocate*. Called into the U.S. Army in 1943, Williams spent a year and a half teaching recruits to operate tanks. He later volunteered to be a liaison pilot and flew high-ranking officials around post-war occupied Germany.

Returning to LSU in 1946, Williams completed his undergraduate studies and then followed Cleanth Brooks to Yale as a graduate student in English literature. After earning his Ph.D. in 1952, Williams taught at Yale and received Fullbright and Guggenheim scholarships to edit the first volume of the Twickenham Edition of the poems of Alexander Pope. He later taught at Rice University and the University of Florida.

Williams resigned from the University of Florida in 1986, protesting what he saw as a failing commitment to quality education.

Erbon Wise

[Interviewed by Tara Zachary, 27 December 1995, Collection 4700.0636]

As a finance officer dealing with United States Army payroll, Erbon Wise was among the first American troops in Britain during World War II, and was soon "handling millions of dollars every month, which was quite a responsibility for a twenty-two-year-old."

After the war, Wise bought the *Maplewood Star,* a small newspaper in Sulphur, Louisiana, and built it into a chain of publications. He commanded reserve units until 1964, when he was appointed Adjutant General by Governor McKeithen.

Chapter Two

The Ole War Skule:
The Military Tradition at LSU

Louisiana State University is fondly remembered as the "Ole War Skule" by generations of alumni. Recollections of lessons of self-discipline and pride learned on the parade ground, company triumphs in drills and maneuvers, the feminine admiration a uniform might elicit, along with those of resentment of reveille and resistance to hazing, feature prominently in the interviews recorded by the Williams Center as part of an ongoing series on the history of the university.

The military tradition at LSU dates to its founding as a military academy in 1860 under the direction of William Tecumseh Sherman. Although nearly the entire student body as well as the president soon abandoned the fledgling institution to fight on opposite sides of the Civil War, the pattern was set. Since Sherman's day, most of LSU's presidents have been retired officers, and for more than a century compulsory participation in the cadet corps dominated the first two years of college life for male students.

By 1968 attitudes toward Reserve Officers Training Corps [ROTC] had changed a great deal. Inspired by the antiwar movement and protests against ROTC on other college campuses, many students and faculty joined together in condemning the university's military tradition and in demanding the end of compulsory military training.

An era seemed to have ended when the Board of Supervisors abolished compulsory ROTC, a move that delighted the nearly 4,000 cadets. Although the military tradition at LSU was wounded — enrollment in ROTC dropped to approximately 150 cadets — it was not a fatal blow. The university continues to honor its war heros such as General Sherman; General William E. Brougher, Commandant of Cadets from 1926-29 and a survivor of the Bataan Death March; General Claire Chennault, commander of the Flying Tigers; and General Troy Middleton, war hero and president of LSU from 1950 to 1962. More than fifty years after World War II, the university continues to point with pride to the fact that LSU provided more officers for that war than any other institution. And the tradition clearly lives on, not only in the remembrances of alumni, but in the students and faculty of today. In 1991, more than 250 members of the LSU community — students, staff, and faculty — answered their country's call to arms and served in the war in the Persian Gulf.

Although some of the following narrators predate World War II, we have included them in tribute to the deep roots of the military tradition at the Ole War Skule.

--Pamela Dean

Grover Rees

Class of 1912

Rees: We were awakened by the reveille, of course. We had to get up and be downstairs to answer the roll call. Whenever we went to the mess hall, we had to line up and answer roll call. Our commandant of cadets, Captain Sorley, was just out of West Point. He tried to make a West Point out of LSU, and he had a Marine, retired, to help him. As I've said, we had to answer roll calls about half a dozen times a day, at the bugle, and I just didn't like it. I didn't like it at all. [We wore these uncomfortable uniforms.] Imagine that damn thing with a collar up your neck like this. And you couldn't leave the campus without a permit. Oh, no, Captain Sorley tried to make a West Point out of LSU.

We country boys, including myself, didn't like to be called early in the morning to take exercise or to answer roll call. I didn't like it, so I quit, or maybe they quit me, I don't know. [No longer eligible to live in the Pentagon Barracks, Rees joined an informal group of ex-cadets known as Hobos.] The Hobos lived in the Pest House. The Pest House was a two story frame building. The top floor had rooms that were used by the scientists or agriculturalists.

T. Earle Johnson

Class of 1926

Johnson: I was living in the room with the company commander [Ambrose Warner], and he called all the freshmen together and announced to us that we were living, basically, under the same rules as those at West Point. He expected us to act accordingly. The least little thing, and we were hazed. By hazed I mean, usually, beaten with a broom. He had a philosophy that a freshman was not properly oriented until a broom handle was broken when he was struck with it. And I didn't like it. I was wondering how I could avoid some of it.

So, I had my own broom, and I was holding it. I had it with the handle pointing down and the broom part up. I took about two steps towards Captain Warner, and then, I stopped and looked down at the broom and said, "Hello darling," then started making love to it. Talking to it very sweetly and carrying on anything that I could think of. He looked at me of course just in amazement at first. I noticed that he was smiling, and suddenly he started laughing. When he started laughing, everybody else did. So, I don't know how I kept a straight face, but I did. I went right on and did my act for several minutes. In the meantime, they were all just laughing and laughing and laughing.

Well, Captain Warner stopped and looked at me, and he said, "I have never seen anybody sling it around the way that you do. I think you deserve a nickname, and I am going to call you 'Bull' from here on out." So "Bull" is my nickname. All the others picked it up too. I was "Bull" Johnson on campus. Boys that I didn't [know] from other companies would speak to me. "Hey, Bull. How are we doing today."

[I got to be pretty famous] because I was getting out of hazing by making love to a broom. Well, then came the big hazing event when the freshmen had their hair cut. This happened, I think, right after the Christmas holidays. The sophomores would come around with clippers, and they would just clip a swath of hair right down the middle of the top of your head. Then we went with them to their rooms where they finished the job. We were completely [bald]. We took the next day as a freshmen holiday. This was completely unofficial, but that's what sophomores said they had done as freshmen. And, with that, we took off.

We assembled out near the Pentagon, and some of them raided the university paint shop and got some buckets of paint and painted all around on some of the buildings and lamp posts and the light. Well, I was in the group, and I guess [I was] one of the ring leaders of the group [that] headed down Third Street. We went there, and there was a fruit stand in the first block. [The vendor] was just setting out this fruit, fresh fruit and so on, when we got there. But we turned over all the crates of fruit; we picked up some, threw some in the gutter, and kept on going.

We [were] just raising hell. Merchants heard us coming, I guess, and started locking their doors. So, we continued all the way up Third Street, all the way up to the capitol, the old capitol building. Then, [we] turned around and went back. [It] took us about two hours. Some of the boys went back home and went to bed or just didn't go to class. But I went to some of my afternoon classes. Of course, I was sort of an object of concern, pity, and what have you with my being bald-headed. But that was it.

Well, at that time, if anybody in the university needed to get in touch with a student, they had the secretary look up the schedule, write the professor a note, and send the note over by another student, by a runner. So, about three days later I got a note that the president wanted me to come to his office at three o'clock that afternoon. I wondered what on earth was the matter. I was not a class officer. I think I was on the Honor Council, but I am not sure. But I know I was not a class officer.

So, when I got there, the president of the freshman class was there. I think maybe a couple of others came in a little bit later. And the four of us were escorted into the president's office. Colonel Thomas Boyd was president then. He was a small man, rather short, bald-headed, and was a very severe, you might say, a severe disciplinarian. Well, he really let us have it. He told us we had done something that was very disgraceful on our rampage of a few days before and that the university was beginning to get bills of damage [for what] we had done. And it was going to be up to us to pay it. So, he talked on a few minutes, and he said, "When I get all the bills in," he told the group, "I'll get back in touch with Cadet Johnson, and we'll let him know how much it is. Then you all have to do something about it." Well, with that, he dismissed us. But he was very severe with us — particularly severe with me because he had said something about my being on the Honor Council too.

Well, we went outside and looked at each other wondering how are we going to do it and so on. But I was most concerned of all. I said, "Why does he pick on me? Why does he give it to me?" I said, "I am not a class officer." The president of the class looked at me and said, "You are now. He just made you treasurer of the freshmen class. The president just appointed you treasurer."

Several days later, I got a note to come to the president's office at my convenience. Well, I went over, and the next class, I think, I had a vacant period. So, I went over as soon as I could. This time he was very nice to me, though. He was much nicer than he was before. He said he had most of the bills, practically all of them. The total was over seven hundred dollars. Well, I was just appalled at the idea of seven hundred dollars. That was an enormous amount of money. That was probably more than twice what it cost me to go to the university, go to LSU, for a whole year. Then he told me to go down to a bank — I think it was the First National Bank — and to see a certain officer there. He was very nice to me. He told me that they had set up a special account for the freshmen class, and they were paying all of the bills. Then we would owe only the bank. Well, it turned out that he [the bank officer] had a son who was one of the ring leaders also. He was one of the ring leaders who had raided the paint shop.

So, I went back and got in touch with the president. We had a meeting of a group of us, including all the officers. I told them what had happened. And we had to decide how we [were] going to pay for it. Some of them said, "Well, let's just assess every freshmen five dollars. That will pay for it." But several of us argued. I was one who argued against that saying, "No, that means our parents would pay it for most of us." I said, "We did it. We need to take the responsibility for it." So, we agreed to meet again. We had that meeting, and it was at the third meeting when we got the idea of putting on a review. We decided to call it the "Bald-Headed Revue."

We called the whole freshmen class together and presented the idea of the "Bald-Headed Revue." We told them what we were going to do and the like. I was explaining it because I had been the one in contact with the president and the bank. So, then when I finished, I asked if there were any questions. If anybody wanted to know anything. Nobody said anything. But, they were watching each other, and finally one boy raised his hand, got up, and said, "Bull, if . . . " — I didn't know who he was; didn't have any idea — "Bull, if we put on a revue will you do your love act to a broom?" I said, "Yes, I will." "All right. Good." He said, "I'll sing a solo." I said, "Can you sing?" He said, "A little." And I said, "Well, I don't know." The boy next to him said, "He's too modest." He said, "He has a marvelous voice." I said, "Well, good. Now we have two acts. We need more." So, we set up a committee and then we worked on it. It was quite a success. We charged a dollar admission. We took in, I think, eight hundred dollars. More than paid for all of our bills. Well, I know that some of the men who bought tickets would give five dollars for two tickets and say, "Keep the change."

One other thing that Colonel Boyd told me, he said, "In a way, you all have done us a favor." He said, "You have given us a real good excuse to stop all of this hazing." He said, "We are going to put a stop to it." He had the Board of Trustees pass a resolution [and] made it an expelling offense to have your hair cut, either the person doing it or the person who it was done [to], the freshman. And, that stopped it.

Thomas Blakeney
Class of 1939

Blakeney: [The first two years at LSU] everyone, every male student was a member of the ROTC; that was part of the deal at that time. I've forgotten how many times a week, but three or four times a week, we would have drill. And, we had ROTC classes too. I got to know a quite a few of the ROTC instructors. They were regular army majors and captains at that time.

Your freshman year, you're just a private. Your sophomore year, you become a corporal, or some people do. Your junior year, you become a sergeant, and your senior year, you become a cadet officer. So, I went all the way up, and my senior year, I was a lieutenant colonel battalion commander of the ROTC battalion. I was a company first sergeant my junior year, and we were picked some way by what we did for our promotions to higher grades.

For me [ROTC was sort of the focus for college life] because I liked it. I liked being a soldier. I liked being an ROTC cadet. It gave me a lot of pleasure to do the things that we were doing. This is where I lost interest in becoming a doctor and decided that I would go into the service. I went in the service, of course, directly from LSU in 1939. When it came time for me to graduate, General Troy Middleton, who was Major Middleton at that time, offered me two things. He offered me a commission in the army, a competitive tour, or a commission in the Marine Corps. The reason I took the army instead of the Marine Corps was that in the army I was on probation for about a year. The marines [would have] had me on probation for two years, and we [my fiancée and I] couldn't get married. I decided I wanted to get married. So, I decided on the army over the Marine Corps because I could [get] married in the army and I couldn't get married in the Marine Corps. It was that simple.

Robert Barrow
1939-1941

Soderbergh: You had some thoughts originally of going to West Point?

Barrow: I read a lot of things related to the military. Again, I'm probably part of that Southern spirit that has a certain martial feature to it that comes out of the Civil War experience. I read a lot about that and other kinds of military things which moved me to be interested. I would send off every couple of years for the [West Point] catalog, look at it, fantasize, and think about going there. I wanted to go, but you had to be right politically. In those days, it was much more important than it is today. There were not that many appointments, and they were highly sought after.

Much of what happened, that took me to LSU, was the determination on my part that I would do it. The tuition, general fee, room, board and all [those expenses] were very modest, but you still had to have whatever it took. You had to have it.

It has to be told that my experience at LSU, while a happy and pleasant one for me, was not satisfactory in terms of the objective for which one goes to school. I will not make any excuses for being a poor student, but there were some mitigating circumstances. I will not use the excuse of being busy, busy, busy with two jobs and that sort of thing. I would say this — and this is not an excuse — I discovered girls. I discovered the happy good time life of the university campus. For a seventeen-year-old coming out of a very rural, provincial kind of life, it was almost too much. I enjoyed it to the fullest.

I enjoyed some of the classes I took. I enjoyed literature, history, and, particularly, the ROTC part of it, and was good at it. But also I became very mischievous. The kind of harassment that freshmen took from upperclassmen was a given, and it was pretty severe. You could get paddled. There was a lot of hazing. The freshmen had all their hair cut absolutely short, short like you were going to Parris Island, almost — skinheads. You wore a little cap with the bill turned up, and you had your name on it preceded by the word "Dog." In my case, I was "Dog Barrow." We were called "dogs." You did the bidding of the upperclassmen. For the fellow who showed a little spirit, a little resistance was an invitation to visit more of the same. So, I was fair game to the upperclassmen.

I became a retaliator, without fear. I still run into some old friends, this being fifty-five years later, who said, "You know, I remember you as a freshman at LSU. You used to give those upperclassmen fits." My favorite technique was to give them a barber pie. Have you ever heard of a barber pie, Dr. Soderbergh? I shouldn't be talking about this, but it's part of my early life and what happened, so I'll talk about it.

You wait until the victim is sound asleep. The rooms all had three people, usually a freshman and two upperclassmen, sometimes one upperclassman and two freshmen. The doors were not locked; they didn't lock doors. So, you would go in. Maybe you had an accomplice and maybe you didn't. You would go into the common bathroom and [take] heavy paper, even good newspaper would do it, fold it up so it was like a dunce cap, turn it upside down, and you've got this triangular shaped receptacle. You whipped up a concoction that knew no limits in terms of imagination, most of it soap suds and maybe some shaving lotion. If you really wanted to get with it, you might to put a little ammonia in it. You go in, and if you really showed full courage, you just didn't administer the barber pie, which was just put it over his face. You shook him gently so that he got the full benefit out of it while it he was coming out a deep sleep, and then you high-tailed it. I shouldn't be talking about all of this, but it was part of what I did. I was just terrible. Giving short sheets, I could put a short sheet on a bed before you could turn around. So, I did all of that. It was sort of like guerilla warfare with me.

Soderbergh: Who won that campaign against the hazers?

Barrow: They won. I guess I left a tell-tale sign; I was about the only guy that would do those kind of things. So, it was understood that if anyone received a barber pie during the middle of the night, I had to have been the one to administer it. As a consequence, I spent a lot of Saturday afternoons marching off demerits. I got none on the field, in terms of my appearance, in terms of being good at drill, and the things that you did in the ROTC, but it was [only in] the ROTC living barracks [that I got into trouble]. You were assigned to the barracks by company. You had the company commander and company lieutenants living in the barracks. So, I had to march off demerits. We had night football games, but we also had some afternoon football games. I missed most of the afternoon football games because I was north of the stadium there, with a few other bad guys, marching off demerits, four hours every Saturday afternoon.

Soderbergh: Not a very promising beginning for a person who ended up devoting four decades of his life to one of the most organized military groups in the world. What happened in between? How did you break out of that mode?

Barrow: I was a failure at LSU. I made A's, B's and F's. I just was not a good student. I was capable of being a good student, but I just went for too many other things. I didn't have my priorities straight. I stayed out one semester as a consequence. I'm not very proud of that; it's embarrassing. As a matter of fact, when LSU bestowed an honorary degree on me in 1990, the first call I got, I said, "No, this is a mistake. You can't do this." [They said,] "Why?" I said, "Because you'd be giving a degree to a fellow who didn't make it when he was there in school." And they said, "Well, we are honoring you for what you became and not for what you were when you were here."

People today cannot possibly understand fully what LSU ROTC represented in those days. It was a super good institution. It was called the Old War Skule, spelled S-K-U-L-E, and it had a tradition. It produced more Army officers, albeit reserved, than the military academy did. Sort of in the same category as Clemson and Texas A&M. A lot of people went [to LSU] because it had an ROTC commitment. It was one of the land-grant colleges that required it for at least two years — unless you had some infirmity and couldn't do it. The parades on Friday afternoons [were] as fine parades as I have ever seen — particularly in the spring months. You had white-gray-white. You had the white color for your cap, your gray tunic, and then white trousers and black shoes.

Soderbergh: That sounds very much like a West Point uniform.

Barrow: It did in many ways look like a West Point uniform. You had a large cadet corps. It was really quite something. As I said earlier, a fair number of people from the North attended LSU, and the great trick question that the upperclassmen would give one of these freshmen from Illinois or wherever: "Who was the greatest, William Tecumseh Sherman or Robert E. Lee?" Well, this fellow would not be a dummy, you know, and he would think, "Gosh, I'm down here in Robert E. Lee country. That's an obvious answer." So, he would say, "Robert E. Lee, sir." To which the upperclassman would say, "You dog, don't you know that William Tecumseh Sherman was the president of LSU!" and he would get his butt beat. If you thought that you'd smarted up and say "Sherman," then of course, they would tell you, "Don't you know Robert E. Lee was in . . ." So, it was a no-win question. But, I think the ROTC was absolutely superior.

John J. Capdevielle
Class of 1942

Besch: Did LSU just have Army ROTC?

Capdevielle: Army was all we had, but they had three branches by this time: infantry, engineers, and artillery. The infantry was housed up in the Pentagon Barracks, the artillery was in the North Stadium, and the engineers were in the East Stadium. The West Stadium was civilians. That's people who weren't in ROTC. Now you had to take two years of ROTC, and you applied for the next two. Thank goodness I went on and applied because, boy, it was about the wisest move I ever made, coming out of there with a commission.

Besch: When you went in did they shave off all of your hair?

Capdevielle: Oh, yes.

Besch: Were you in uniform all of the time?

Capdevielle: No. You had to wear a uniform on drill days, and my drill days were Monday and Thursday. We drilled at noon, [from] twelve to one. If you didn't get a chance to eat, that was tough. Nobody seemed to worry about it. I remember taking freshman chemistry, and I think I had it on Tuesdays and Thursdays. You had a lecture, and then, you had a lab. So it went quite lengthy into the afternoons. You had drill, which meant you reported in and you missed lunch. We'd pick up a Coca-Cola and go by and see if we could pick up some grain alcohol to spike the coke up, and that would help us get through the afternoon. It made it pass faster. [Capdevielle and Besch laugh]

Besch: Did you have to wear your uniform all day long on drill days?

Capdevielle: Most everyone did. You didn't have time to go change, you know. You had a lot to do so you went on and just wore your uniform. We had an outfit out of New Orleans that came up and measured you during registration, and within two weeks they had you in your uniform. And the things fit. The cadets wore gray. They had a pair of grey wool trousers with black stripes down the legs. We had a gray cotton shirt, a gray wool blouse, and a gray cap with, you know, a bill cap. You had a white cap cover that you could put on for summer use. You also had a black leather belt to go on your blouse, and you had a white belt for summer use. You had a pair of white gloves, and you wore the white gloves with the white other stuff. And, I don't recall we ever thought it was hot. When you got to be a junior, if you went into the advanced ROTC, you got khaki stuff. Now, the earlier [uniforms] used to have the choker collar blouses, and we didn't. We had the ones with the lapels.

Besch: Did they pay you when you were in ROTC?

Capdevielle: Nope. No pay. And you bought your own uniform. There was a lot of trade that went on. People would sell uniforms. So, if you came in and were lucky enough before registration to find some junior who was getting out of it, and he was your size, you bought his uniform. Then you didn't have to buy so much when you went in there.

Besch: What did you wear on non-drill days?

Capdevielle: Just regular clothes.

Besch: Did you have to wear a beanie?

Capdevielle: The freshman wore beanies until their hair grew out which [was] sometime around Thanksgiving, and then [they would] throw that thing away. They called them "dog" hats, and you'd put your name Dog Besch or Dog Capdevielle or whatever it was [on the bill]. You know you turned the bill up and wrote it on the bottom of your bill. It was purple and gold.

Besch: Was there any hazing in the corps?

Capdevielle: Oh, yes. They used to play games in the barracks called "cuckoo," and they also made things called barber pies. "Cuckoo" was to take a freshman and put him on the table with a rolled up Sunday paper, a [New Orleans] *Times-Picayune.* They'd put another freshman under the table with another paper. The one under the table was supposed to come out and swat the one on top without getting hit himself and holler "cuckoo" when he did it.

When the draft came up, they said we didn't have to go sign in the draft because we were already in advanced ROTC, so we didn't. I've never signed up for the draft board. When we graduated, they just gave us some orders. Some got orders right away; others were delayed. I had to ask for a deferment, and Colonel Hill gave me a deferment to finish summer school because I could get a degree if I could wait that long.

Besch: Did they commission anybody in the regular Army out of LSU?

Capdevielle: Oh, yes, yes. Louie [Reinberg] got a regular commission. They take the honor graduates. They still do, as I understand it. The honor graduates get a chance at a regular commission. Right now with them trying to downsize everything, you may have a problem with it, but I don't remember anyone in our group taking a regular Army commission from LSU. With the war coming on, I don't believe anybody in our class was even offered anything like that, but they were offered this later on. In 1946, just before I got out, I was offered a regular commission, and I told them they would have to issue a regular divorce along with the regular commission if I was to take it. I had to turn that down.

In '39 LSU got its first flying school through civilian pilot training. The government gave them the money, and the College of Engineering acted as the recipient of the grant. They bought the airplanes and hired teachers that taught the students to fly that wanted to learn to fly. The only condition with learning to fly was [the students] paid a little bit of something in `39. In the summer of 1940, they offered it just to any enrolled student, and there was no cost. I could enroll for two dollars in the summer term. So, I borrowed two dollars from my father. I told him I wanted to enroll, and I didn't tell him what for. He was delighted that I had enough interest in going to school that I wanted to go a summer. So, he gave me the two. A couple of weeks later he asked me what I was enrolling for, and when I told him, he went higher than most of those airplanes would go. But, he decided finally that if LSU taught it, it was all right, leave it alone. We signed a paper that said that in the event of a war, we would attempt to get into something that did involve flying. So, that's how I got into that.

I signed up for pilot training and officer's grade. I had some problems with the physical, [but] I went on into the service. I was over at Hattiesburg [Mississippi] at the camp there. I've forgotten the name of it. But, I was with the 321st Infantry Division.

Louie Reinberg
Class of 1935

Hebert: Was there a military ball once a year?

Reinberg: Oh yes, the military balls were every year. We used to all go in uniform, and the girls always wore evening dresses. We used to have a great big parade. It wasn't [exactly like] a cotillion, but you would parade with your dates up front, a big line of boys and girls in uniform and evening dresses. I have some pictures of that there in my *Gumbos*. It was quite a nice affair. The funny part about it, the boys that were not in ROTC, that had dropped out, used to scrounge up a uniform and go to the dance.

Hebert: It was that big.

Reinberg: That's right. It was that big. And, people enjoyed it. We used to have a pretty good name band. I mentioned Guy Lombardo and those others; they were name bands. They were extra. I think student government had paid for those. They used to have good orchestras around.

The boys in Africa relax this way, too.
1943 Gumbo, page 110

Hebert: Did the cadets march at the football games?

Reinberg: I only remember marching in the stadium once as a cadet. I've forgotten what game it was, but they'd march the whole cadet corps on the field. We all went up and sat in the stands. There was nothing but an infantry; I mean, there was no supporting arms. Before the stadium was bowled in, we'd form on the south end of the stadium and come into the stadium and go up in the stands. Then my junior year, they finished building rooms on the east and west side of the stadium where they put other companies. We used to have lettered companies. We used to have three battalions of A,B,C; D,E,F; G,H,I. Then, the K, L, and M was down in the stadium, that was the fourth battalion. It was all infantry.

Hebert: You lived in Pentagon Barracks at that time?

Reinberg: I was living there in A Barracks, in the Pentagon. The ROTC used to have to maintain those things. We'd have Friday inspections, and we'd all have to put plain sheets on the beds, make sure that the rooms were cleaned up, the bathrooms were clean. We'd sweep it all out into the landings, to the hall, and the janitor would remove it. It was a ritual every Friday morning to have inspections. When I was a first sergeant and then a company commander my junior and senior year, it was my job to make darn sure everybody got up and got working. You'd hear a whole lot of grousing and fussing, but everybody seemed to get along all right.

Hebert: Did [Major Middleton, as he was known then] handle the disciplinary problems within the cadet corps?

Reinberg: No, he didn't. When he said something, the cadets knew he meant it and that was the end of it. In other words, we used to have some kind of hazing on the campus, not anything bad, but he'd get word of it. He'd say, "Gentlemen, this has got to stop." And, that was it. That was all that was said. Nobody argued about it. When the major said it, that was it.

Hebert: Was Middleton well respected by the cadet corps?

Reinberg: He was extremely well respected. I respected him.
      Before I came back to work for the university, I came back here on leave and stopped by to see him and pay my respects. [Middleton] had built a big hole in the ground out there where the library is today, and I said, "General, what in the God's name are you doing to the campus?" I said, "You have a hole out there big enough to put a horse in." He said, I'm building a library." He said, "Nobody can say they can't find it. You've either got to go through it, around it, or over it. But, that's the library." And, I'll never forget it. That's the way he explained it to me.

Hebert: When you were company commander did you keep some control over [hazing]?

Reinberg: Well, I didn't encourage it. Of course you can't ever stop it. But, as far as I was concerned, we had very little hazing, and I didn't have enough to concern myself with it.

Hebert: Could you describe the head shaving ritual? When did that happen?

Reinberg: Oh, that happened before I was a freshman. A freshman was fair game. When he came on the campus and he had the full hair, he got clipped. Some of them beat them to it. They had it shaved at home, in odd shapes, and stuff like that. I've forgotten who shaved mine, but I got peeled too. But, by the time Thanksgiving came around, everybody had enough hair on their head so they wasn't bald or anything. And, we all had to wear pajamas [to the] first football game. They would put us out on the field with our shaved heads and pajamas, run us around the field, and put us back in the stands. But it was all in fun. Nobody got hurt.

Hebert: How were you selected to be company commander and first sergeant?

Reinberg: I don't know. That was done by the powers that be, [by] Major Middleton and his staff. You could apply for advanced military.

Hebert: How often did you drill?

Reinberg: We used to have parades once a week. After everybody got outfitted in uniforms and learned how to drill, we'd have a parade out on the parade ground. The parade ground [would be] full of cadets. It was well received. Baton Rouge would turn out en masse to take a look at it. The sponsors would be there for the company, and the ROTC group with the major. The governor, and sometimes the president [of the university], would show up or something like that. It was on Thursday noon that we had our parades.

Jack Gremillion
1931-1933

Gremillion: Well, when I entered LSU as a freshman, I was obligated to take and participate in the ROTC program, which was designed to qualify you as a soldier. If you decided to, you could pursue becoming an officer in the Reserve Officers Training Corps. That's what it was for. We used to march during the noon hour, three times a week. We had a class once a week, usually in the Gym Armory, and I participated in it. I rather enjoyed it, and I passed it, of course. I found out that it did help me a little bit in later years to come when I was drafted in the army of the United States.

Hebert: Tell me about the initiation.

Gremillion: Oh, let me tell you. I think people are confused about an initiation. I had no initiation in ROTC. When [a] freshman came to LSU, they usually made him shave his head, and they hazed him — made him wear pajamas to one of the football games. And, it was a sort of initiation that gave you a mentality and your courage a little test as to what you will have to face in the future. But, that initiation was never associated with or a part of ROTC. That initiation was strictly something they called hazing. It went on in school as a result of tradition that existed over the years. It really had nothing to do with your ROTC training. However, it probably was associated, just by coincidence, with being a freshman and living in the dormitory because all of the freshmen were obligated, as much as possible, to live in the dormitory. I lived in Building B-59. I stayed there for the first semester. And you were obligated to stay there at least for one semester.

After that, I got a job. I was poor, didn't have any money coming from home, and had to get a job. So, I got a job downtown opening oysters in the old A&W Root Beer stand. I had a room in the old Baton Rouge Athletic Club. So, I went down and started living in Baton Rouge proper, which is right off Third Street and was commuting back and forth from LSU. But to answer your question specifically, I never associated an initiation with ROTC. In fact, I don't think they had any, and I hope I'm not considered as an authority on that because honestly there was none.

Hebert: Was there any corporal punishment?

Gremillion: No, oh absolutely not. Oh, a couple of upperclassmen, like football players, might catch a freshman and tease him a little bit and take a broom and make him bend over and hit him on his fanny three or four times. I had that happen to me on several occasions, but that wasn't part of any ritual. That was strictly something that was personal, more or less.

Now, in the ROTC, if you didn't comply with your assignments and you messed up, let's say, on some of your projects or whatever it was, you would be sentenced by the upperclassmen to serve a rifle duty around the flagpole. The flagpole in those days sat in the middle of the campus. It's not there anymore; buildings now occupy that place. But, if you were late for something, and you didn't do your assignment correctly or something like that, you'd get sentenced — I believe by the company commander — to serve twenty-five strolls, or whatever it was, along by the flagpole, usually on a Saturday when free time was afforded to other students to make the penalty a little more severe to you. Now, that's the only punishment that I knew of that was associated with ROTC. I judged it [as] being consistent with ROTC and military regulations.

Robert LeBlanc
Class of 1942

LeBlanc: The Pershing Rifles were a drill team. They're still there, by the way, I was checking, and they are still at LSU. I'm one of the charter members of the Pershing Rifles. They were organized, I think, in 1940. A team from up north came down and wanted a bunch of cadets who were interested in being on drill teams. We had been in a firing squad. The commander of my company had recruited a bunch of us to do the ceremonial firing, and they asked if we would join a special drill team organization, which we did do. From there, we went various places and performed at the football games at the half-time as special drills team.

Now, one of the events that the Pershing Rifles took part in was we went to New Orleans to the opera. One of the operas needed a firing squad, and we went over there and performed in an opera.

Hebert: Did you have room inspection?

LeBlanc: [Your bed had to be] perfectly made, and everything had to be just so, or you got demerits. You had study hall periods every night. It was discipline, and I'm sorry to say that it's gone, gone, gone, gone. Because, I think it was very good for young people. I was only sixteen years old when I went to college. But, it certainly instilled in me the need for education, the need for discipline, organizing time in the way that you could get your tasks accomplished.

Hebert: How were the ranks determined within the cadet corps?

LeBlanc: Your first year you were basic, your second year you were squad leader, third year you were sergeant of some type, and your fourth year you were an officer of some type.

Hebert: Did you have to do all four years?

LeBlanc: No. You were required to do the first two years because [LSU was] a land grant college, and the law required you to do it. But you applied for the third and fourth year.

Hebert: Did ROTC prepare you for war?

LeBlanc: [It did] not prepare you for war totally. You ended up at Fort Benning [Georgia] for the actual tactical knowledge that you needed. You had a military background in ROTC, but it was mostly close order drill and that kind of thing. For tactical training, you needed the field activities; you needed a training at Fort Benning. You didn't get your commission at LSU. You had to go to Benning before you could get your commission. And, it was a good thing you did, because you really needed Benning, for the training that you needed in war — for the coordination of gun fire and that type of thing. In other words, you need to know how all of the instruments of war work together. You need to know all of the communications. You need to know how to call for supporting fire. And, all of this, you get at Benning without so much classroom training. You learn how to read maps one end to the other. You learn to take a map and see the terrain on the ground and know where you're at. You learn land navigation. You learn all of the things that you really need as a soldier on the battleground.

Hebert: You didn't get any of that at LSU?

LeBlanc: You get the map reading at LSU. You'd get some of those courses, but it's not like doing it in a combat situation. And live firing, the only time we did live firing at LSU was when we went to that six weeks ROTC camp. It's not like going to Fort Benning where there's a regular Army unit [with a] demonstration team and sarges and lieutenants that teach it every day, who are experts in it. In other words, when you took mortar training at Benning, you started just like you were a basic cadet and were the assistant gun loader.

[You had to learn] every aspect of what every man did. Just like communications, you had to learn all the different types of radios. You had to learn how to operate them, you know. How to have to take immediate action on all the weapons and that type of thing because you will end up being an instructor in this.

Hebert: But the LSU experience was helpful for you?

LeBlanc: Very much helpful. The LSU experience was primarily helpful in interpersonal relationships, of knowing how to lead cadets. You understood more closely the relationship between your soldiers and yourself.

Wiltz Segura
1940 (spring and summer)

Segura: LSU had a couple of other boys from New Iberia. We had always gone together, and we kind of got away without having [our hair cut] for about maybe three weeks or four weeks until I met one of my [older] friends from New Iberia who had been at LSU. He looked at me and said, "Didn't you get your hair cut yet?" I said, "I'm not getting my hair cut." He says, "Okay." So, about three days later, there was a knock on the door, and there was about fifteen guys, about ten of them from New Iberia. I've never forgiven him for that. 'Cause I don't have a head that lends itself to shaving. [laughter] I mean, you know, I'm sort of like Samson, you cut my hair and there's nothing left.

They took us into the bathroom and shaved us, and that was horrible, horrible. [My future wife,] Joy and I were going out together. So, I didn't want to come home. I still have some of those pictures. Anyway, you get those little beanies that you put on. And, of course, then when you got around the campus, everybody recognized you. But, it wasn't that bad; it was kind of fun.

A couple of times in the stadium, some of the smart-aleck guys from the city — most of the guys from the city were the ones that would cause the most trouble — they were going to make me assume different positions, and I just wouldn't do it. It got down to a confrontation one time, and we were ready to go at it. Somebody with a cool head stepped in, and there was some sort of face-saving on both sides, and they [said], "Well, we'll get you later." But, anyway, I had tried to avoid those hot spots, but I never did like hazing, not even in the military.

There's always a few of these guys who carry it too far. I think it's a lot of fun if its done intelligently, and with some purpose in mind for discipline, and so forth. But, some of these guys are just out of control, and someone needs to step in and stop those things. When I got to be a commander, I made sure that [it] didn't happen. I think we can teach discipline in other ways than having to humiliate people. But that was the system, and you just got to swim with the current sometimes.

Every time I had any free time, I would hitch-hike back to New Iberia. You know, those sweet little girls from South Louisiana really have a magnet. They would draw you back. So, I was promised, and so, I had to come back here [to New Iberia]. In that uniform, I could leave LSU and get back to New Iberia as fast as if I was driving a car. You could go anywhere with your uniform. If you were a young man and neatly dressed, they would pick you up. People trusted each other. I did a lot of traveling in that uniform, and everybody picked you up. That was good. I remember that.

I lived in the stadium on the third floor. My roommates were two boys from New Orleans, so I had a hard time at the beginning. Nice boys, but they were always kidding us about being country bumpkins and Cajuns and so forth.

We all had our pictures of our girlfriends on the wall. You would come back, and there would be a note pasted on your girlfriend, something about "must be related to the swine family," or something like that. So, [my roommate from New Orleans] used to do that, and he had a picture of his girl on the wall. So, I would reciprocate. One day he comes back from a visit to New Orleans, and he is all grins. I said, "What's the matter?" He says, you know, "I was talking to my girlfriend, and she tells me she's your girlfriend's second cousin." [laughs] And he's been saying all those derogatory things, you know, about her. It was a good joke.

About thirty-five years later, I had retired and was coming through New Orleans. I said, "I got to look this boy up." So, I looked in the telephone book and found his name. I stopped in, and we had a big visit, laughed a bit. He never did marry that girl; I married mine, but, he didn't marry his. I told him he couldn't qualify.

Hebert: Did [the upperclassmen] use brooms as paddles on you?

Segura: They did worse than that. They would take a coat hanger and put a question mark on you. Make you bend over, catch hold your ankles, and then hit you in a very embarrassing place. But I think all of those things, even though I didn't like them and don't approve of them, they prepared you and hardened you for life after that. You can take almost anything. You have to learn how, sometimes, to hold your feelings, especially in the military, you know. There's always somebody above you in the military, and you can't get revenge against somebody that's got authority over you.

Aubrey Williams
Class of 1947

Pleasants: How did you meet your wife?

Williams: At the Sigma Chi house there was an annual dance. I saw this young woman dancing with a fraternity brother of mine. I only saw her from the back, but I thought I had met her and knew her. So, I went and tapped my fraternity brother on the back and broke in. This gal turned around, and I realized I had never met her before in my life. So, that's how we met. Then, we started dating.

Pleasants: And when did you get married?

Williams: In 1943, just before I went in the army. There was a girl named Mary Carolyn Bennett, who was the editor of the *Daily Reveille*.

She was the editor, and I was campus editor. My wife was one of the few girls back in those days who had an automobile. She had a green Mercury convertible. One of the exciting things in my life was that she would pull-up outside the stadium and honk the horn, and I would see her from the window in my room. I'd march down, and I'd be the envy of everyone on campus because I had this beautiful young woman picking me up in a Mercury convertible.

One day, we were riding around with Mary Carolyn Bennett. I was about to go into the army and Mary Carolyn Bennett says, "Why don't you two guys get married?" Well, I knew I wanted to get married, but I thought I was going to go off and get killed. So, I thought this was a bad idea. But at any rate, we were riding around, and all of a sudden my wife, Betty, wanted to get married.

I didn't know how to get married. It was a Saturday, and we drove over to a place called Magnolia, Mississippi. There was a sign for a church of a certain minister so we went to him and asked him if we could get married. He said, "First you have to get a license." He said, "I'll take you downtown, and I'll get the clerk to open up and give you a license because I think you young people need to get married." So, we went downtown, got the license, and went back to the church. [The minister] said, "Young man, you need a shave." He loaned me his razor. I shaved.

I remember walking down the aisle of the church, shaking all over, thinking, "God, I'm too young to get married." But at any rate, [we] got married [laughs]. That's how I got married. Nothing formal about it at all.

Nina Nichols Pugh
Class of 1945

Campbell: Why did you choose to attend LSU?

Pugh: It was the obvious thing to do. Most people in Baton Rouge went to LSU. I don't know that I ever gave it much thought, and Mamma didn't particularly push Newcomb. Everybody knew LSU was a heap better school than the University of Mississippi, where others in my family have gone to school. Then, World War II came along, you see. My years at LSU exactly parallel those of World War II. I entered in '41, Pearl Harbor year, and I graduated in '45, which was when the war was over. The war was building before I went there. The United States was increasingly involved and chaos was building.

We really didn't think of going off to school. I can't remember having friends who went off. I think we had a couple of girls whose parents sent them to a girls' school somewhere for a year. You went from Baton Rouge High to LSU. That was just the thing to do.

Campbell: What was your first day like on campus? What are some of the memories you have of entering as a freshman?

Pugh: I can't remember anything much, but registration was a big deal. You didn't pre-register. You didn't do anything "pre." I came up for rush week; I believe rush week and registration were all at the same time. We were on the eve of World War II which made a tremendous difference in college life. People were talking about going off to war. This was before Pearl Harbor.

I shall never forget it. It happened to be December the seventh, which was my mother's birthday, and Mama always contended, you know, why did they have to ruin her birthday like that? But, at any rate, it was a Sunday, and we were off at the old Boy Scout camp, way out from town, at a Chi Omega-Kappa Sig party — way out at the old Camp Istrouma. Somebody in a car must have had the radio turned on and heard, "War!" Somebody heard it and ran and said, you know, "War! War!" Of course it had been building up all this time. And so, without any decision-making, people just immediately got in cars and flocked back to the campus. I guess we still were with our dates, but they must have taken the girls to the dormitories.

The men, *the boys*, they were kids — we were sixteen when we entered LSU — they all converged on the president's house, which was on the campus. You know which one that is? It's the building on the side street by the Faculty Club, across from the Union. Campbell B. Hodges, who was president then, was a general, a Louisianian and a

1943 Gumbo, pages 6-7

former Tiger, but a West Pointer and a military man. All the boys, everybody was just stunned. I mean, just as you'd expect, it was stunned silence, and the boys all converged there.

They all marched over to see the general — what to do? Everybody wanted to rush off to war. The general, General Hodges — a very, very fine man — he said no, they could best serve their country by going back and studying. He tried to calm them down and that sort of thing. But I shall never forget it, I mean, there is no way that I can tell you the emotion involved in all of this. Because of course, it meant a complete new way of life for everybody, particularly the boys. Some boys left and went off to war — volunteered. Many stayed to get more military training. Well then, they were drafted — at eighteen they were drafted, you see.

The high upperclassmen, who were maybe going to be commissioned, stayed on because they would be commissioned as officers when they graduated. They had an accelerated program so they'd graduate early, and I think we must have very soon gone on the quarter system to accelerate graduation at that time. But, everything changed. I think, as I see it, I had one good year of college, one good typical collegiate year. After that, the boys were leaving constantly. The mood was different.

After my freshman year, the war effort took over. You did not celebrate and socialize as much. Everything was scaled towards the war effort. It was unpatriotic to spend money on decorations for dances or anything like that, you know. Everything was scaled back. And then, the boys were always leaving.

Mary Frey Eaton
Class of 1947

Eaton: The day of Pearl Harbor, the Chi Omegas and the Kappa Sigs had a party together [at] Camp Istrouma, which was the boy scout camp. You could rent it for a day, and we just had an all day picnic out there. We didn't have dates. All the girls went, and all the boys went.

I remember calling home and asking Daddy [Dean Fred Frey] if I could take our car, and he said "Yes." He was going to be working in the yard that day. He came out to the campus, and I can remember running out to the car. I never had seen him look like that. He looked sort of gray and was listening to the radio. He said, "The Japanese have bombed Pearl Harbor." I had no concept of what that meant. I didn't know what Pearl Harbor was. I was kind of like, "So?" You know. But he understood. I never have forgotten that expression on his face. It was just very grave and distressed.

Chapter Three

Pearl Harbor: The War Begins

The Japanese attack on Pearl Harbor was a defining moment for the American people. For over two years the administration of Franklin Roosevelt had been waging a two-front "war" on the Axis powers. At the outset of the conflict in Europe, FDR's earnest hope had been that the United States could remain at peace, although he considered Nazi Germany a significant potential threat to the security of the Western Hemisphere and persuaded Congress to revise the Neutrality Law to permit the sale of weapons to the Allies on a cash-and-carry basis. The Wehrmacht's stunning conquest of Western Europe in the spring of 1940 convinced the White House that the Third Reich represented an urgent threat to the vital interests of the United States. As a result, Roosevelt and his advisors crafted a "Germany-first" strategy that involved a wide array of public and behind-the-scenes measures designed to help bring about the destruction of the Hitler regime. With the signing into law of the Lend-Lease Act in March 1941, FDR had gained a potent weapon. Having declared his goal to be the transformation of the United States into an "arsenal of democracy," he had used his authority under that historic law to spur domestic production and accelerate delivery of military supplies to beleaguered Great Britain.

American neutrality by this time was a fiction, and it became increasingly so as 1941 wore on. While American and British military planners secretly discussed a joint effort on the European continent against the Wehrmacht, Roosevelt told the nation that Germany was bent on world conquest and proclaimed an unlimited national emergency. To assist British convoys the chief executive ordered aggressive patrolling by the American navy in the Atlantic and dispatched troops to occupy Greenland and Iceland to forestall any German intrusion. The result of the administration's policy was an undeclared naval war with the Reich. FDR took the gloves off when he announced in September that he had issued shoot-on-sight orders to American warships that encountered Axis vessels in the hemispheric neutrality zone. Following a clash between a U-boat and an American destroyer in November, Roosevelt got Congress to repeal the Neutrality Law altogether and began arming merchant ships heading for the European war zone. By December 1941, the United States seemingly was on the verge of formal war with the Third Reich.

By definition, the Germany-first strategy meant that Roosevelt and his counselors considered Japan to be of secondary significance as a strategic threat. The Philippines and the Hawaiian Islands, along with Midway, Guam, and Wake, did give the United States a stake in the peace and security of the Central and South Pacific, but Japan was waging war against China on the Asian mainland, where America had no real interests, economic or otherwise. The Pacific Ocean, furthermore, is vastly wider than the Atlantic, so German submarine pens on Europe's Atlantic frontier had one meaning for American strategists, while Japanese bombing raids on Chunking had quite another. From the standpoint of Realpolitik, therefore, the logical course for Washington was to avoid a clash with Tokyo. As Roosevelt confided to a cabinet member in mid-1941, "it is terribly important for the control of the Atlantic for us to help keep peace in the Pacific."[1] But Japan's brutal aggression in China, images of which had reached millions of Americans through newsreels since the 1930s, aroused public opinion in the United States to a degree incommensurate with the actual threat posed by Japan. The effects of Japan's aggressive foreign policy, belligerent propaganda, and battlefield conduct spilled over into the American political arena and promoted divisions within the Roosevelt administration itself, making any compromise with Tokyo extremely difficult. Race, culture, moralistic considerations, and mutual ignorance and suspicion ended up diverting Roosevelt's policy from the course of cold calculation.

The decisive moment came in July 1941 when, in response to Tokyo's decision to move troops into southern Indo-China, FDR froze Japanese assets in the United States, a step that resulted in an embargo on the sale of oil to that country. With stocks dwindling and Japan's major source of oil imports now closed, strategists in Tokyo made the fateful decision to seize the petroleum-rich Dutch East Indies — even if it meant war with the United States and Great Britain. While special Japanese envoys endeavored futilely to reach a political settlement in Washington that would obviate military action, the Japanese navy made preparations for the day that, in American eyes, would indeed forever "live in infamy."

Few Americans could have been unaware of the general crisis facing the nation in 1941. Newspaper headlines, radio news programs, and newsreels had kept the deterioration of relations with the Axis firmly in the public mind. FDR had made a consistent effort to mobilize national opinion for the crusade he increasingly thought inevitable. With his "Four Freedoms" speech in January, the national emergency address in May, and his widely publicized meeting in August with Winston Churchill off Newfoundland where they proclaimed the "Atlantic Charter," he had defined for the nation the momentous issues at stake. Still, the Japanese attack on Pearl Harbor on December 7 — part of a simultaneous offensive that included the Philippines and other American-owned islands as targets and that sought to neutralize American and British naval and air power in the Pacific — was a profound shock to the American people. Stunned, disbelieving, angry, many unsure about just where Pearl Harbor was, Americans reacted swiftly, stirred by FDR's historic war message to Congress. "No matter how long it may take us to overcome this premeditated invasion," he solemnly vowed, "the

American people in their righteous might will win through to absolute victory." When Hitler declared war on the United States on December 11, the war became a global one.

As the shock waves of Pearl Harbor rolled across the country, Americans rolled up their sleeves and prepared to wage total war. What took place in Louisiana was a microcosm of what occurred on a national scale. Simply put, the citizenry wanted action. In New Orleans, a crowd of several hundred demonstrated outside the Japanese consulate, booing as consular officials burned papers; local police intervened to stop further destruction and seized what documents they could. On the Louisiana State University campus, "several thousand" students marched to the residence of Major General Campbell R. Hodges, president of the university, on the night of December 7. "Our navy has been prepared for some time to blow the Japanese navy out of the water," Hodges told the crowd, "and now we have the chance." Everywhere young men rushed to army and navy recruiting stations when they opened on Monday. "Four times as many applicants as usual have come to the office," the head of the Naval Recruiting Office in Baton Rouge told the press on December 8. "We can't take care of them we're so busy."[2]

The arrival in Baton Rouge and New Orleans of army troops from Camp Claiborne the day after Pearl Harbor to guard key installations focused attention on the potential problem of fifth-columnists, and officials throughout the state took steps to meet the perceived challenge. Sheriff Newman de Bretton announced in Baton Rouge on December 9 that ten companies, with secret membership and each led by a member of the American Legion, were being organized in the city. "The men will be well equipped and qualified for their duties, which will be to get information concerning subversive activities and other suspicious acts," he explained. "There will be a secret office set up. Only the membership of the companies will have the telephone number and reports will be made night and day."[3] FBI agents, meanwhile, were busy rounding up twenty-one aliens, the majority of whom were Germans from the New Orleans area. J. Ellis Clegg, the Bureau's special agent in Louisiana, urged the public to be "constantly on the alert" and to serve as "eyes and ears" for the FBI. In large towns and small, there was applause for the call for special vigilance. "There is no room in this parish for a man or woman unsympathetic with the American plan of liberty and freedom," the *Bunkie Record* bluntly proclaimed. "If you locate such a rat, come to this office and we will supply you with the necessary information to get action." President Hodges of LSU summed up what was probably general opinion. "My only regret about this war," he affirmed on December 16, "is that saboteurs and fifth columnists are not given a punishment of quick and sudden death."[4]

Mobilization for general civil defense was intense. Governor Sam Jones on December 12 called for statewide registration of volunteers, and the citizens of Louisiana responded. The spirit of residents of New Orleans seems to have been typical. Turned down for being too old, an elderly man was leaving a civil defense volunteer office when he spotted a sign urging people to register. He wondered why he couldn't at least walk up and down the street carrying the sign. "My grandson is in service and I don't want him to be ashamed of me doing nothing," one woman explained as she volunteered. It was common for office workers to show up offering to serve in their off hours, and one young woman even wanted to help organize "guerrilla bands of sharp-shooters." Another unusual bid came from a robust young man who "said he had a good baritone voice [and] asked if he could sing at war benefits."[5] In other parts of the state there was a similar rush to serve in some capacity. In Lake Charles, for example, some 3,000 persons volunteered within a week of the Japanese attack, while in Morgan City "hundreds" of people lined up at voting precincts to become what Governor Jones called "a warrior for victory in Louisiana."[6]

Fear of air attacks drove much of the initial civil defense fervor. Curtis Mitchener, defense director for Baton Rouge, quickly worked out a provisional air-raid warning system for the capital based on use of sirens on police vehicles, ambulances, and fire trucks. The press on December 13 carried his simple advice to residents in case of air attack: "When bombs fall, lie down, whether at home or outside." City authorities mobilized school officials to implant a program of drills and safety measures in public schools. Chief Bogan, calling for several hundred volunteers for fire crews, warned people to clean out their attics in case the enemy dropped small thermite bombs.[7] Mayor J. Maxime Roy in Lafayette echoed Bogan, promising to organize an effective fire-fighting force. "It may mean the difference between a city saved from fires caused by bombing attacks, and a city lost because of inadequate manpower to handle the situation," he said.[8]

And so it was that Louisiana, like the other forty-seven states, prepared to go to war. Gone was the national indecision of the previous two years. Pearl Harbor had shaken many Americans out of their complacency, welding an outraged population into a cohesive whole. Japanese leaders had completely misread the American people and their potential for self-sacrifice and ferocious determination — and never was the Japanese high command more misguided than in its calculation that the United States would accept a compromise peace after suffering military setbacks.

Robert LeBlanc

December the seventh, 1941, I was on the Indian Mounds listening to a portable radio with a group [of friends]. That's when we heard the news of Pearl Harbor being bombed. Naturally, the entire cadet corps reacted, knowing they were going to be called, and it made them very patriotic. They wouldn't let us [leave immediately]. They [the military] told those that were in advanced ROTC to stay in. They didn't want us until we got our commissions. In May, we graduated and went to active duty.

Steve Chappuis

I had come back from Hawaii and was at a station in Arizona called Fort Huachuca. Well, as Roosevelt said, [it was] an act of "infamy." I think everybody else felt the same way, particularly when all the casualties were announced. It certainly set the stage for the army to begin a real expansion program, and I think a lot of people were very enthusiastic about what the future held.

Celine Ganel

Oh yes, I remember exactly where I was. It was a Sunday, and I was supposed to go to a sodality meeting at the Catholic school right across the street from where I lived. I never did get to the sodality meeting. It was a shock. I guess we should have foreseen something like it, but we didn't. We heard it on the radio. There weren't any televisions; we heard it on the radio. I think that Sunday afternoon, everybody knew about it in no time at all. It was just, as I say, it was a shock.

Charles Titkemeyer

I was sitting there one Sunday afternoon studying, and suddenly, the radio began to blubber saying that the Japanese have attacked Pearl Harbor. That was on December 7. I lasted just until the end of the semester which was in January. I got out of Purdue on about January the 14th, and on the 16th, I was going hut-to, hip-ho in the air force.

Wilbur Joffrion

I was in high school. In fact, I was working at the drugstore, Avenue Drugstore, on that Sunday morning when the attack on Pearl Harbor [occurred]. I was a senior in high school, and I never will forget it. It was mid to late morning when we got word about the attack, and of course, it surprised all of us. I worked the rest of the day and went to school the next day. It was the only time I remember during school that our teacher let us bring in and use the radio. I heard the famous speech by President Roosevelt in which he asked for war against Japan and said, "This is a day that will live in infamy." A very famous radio address of his.

I remember in detail Mrs. Longmeyer's trigonometry class, one of our math classes, when we listened to this. A few days after that, we organized a home guard at Bolton [High School]. They did not have ROTC in high school, but several of us went to see the principal.

I was very interested in the military even in those days, even though I was too young to be in the military. Alexandria was the base location of all these camps that came up: Camp Livingston, Camp Beauregard, Camp Claiborne and Camp Polk. There were literally hundreds of thousands of troops there. We went to see the principal and wanted to organize the home guard, and he said that would be fine. So, we did organize a little home guard and started drilling. In fact, we went up on top of the school building, which was flat, and we were looking for Japanese airplanes. You know, there was a real fright in the country then about the Japanese. That's when they moved the Rose Bowl from the West Coast inland and when they transplanted all the Japanese

Americans. We wanted to be sure there were no Japanese airplanes coming into that area.

Dupuy Anderson

December '41, Pearl Harbor. I was in church at Fisk University and an announcement went out: "All students report to the artist's school auditorium immediately." We went over there, and by the time we got there, they started issuing papers for us to sign. We are in the army now. Everything was prepared and ready to go. So, that made me think they knew something was going to happen. After we signed up, it was about two or three months before we [went into an] army training program. We all left and went to Fort Benning [Georgia] for our exam, to be issued clothing, and everything.

Anthony Palumbo

We were still at Camp Dix, New Jersey, [in the Civilian Conservation Corps] on December 7, 1941. We were out that day working on an old log cabin that was supposed to belong to our landlord, and we got back that night and some one said, "Anthony, have you heard the news of Pearl Harbor being bombed?" I knew about Pearl Harbor being a big navy base; I didn't know that they had been attacked by the Japanese. I remember [FDR's speech]; I can hear it just as clearly as I was there: "Yesterday, the day that will live in infamy."

Robert Barrow

I was in Yazoo City when I heard about [Pearl Harbor]. I think anger was the number one reaction that most Americans demonstrated

— not at any of our officials, but at the dastardly act. It clearly left the impression on everyone that there be no doubts, and we entered [the war]. That's one thing about Pearl Harbor: there was no debate.

The thing about Pearl Harbor, it probably worked more to the disadvantage of the Japanese than any other single thing. That single act, on the face of it, seemed so dastardly, so beyond what one expects in the way of how you start a war, that it awakened the whole country to just a fever pitch of response. Unlike one in which you would debate whether you go to war or not — the longer that lasted, the more you had those who said "no" and those who said "yes" and some in between. But, Pearl Harbor, that single act, I would say, compelled ninety percent, hundred percent, I don't know, certainly an overwhelming majority of Americans to be fully committed to dealing with the problem.

I probably didn't think it at the time, but had the Japanese not done Pearl Harbor, I doubt that we would have gone to war. We would have come closer and closer. We would have been more supportive, even to the point of, perhaps, being dragged into it somehow. There was just a large segment of the population that didn't think we should have been in the war at all. We weren't too far removed from World War I, with all of its horrors, a lot of which we didn't experience ourselves to the degree that the Germans, the French, the English and a number of their colonials and people like that did.

Louie Reinberg

I was at Pearl Harbor. I was in the harbor. I was with one of the defense battalions that had been sent back from Midway. So, I'll never forget there was a friend of ours came over one night visiting my wife and myself, and we had our new baby. This person made a remark, "Tomorrow would be a real good day to start a war, wouldn't it?" You know how prophetic she was. [The next day] my wife mentioned to me,

"I wonder where all that rumbling is coming from." I says, "It's nothing. It's just the navy doing target practice." She said, "On a Sunday?" I said, "Well, they got to be out at sea. What the heck's the difference?" We were all waiting for something to happen, you know.

There was a fellow, a neighbor of ours, he'd gone to church that Sunday morning. His mother came over, and that's the first time we knew the war was on: "They've shelled Pearl Harbor, and I don't know where Johnny is!" So, I said, "Well, I'll go get Johnny." I got in the car and went down about two blocks, and there he was walking along. I brought him home. About that time the telephone rang, and my friend from longstanding said that the island was under attack. He said, "I haven't got time to talk to you. You listen to the radio." So, my wife turned on the radio, and sure enough, we heard. The phone rang again, and it was a real good friend of mine whom I've stayed in touch with for years, and he said, "You bring Carrie and the baby up here and stay with Marian. You and I will go out to our base in your car." I wouldn't leave Carrie down on the beach or anything like that. So, I went to Pearl with him. We got out there, and things were in a chaotic state. It was just after the bombing and sinking of the ships. There was a lot of fire and smoke.

I was told to take my battery and go up to what they call a fuel depot and secure it. I had never been up there before. By the time I got up there it was dark, and I didn't know what was what. So, I fumbled around there, and we finally made out what it was we were supposed to do. [Later,] they put me on a telephone watch with several other people that I knew. That's the way I spent about the first few days of the war, in the command center answering phones and stuff, then relaying messages.

Murray Hawkins

[I was a civilian employee at Pearl Harbor and was aboard a launch off Ford Island when the first explosion sounded.] I said, "That must be a gasoline explosion." The coxswain of the boat says, "Hell, no gasoline explosion, them's Japs." I looked up and saw airplanes over there with that orange spot on their wings, and I'm ashamed to say, I didn't know that was the Japanese emblem at that time. Then, all hell broke loose. We were right by Ten-ten Dock where the *Pennsylvania*, the *Cassin* and the *Downes* were later bombed, and we continued on out toward our operation in West Lock. We got in the main channel heading out of Pearl Harbor, and there were destroyers and cruisers trying to get out. The Japanese were evidently trying to sink a ship in the harbor entrance, which would have been a terrible thing.

The bombs were pretty heavy around there. So, we put ashore and got [inside] some huge cast iron sewer pipes. I guess they were about an inch thick and five feet in diameter, and then the bombs started dropping all around us. So, the rest got back in the boat and went on out. A friend of mine and I went on back into the harbor. We went about a block, then ran into a jeep with a Marine officer in it, and we asked him what we could do. He said, "Come with me." He took us to an ammunition warehouse where they were unloading the ammunition, lest it be bombed, and we spent the rest of the morning there. That was the main part of the attack.

Later on, in the afternoon, [I went] out on the docks and saw some thousand sailors laid out there that had been killed in the attack. It was a pretty dreadful thing to see.

1. FDR, quoted in Eric Larrabee, *Commander in Chief: Franklin Delano Roosevelt, His Lieutenants & Their War* (New York, 1987), p. 66.

2. *Baton Rouge State Times*, 12 Dec. 1941, pp. 1, 12.

3. *Baton Rouge State Times*, 9 Dec. 1941, p. 1.

4. *Lafayette Daily Advertiser*, 10 Dec. 1941, p. 1; editorial: "Don't Lose Your Head," *Bunkie Record*, 12 Dec. 1941; *Baton Rouge State Times*, 16 Dec. 1941, p. 3.

5. *Baton Rouge State Times*, 15 Dec. 1941, p. 1, 12 Dec. 1941, p. 12-B.

6. *Lake Charles American Press*, 13 Dec. 1941, p. 2; *Morgan City Review*, 19 Dec. 1941, p. 1; Sam Jones, quoted in *Baton Rouge State Times*, 15 Dec. 1941, p. 1.

7. *Baton Rouge State Times*, 13 Dec. 1941, p. 7, 16 Dec. 1941, p. 7

8. *Lafayette Daily Advertiser*, 11 Dec. 1941, p. 2.

"Come hyah boys! Woo woo."
Celine Ganel, Margaret Woods, Mary Jane Larson
(Philadelphia, 1944)

Chapter Four

Stateside: Preparing for War

The international crisis of the late 1930s found the United States ill-prepared for the task of national defense. A massive drawdown at the end of World War I had left the army with little but the shell of an effective fighting force, and successive budget cuts in the 1920s had hurt not only recruitment, but training, the acquisition of equipment, and research and development. "The army as a team," Chief of Staff George Marshall recalled of that period, "was gradually being starved into a condition almost comparable to its pre-Spanish American War condition."[1] The stock market crash and onset of the Depression dramatically reinforced the resurgent isolationism of the United States and augured ill for the armed forces. When Franklin Roosevelt took office, the army ranked seventeenth in the world in size. Although the National Defense Act of 1920 had authorized a peacetime strength of 280,000 men, its average level during 1925-1935 was less than half of that. Under the pressure of international events, army budgets improved slightly in the late 1930s, but when war broke out in Europe its troop strength stood at 174,000, and its world ranking had dropped to nineteenth, "ahead of Bulgaria but just behind Portugal."[2] The navy, considered the country's first line of defense, fared somewhat better in budgetary terms and remained world class in the 1930s. However, late in the decade its personnel numbered only 132,000 (including 18,000 marines), and the fleet, at least as far as destroyers and submarines were concerned, was largely overage.

When Marshall became chief of staff in the summer of 1939, he immediately launched an innovative program to reorganize and modernize the army from top to bottom. The swift pace of events in Europe after the Wehrmacht's invasion of Poland in September 1939 and Japan's redoubled efforts to subjugate China provided American military leaders with valuable lessons and aided Marshall in his efforts, although isolationist sentiment still dominated Congress. It was the Blitzkrieg against the Low Countries and France in the spring of 1940 that finally galvanized legislators. Congress now voted the largest peacetime military budgets in United States history to that point, and FDR, after the fall of France, boldly announced the government's intention to build a two-ocean navy and the largest air force in the world. The army received more funds in 1940 than it had over the previous two decades, and Marshall and his advisors could set to work in earnest. Before Pearl Harbor his accomplishments would be many, among them: the creation of the first American armored divisions and airborne units; extensive motorization of the army; strenuous efforts both to expand and improve the officer corps, in part through the creation early in 1941 of a system of officer candidate schools; and the execution of large-scale maneuvers, including those in Louisiana in May 1940 and September 1941, the latter being the largest the army had ever held. "Throughout the Louisiana affair the men bore the hardships in great shape," Marshall wrote privately following the 1941 exercise. "It was very impressive to find a maneuver covering practically an entire State."[3]

Passage of the Selective Training and Service Act in September 1940 set the stage for dramatic manpower expansion. The law authorized the call-up of nearly a million men for one year of service and federalized the National Guard. On October 16, nationwide registration occurred, and by the end of the day 16,000,000 men had registered. Starting in November, the 6,500 draft boards across the country began the job of calling up single males, all designated for service in the army since the navy, marines, and coast guard insisted on recruiting their personnel. The War Department initially enforced its standards: draftees could not be less than 5' tall or over 6'6"; they had to weigh a minimum of 105 pounds; possess at least a fourth-grade education; and had to speak English. The average inductee was slightly taller and heavier than the doughboy of World War I, and he had a different name: GI. The law gave special protection to African Americans, who could not be drafted in numbers disproportionate to their percentage of the nation's population, at the time less than 11 percent. The minimum age for a draftee was then twenty, but local boards usually did not dip below age twenty-three. The navy and Marine Corps, on the other hand, recruited freely from men as young as eighteen.

Institution of the draft and federalization of the guard created an immediate need for training facilities. The result was a crash building program, especially in the South where weather was better suited to year-round training. Between the first call-up in November 1940 and mid-1942, nearly fifty new camps appeared. Camp Claiborne in Louisiana, home of the 82nd Division, which became the army's first airborne division in the spring of 1942, was one of them. By the end of the war, the army would be utilizing more than 240 training centers in the continental United States; of the major ones, i.e., those handling 50,000 troops or more, only one (Fort Lewis) was located outside the South.

By mid-1941, the strength of the army stood at 1.5 million officers and men, almost a nine-fold increase since the outbreak of the European war. The unique experience of a peacetime draft and the scale of the army's expansion had an enormous impact on American life, affecting not only individual lives, but local economies and even popular culture. While radio stations across the country played the new novelty song *This is the Army, Mr. Jones,* Paramount Pictures quickly capitalized on national discussion of Selective Service to produce a film, *Caught in the Draft,* starring radio and screen personality Bob Hope, which was released in May 1941. Box office favorites Bud Abbott and Lou Costello also played in three films in 1940-1941, *Buck Privates, Keep `Em Flying* and *In the Navy,* dealing with the theme of hapless civilians trying to adjust to the shock of military experience. But the subject was not a laughing matter for hundreds of thousands of young men and their families. When Congress in the summer of 1941 extended the term of service by a year and half, morale plummeted within the ranks, especially among National Guardsmen; the army contained the situation by granting early discharge to soldiers over twenty-eight years of age. A confidential investigation of the sources of discontent by a *New York Times* reporter, who had the full cooperation of the army, revealed that many men were not yet convinced of the necessity of their mission. "They compare it to a football team in training but without a schedule of games," the reporter wrote.[4] December 7 changed all that.

The pace of military preparations accelerated dramatically after Pearl Harbor. Although the number of volunteers for military duty rose abruptly, the overwhelming majority of the new soldiers were draftees. Within weeks of the Japanese attack they were arriving at reception centers or training camps at the rate of several thousand a day. Reflecting the gravity of the challenges facing the country, interesting changes occurred in 1942: the army started using live ammunition in basic training; the draft age dropped to eighteen; and a private's monthly pay jumped from $21 to $50.

The production of combat infantrymen was the main purpose of the army's assembly line. The navy and Marine Corps, of course, siphoned off part of the draft pool, and specialized branches of the army, such as the Army Air Forces, did likewise. One program popular with college students was the Army Special Training Program (ASTP), which allowed draftees who scored sufficiently high on the general classification test to continue their studies in fields of value to the armed services, such as medicine, engineering, and critical foreign languages. At the end of 1943, there were approximately 140,000 student-soldiers in the program. But from the beginning, the vast majority of the inductees were slotted for the infantry. The philosophy of General Leslie McNair, head of the Army Ground Forces, was that the traditional practice of separate training methods for the various combat arms was misguided and that all soldiers should receive the same basic training designed to accomplish one fundamental objective. "We must lust for battle; our object in life must be to kill; we must scheme and plan day and night to kill," he declared in a nationwide radio broadcast in 1942.[5] As the need for infantrymen rose progressively in 1943-1944, the government reluctantly took steps to broaden the draft pool. It waived education and language requirements, for example, to permit the induction of some 800,000 illiterates and aliens who were then taught to read and write English by the army. Fatherhood after mid-1943 no longer was a shield against conscription; by then the draft boards were rapidly exhausting the supply of single men and had no option but to call up fathers, who constituted more than half the men being drafted by the spring of 1944. The ASTP also suffered gradual reductions until the army abandoned it altogether late in the conflict.

Socially, the wartime armed forces mirrored American society at large, its strengths and virtues — and its defects. The treatment of black GIs, for example, reflected the segregationist attitudes that prevailed in much of the country. From Marshall and Secretary of War Henry Stimson down, the dominant sentiment among military leaders was that African Americans did not make good fighting men. The army carefully segregated black troops, placed white officers in command of black units, and refused to permit any African American from holding a rank higher than a white officer in the same unit. By the spring of 1943, of the slightly more than 500,000 blacks in the army, less than 16 percent had been sent overseas because of the objections of theater commanders. The overwhelming majority of black soldiers served in support units. The single African American division employed in combat did not, in fact, do well, but the conclusion of a post-mortem conducted by the army itself was that the problem had been one of morale caused by segregation. The all-black 99th Pursuit Squadron, on the other hand, performed with gallantry and efficiency, as did various smaller black infantry units. The war ultimately did result in progress toward integration of the armed services: by the end of the conflict, the army had allowed blacks into combat and ordered the desegregation of training camps; the navy had integrated more than a score of ships; and the Coast Guard had commissioned hundreds of black officers.

American women made an enormous contribution to victory in World War II. The "Rosie-the-Riveters," whose numbers ran into the millions, gained fame for their vital role in defense production, but thousands of women also performed important tasks for the military through service in auxiliary groups. Had it not been for Pearl Harbor, women probably would not have been given the opportunity. A bill introduced in Congress in the spring of 1941, partly through the influence of Eleanor Roosevelt, the president's wife, called for the creation of the Women's Auxiliary Army Corps (WAAC), but the army initially had little enthusiasm for the project and congressional leaders declined to act on the bill until after the Japanese attack. As defined by the law of May 1942, the WAAC was not part of the army, but the national emergency at least had given women a chance to prove themselves capable of a more direct role in national defense. Tens of thousands took up the challenge, and a year after Pearl Harbor enlistments stood at 60,000. The idea of women's service now accepted, Congress, with Marshall's support, in mid-1943 created the Women's

Army Corps (WAC) as a formal part of the army attached to the General Staff. Members of the WAAC transferred en masse to the new organization, and by 1945 the WAC had a force of 100,000. WACs performed clerical tasks or became technicians of various kinds; almost half of them served in the Army Air Force and more than 15,000 WACs would see duty overseas.

Robert Barrow

Barrow: The only chance that you had of visualizing the war was if you went to the movies. [There were] black and white films in 1940 of the U.S. Army getting ready to build up. Soldiers [were] drilling with wooden rifles and maneuvers in which there were no tanks. But there would be a big truck [that would] come by with a big sign hanging on the side, "T-A-N-K." There was a double-spread page in the Baton Rouge *Morning Advocate*, sometime in `42, showing a World War I marine in his tin hat and leggings jumping out of a trench, not a fox hole, with an 03 rifle. The caption said, "Join the Marine Corps, and we will have a rifle in your hand and a man to show you how to use it within forty-eight hours."

Jack Gremillion

Gremillion finished two years of ROTC training during the time that Troy Middleton was Commandant of Cadets at LSU. "That helped me a lot when I went into the army," he recalls. When he was drafted, Gremilllion acted quickly, "You knew your number; you knew you were going to get called within 30 to 40 days."

Gremillion: I tried to get in the navy. I wanted to do something that I knew a little about, and frankly, I didn't care about getting into infantry because they suffered the most casualties. But anyway, I tried to get into the navy. The induction office at that time was in the St. Charles Hotel in New Orleans. So, I had a friend who was in the induction center, and I went down to take the exam. The navy was looking for lawyers for intelligence work. That doesn't mean I'm intelligent, but they were looking for navy officers particularly in intelligence, not necessarily aviators.

I went down and took the exam, and this friend of mine said, "You look mighty good; you're going to make it." But then [I had] to take the [physical] exam, and you had to be at least five feet five. I was five feet four and a half. And hell, they turned me down on account of that.

Hebert: On account of a half an inch?

Gremillion: That's right. They turned me down. Of course, if I could've waited about another six months, they'd have gladly taken me because that's when [World War II] started escalating, and they needed men. They were waiving those little deficiencies.

And I said [to my friend], "Well let's ask them for a waiver." So, we went to see the admiral or whoever he was — the captain — and they refused; said that there were strict [rules], that the navy had to abide by.

This friend of mine had a scheme. He said, "Tell you what you do. You're staying in the hotel, aren't you?" I said, "Yes." He said, "Well, you go on up to your room, and you get in your bed tonight and get you two or three bricks and tie them around your feet and sleep with your feet out the end of the bed. And maybe we can stretch your legs long enough. [When] we open the office, you come down there, and I'll get you in [to see] the doctor and see if you have gained that half an inch so we can make it." He had been assured that if I could make the five-five they'd take me.

So, I went upstairs and my wife was with me, and I had a good friend — another friend of mine was a lawyer down there — he went and got some bricks and ropes. So I slept most of the night with my feet hanging out of the end of the bed praying that my legs would increase. So next morning, boy, I got up at eight o'clock. I went right to that office, and the doctor put me on the scale and everything, and I was five feet, four and three quarters inches.

I asked him, "Look, give me a waiver." But they still refused to do it. So, within a few days, I was drafted. I was sent to Camp Walters, Texas. It was an infantry training center.

I spent sixty days there and during that time, I was made a corporal. They called me in, and they said, "Now look, you've got a pretty good record. You're at the point now you're going to have to determine your choice of service." I couldn't go to the navy, and I couldn't qualify as an army pilot for some reason — I don't know — some ridiculous reason. So I said, "Well, I'll just go ahead and take the infantry." I said, "I've had two years in it, and it looks like I'm sort of stuck for all these numerous reasons." I went ahead and went to infantry training school.

[After I'd gone through infantry training and been promoted to first lieutenant,] my wife had a baby boy who we called Junior. I had a leave coming to me, about a twenty day leave, and I came back to Baton Rouge. While I was in Baton Rouge, I got a telegram to report back to my unit. Well, I knew what the hell that was. So, I went on back and when I got to camp, I didn't even have time to change my clothes. In fact, I left my leggings there.

I was taken out of the 106th and was put in this assignment for replacement officers. I was real glad of it because the poor 106th was mauled in the Battle of the Bulge.

John J. Capdevielle

After graduating from LSU, Capdevielle was commissioned as a second lieutenant and entered the United States Army in August, 1942. In his first assignment at Fort Bragg, North Carolina, Capdevielle trained new recruits.

Besch:　　　You said [while you were at Fort Bragg,] you had to teach recruits how to write?

Capdevielle:　That was one of the things I taught.

Besch:　　　Back in those days, people were not mobile. You lived in an area and probably would die in that area, unless something drastic happened. The war changed all of that. So, you had a different kind of recruit. Do you recall any peculiarities about [your] recruits?

Capdevielle:　Yes, we had a whole bunch [of recruits] out of the Appalachian area, and those were the ones that couldn't read or write. And they were just good old boys, and I would certainly have hated to be on the other end of a rifle from them because they were good shots. In drilling, you had to try to teach them which was their left foot and to step off on that left foot. We didn't even have cannons in these regimental batteries because we were trying to make soldiers out of them first. [We had to teach] them to march, wear a uniform properly, and get their hygiene up to snuff, and [we] had about six weeks to get it done in. Then, they shipped out somewhere else for more training.

　　　You had all kinds of people in there. Some of those people, we wondered why they were ever sent in. They were drafted, but I mean, they were cripples. People who had deformed limbs that impaired their walking or impaired their doing something with their hands, but they were sent in.

　　　We were trying to keep the payroll. If you [were] paid, you had to sign against the payroll that you had received this pay. And if you couldn't sign your name, you had to have two witnesses to your "X."

Well, that made three people fooling around with that payroll. I mean it took all day to pay a battery off. So, we worked on getting everyone to where they could sign their name, or draw it, not really sign it, they drew it. I would ask a fellow, "What's your name? Give me your dog tag." And I'd take it off of his dog tag, and if his name was "Everett Besch," well, I'd write it down at the top of the piece paper. I'd give him a pencil, and I'd say, "Now, practice writing your name just like I wrote it." And that's what they'd do.

Aubrey Williams

When asked if he volunteered for service in the army, Williams replies, "I enlisted in the army when I became a freshman at LSU. As a member of the ROTC you were in the Reserve Officers Training Corps." Williams' unit was called to active duty in 1943.

Williams: I went to a camp in north Louisiana as a corporal for a month. And somehow, I offended the first sergeant and found myself assigned every other day to what was called the boiler room, right outside the mess hall. They made the food in these huge pots that you'd have to crawl inside to clean, and that's what I did. I had to get up at three o'clock in the morning and go clean pots. I got out of that and had to go to Fort Knox, to Officer Candidate School.

Pleasants: Why did you choose the tank corps?

Williams: Well, I hate to admit it, I thought it [was] something like the cavalry and [was] much more dashing than going into just a regular field artillery unit. I thought it was going to be like a mechanical horse of some sort. Of course, I was an idiot, not knowing what death traps tanks were at that point.

Pleasants: When you finished officer training school, what rank did you have, and where were you assigned?

Williams: I was a second lieutenant assigned to a place whose name actually was Battle Training, near Elizabethtown, Kentucky. It consisted of a headquarters, barracks, and big latrines out in the woods. I was put in charge of a platoon of draftees. Every two weeks, we'd live out there and be on maneuvers. [We had] a weekend in town then it would start over again with a new group.

In '43, I was twenty-one years old, and many of the men who were being drafted were much older than I, from all parts of the country. Even though I was just a young shavetail, these older men would come to me for advice on all sorts of personal problems just because I had on a gold bar and because I was in charge. It was amazing that they would trust me so much to confide in me.

I'm sure that the most important thing [I learned] was how to run a tank. When I was on maneuvers with these guys, I would be up in the turret and there would be four men down in the Sherman tank, [which were] medium tanks. There would be a driver and a gunner to his right and [one or] two other guys.

A lot of people don't understand how hazardous training is, how many soldiers and sailors and marines are killed every year in training. But you take a tank, weighing I don't know how many tons, and you start down a Kentucky hillside in that thing. If you hit a ravine or a ditch, that tank can roll over. Can you imagine a Sherman tank rolling end over end down a mountainside? By the time it gets to the bottom, there's not going to be anything in there but hamburger.

On a cold winter night, it's difficult to keep in communication, especially in those days. Just for me to communicate with the driver, from the top of the tank down to him, I sometimes had to climb down and kick him on the back and say, "Stop! Stop!" I remember one day, we were heading towards a river. I was in the lead tank, [and] we were heading right to a bank with a drop-off. I kept saying, "Stop!" But [the driver] couldn't hear me. [I] had to climb down and pull down on the levers myself. I said, "Open up the turret." He opened up the turret. The front of that tank was practically over the side of that river.

Sometimes you'd be in a trench with a guy, trying to teach him how to throw a grenade, and you'd say, "Okay, now you pull the pin." You'd do it first and then would say, "Don't release that spring until you throw it." And sometimes a guy would just freeze. He'd be so petrified, you'd have to take his hand and make him throw the damn thing. You didn't know if he was just going to drop it right between your feet.

It was hard, boring, dreary, and frightening work at times. I'm not trying to exaggerate. It's not like combat at all. You do it month after month after month and get a night in town every two weeks and then have to go back out and live in a barracks and share a community latrine with guys. Finally, I'd see these airplanes flying over, and I would think, "I'd like to be up there instead of down here in the mud and the dust." So, I kept trying to transfer out, but Colonel Steel would block all such letters.

One day I noticed on the bulletin board that you could write directly to the commanding general if you would volunteer to be a liaison pilot. So, I wrote. I was so anxious to get out, and I was scared to write to the commanding general and skip channels, but anyway I did. Two weeks later, I was in Sheppard [Air Force Base], Texas, going to flight school. So, that's how I got out of Battle Training, [Kentucky].

Louie Reinberg

"Well, I'll tell you, lady, when I graduated in '35, careers were not very promising," Reinberg tells interviewer Mary Hebert. "And the marines looked like a pretty good job to me, if I could make it." Reinberg recalls that there were only 1,500 officers and 15,000 men in the marines when he enlisted.

Reinberg: I went in the service right after graduating from LSU and was given a commission in September of 1935.

Hebert: What was your training like?

Reinberg: Well, I went to the basic school, the Marine Corps school of indoctrination, or whatever you want to call it. We had classroom instruction in naval gunnery, courts and boards, and administration and things like that.

After I'd finished the basic school, I was sent to sea. I went aboard the United States *Mississippi*, a battleship. And you talk about a lost soul. Well, I wouldn't admit it, but I was. [I went] all over the Pacific, a junior marine officer on the ship — Hawaii and Bremerton, Washington.

Most of our work was for naval gunnery, [but I did some work for] naval courts and boards — when we court martialed. In days gone by, whenever a second lieutenant was appointed to a ship he was always a court martial officer. Later on, it was changed a little bit. I had several cases. None of them memorable.

On the battleships that I was on, we were on the secondary battery, [with] five inch, 51-guns which we'd call the broadside batteries. Later on, I was given a job as junior officer of the deck.

One morning I was waked up and informed I had to make a boat trip out to the landing. Well, our ship was way out. They used to have a landing at what they'd call Pecos Street Landing in Long Beach. I was the officer put on this fifty foot motor launch with a navy coxswain and engineer. We took off and went in to pick up sailors from liberty. When there were fog trips, they put an officer in. We got in, got a load, and here was a second lieutenant in charge of the boat. I had a whole bunch of old flea-bitten navy men in there, sailors, and we got started back to the ship.

It was foggy, and you couldn't see a hand in front of your face. We'd listen to the ship's bells. Four-one, four bells and then one was our ship, but there were some that sounded just like it. So, I wound up broadside to the aircraft carrier *Lexington*. [laughs] It was a big thing, and they told me, they said, "We're somewhere off to the right." So, we took off and finally made it back there. I'm sure those sailors never forgot that or forgave me, a marine losing my way.

Robert Barrow

When Barrow entered the military, he never thought of the consequences of going to war. He remembers feeling, instead, the way that many young people felt: "I'm going to do something. I'm going to be a part of something." He didn't know then that military service would become his life-long commitment.

Barrow: My [boot camp] experience was simply tough. Physical conditioning was emphasized, [but it was] not equal to what it is today. The emphasis was on learning how to drill, shoot, drill [as well as] close combat, that sort of thing. Many of the things that we have now and have had since World War II in our recruit training experience were missing. But the fundamentals have always been present. That is, to extract from the individual a total and complete commitment to something called the United States Marine Corps, to become real believers. There's no other way to achieve that as totally as what is done in the recruit training experience.

[When I started boot camp,] I had some vague understanding of what the service [would] be like, [but] you only get the full flavor of it if you become a part of it. It was very regimented, obviously, very disciplined, but fair. I liked it enormously from the very outset. So, I'm one who, in my subconscious and probably my conscious as well, wants discipline; I want to be in a regimented environment. Doesn't mean you can't be a free thinker and a lot of other things, but the routine, the commitment, the structure I found to be very appealing.

The only unusual thing that occurred to me in boot camp, maybe because of my ROTC experience, was that I was singled out by these two drill instructors, who, I might say as I look back on it, were good but a little bit laid back. Towards the last couple of weeks, they would call Barrow out to take the platoon to the evening meal or the noonday meal, which was not as simple as it sounds because the place was so crowded. As you drilled, marched your platoon to the vicinity of the chow hall, you had to be careful that you didn't bump into someone and you fitted into the space allocated to you for the purpose of getting lined up to go in and eat chow.

As a consequence of that when we graduated, I was kept there and made an assistant drill instructor. I had my senior staff sergeant named Mann, who was of the old school, and he was my senior in every sense of the word. He taught me about how to be a drill instructor [and] more about the Marine Corps. I worked with him for some three or so platoons we brought through together. Great experience.

While I was serving as an assistant drill instructor at San Diego, a team of officers came out of the headquarters of the Marine Corps at Quantico to the depot. [They] spent several days in [San Diego] in which they interviewed prospects for Officer Candidate School, gave tests, and talked to people who knew the prospects. I was selected to go to Officer Candidate School.

[Quantico was] perhaps more difficult [than San Diego]. More was expected of you in terms of things like map reading, knowing tactics, knowing more weapons, knowing more about how to fire supporting weapons, how to control direct fires. And you were in somewhat faster company. We're talking about a lot of prospects who were, well, almost all were college graduates; I was one of the exceptions. They were all volunteers, all just first-class people. There were 236 in my class. I think all but a couple finished. The officer candidate class lasted about eight weeks.

I had six weeks of boot camp, a few months went by, I had eight weeks of officer candidate class followed immediately by ten weeks of reserve officer class. Now, all those are much shorter than what we would have today, but in the aggregate, I had become a pretty good fundamental, basic officer, if you will. I was an infantryman.

I should say that, as I've already indicated, that I had a love affair with the Marine Corps from the outset; this was what I wanted to do in my life. I don't think I consciously said, "I want to excel in officer candidate class and reserve officer class." But I was motivated to do well, the antithesis of my LSU experience. I found something I could believe in.

[After reserve officer class] I was ordered to the Naval Ammunition Depot at Belle Chasse, below New Orleans. Went there, and I found myself assigned to a small barracks, headed up by a long, tall, tough, infamous major. Infamous, in that he had enlisted in the Marine Corps around 1910 or '12 under the name Frank Kennedy. Some time after Vera Cruz, which he was in, he was given a field commission, and he had to reveal his true identity. He had enlisted under an assumed name. His name was Herbert Kimeland; he was German.

From early on the Marine Corps has always harbored people who were different from other folks. There may have been an ethnic difference; there may have been a background difference, but it could accommodate them. It could bring them in and they were every bit marine. They might have been just a little bit different. [Kimeland] was like that.

He was tough, but he was never going to go to war. This was his twilight tour. He retired in about 1944. He took me under his wing to teach me the fundamentals of what it's really like after you've graduated from all these schools. But I was not there very long. I was only there, oh, at most about three or four months. Interesting experience mostly because of him.

When I arrived at the barracks in New Orleans, most of the enlisted complement and those who arrived subsequently, were from the Pacific wars. [This meant] they had been wounded in Guadalcanal or they had malaria or if they came out of Samoa, elephantiasis, which was a disease that afflicted those who served in the Samoan Islands. That made it a little hard — to see folks who had come back and you still hadn't gone.

Ellen Bryan Moore

The Women's Army Corps (WAC), formed during World War II, offered one of the first opportunities for women to join the armed services in the United States. Moore, who taught school for several years in Baton Rouge prior to the war, joined the Women's Army Corps and soon became a WAC recruiter herself.

Moore: They said if more women would come into the service, they could do a better job at getting the men out that they needed. And so, I joined the service. In fact, I was the first woman from Baton Rouge to go into the Women's Army Corps with three other ladies from Louisiana. We were in one of the first six companies that went to Fort Des Moines, Iowa, for our initial training.

Hebert: Was there a recruiter that came to Louisiana?

Moore: Well, no, it was mostly talk at that time, but funny thing that you asked me that, that's what I ended up with, recruiting. My first assignment was recruiting to the home town of Oveta Culp Hobby, who was head of [the Women's Army Corps], Houston, Texas. Her husband had been governor there. So, I thought, well, that ought to be a good place to recruit. So, I did, and it was an experience of a lifetime.

I lived at the Rice Hotel, which was about two or three blocks from the recruiting office. We did have many times that we recruited at places when they [had] horses out, cowboys come to visit the city, and rodeos. So, it was an interesting period of time. And the hotel was wonderful. When any of the other [WAC] officers would come to visit with me, they could put up in my room, and it didn't cost them a cent.

Hebert: Were you the only woman recruiter in that area?

Moore: I was the only one at that time, and then, I had three other officers, later.

Hebert: Did you know Mrs. Hobby?

Moore: I did know Mrs. Hobby and dined several times in her home with her. She was a very lovely lady and very capable. You wouldn't have wanted a better head to the Women's Army Corps than Oveta Culp Hobby.

Hebert: What was that basic training like at Fort Des Moines?

Moore: Colonel Darden Faith, who was head of the area at the time, was a perfectly wonderful officer to be under. But a lot of the other officers said, "Oh, these women think they want to be in the army. We'll show them." So, it wasn't easy. Their training was just like the training the men got in most instances. I would say that it was excellent training for any woman that went in.

Hebert: Did you feel that you had to work harder than the men to get ahead, to study harder, to improve yourself?

Moore: A lot of the women there did. I didn't particularly, I think mostly because I was a daddy's girl. My mother had twins when I was seven years old, so as a result of that, I strictly became a daddy's girl. So, I had been used to being around men more, probably more than I was women, in my life, and, it worked out all well for me.

Hebert: Did you have women officers training you, or were you being trained only by the male officers?

Moore: No, all male officers.

Hebert: Were you closely chaperoned? Was your time out in town regulated?

Moore: We didn't take a lot of time out in town, but I will say this, for the rest of my life I've remembered the people of Des Moines because they were so hospitable. Everybody thought, gee, when they send all those women to Des Moines, they're not going to know what to do with them. Really, they were just wonderful. Families invited you to meals, and I just will remember for all my life how nice the people were.

Hebert: How did the men in the officer training corps react to having women come in?

Moore: Well, you had two really diverse types of individuals. You had many of the men that were most appreciative that women were coming to help, and they were delighted to be instructing us. They treated us well, with a great deal of respect. Then, you had some who were just the opposite. The idea was I certainly don't want my wife or my sister in this, you know. But in most cases, we found it was quite easy to recruit the wives and sisters of men who were in service.

Hebert: How did your family react to your joining?

Moore: My family knew — I guess since I was a child — that I dare. I guess they would expect Ellen to do this. So, there was nothing but joy and delight that I was asked to come on in and be one of the first to go. When I would come home, people were just delighted to see me and pleased that I was happy with my decision.

I had any number of interesting things happen, while I was in recruiting. At one time, a gentleman from Baton Rouge was out at Fort Ellington, at one of the bases, and they were looking for somebody to help these six Yugoslavian flyers, who were the last to come into this country to fight with us, before Tito came in there. So, it was an interesting experience when I got an order one morning that said, in addition to other duties, Captain Moore will report to Ellington.

When I got there, here I was confronted with six gentlemen who did not speak one word of English, and they, with a woman, who didn't speak one word of Yugoslavian. But, the reason this officer from Baton Rouge had suggested me was because — like you said, you're a Cajun — all of us can talk with our hands and say anything we want to say. I'm not particularly Cajun, but I do have some French in me.

Hebert: So, you-all used sign language and pointed a lot?

Moore: That's right! In fact, if [I] wanted to dance, I would point upstairs and dance for a while. They would say, yes or no. We had no problems at all. I mean, it was amazing the things you could say [without speaking].

Hebert: You mentioned dancing; did you go to the USOs?

Moore: Yes, we did. The town was great with putting these things on, and they had several clubs that gave dances every weekend. Then occasionally, if I had several of my officers in, we would take them into the hotel area where they danced. So, they had a good time when they'd come in on the weekend.

Hebert: How did you get appointed to be a recruiter?

Moore: I was a teacher, not a stenographer or a office person, when I went into the service. I went in thinking that I would probably be teaching something. I don't know. They just called one day and said, "We think you'd be good on recruiting, would you like it?" And, I said, "Oh, I would just love it, where will I go?" They gave me a choice of about four places, and I was able to choose Houston, Texas. Then, believe it or not, my next assignment was in Louisiana. They were not making their quota, and they needed somebody to come over and help them recruit. So, I got an order from the commanding general of the Eighth Service Command that said, "Captain Moore, we need you in Baton Rouge. That's your next assignment." It didn't read like that, but that's what it said. So, I came on back. I was at Fort Polk.

Hebert: I read this article that said you recruited three hundred women in one day, at a rodeo [in Texas].

Moore: I did that. And gave them each a bag of soil. Anybody that hasn't lived in Texas doesn't know how people in Texas love Texas. This would indeed be the greatest country — I think it is anyway — but it would be even greater if everybody in every state in the union loved where they were like Texans do. Just unbelievable. We got one of the companies that used to sell tobacco to give us the little bags they used, and we filled them up, all three hundred of them, with soil from Texas.

Hebert: I read that the WACS, the first group at least, were some of the most educated people in the army.

Moore: That's right. I was amazed at some of the [WAC] officers they sent me who were lieutenants when I was out recruiting. They had been head of departments in the biggest stores in the country. I'm talking about stores like Macy's, and places like that, and I had two women, at one time, that just had a background you wouldn't believe. They had done so much in their life. So, you were never ashamed of any of the girls that were sent to you, I can tell you. I never had any trouble with any of them, disciplinary trouble.

Hebert: Did you have problems recruiting women, or, did they want to serve their country?

Moore: Most of those that I had were volunteers and wanted to come into the service.

Hebert: Did many of them go overseas?

Moore: Oh, yes. And they got very high praise from the tops of the various companies who were overseas. A lot of them did. While I'm talking about the WACS, I was not a part of it, but I want to really give due credit to the many thousands of women who were nurses in the army, who really were there before WAC came.

Hebert: Did Louisiana start meeting its quotas for WACS?

Moore: Well, we came close to it.

Hebert: What was the quota?

Moore: I really don't remember. In fact, I don't actually remember the exact quota for Texas. But, I know we were meeting it [in Texas]. That was the main thing. I did a lot of speech making to groups of women and also to the men at their mess halls. I would go and speak while they were eating and tell them how important it was then hope they would write home [to find out] if their wife, or sister, or anybody was a person who really should be in the service. Many of them did.

Hebert: Did many married women enlist?

Moore: A great many married women [enlisted]. But they changed WAC. One of the [reasons] for doing that was so the women who did not fit and who went in [WAC] for other reasons, had an opportunity to get out, when they found it was real business. And, a good many did get out. Of course, when that happened a lot of appointments could be made with people who were already in the service, raising them from the rank of second lieutenant to first lieutenant.

In other words, you were dealing with a certain percentage of women who really got in it thinking it would just be fun. All the men were going away, and it would just be fun. And, it wasn't a deal set up to be fun. It was set up to be of real importance and value to our country. So, you did have a good many to get out.

Hebert: Were there any black women recruited?

Moore: Oh, yes. I had several very good ones. In fact, I recruited a good many people from one of the very fine Negro colleges over in Texas, and we had some good officer material from colleges over there.

Hebert: Were they given clerical positions?

Moore: Not always. A lot of times they were put into jobs they had never done before, but they were the type of women who were subject to being trained. Of course, they had programs for them to get advancement, and to be in a better position than they were, and many of them took advantage of that.

Anthony Palumbo

After high school in Rochester, New York, Palumbo went into the Citizens Military Training Corps (CMTC) established after World War I in order to help build up the U.S. reserve components. In 1933, Palumbo joined the Civilian Conservation Corps (CCCs) and spent six months in Lewiston, Idaho. "We were all youngsters, 17, 18, 19 year old boys from the cities," says Palumbo. "It was our first experience out in the country."

I was stationed at various camps in upper New York State. [When we were at Bear Mountain National Park,] we were just a stone's throw away from the U.S. Military Academy at West Point. But we didn't know a thing about West Point at the time. I had just had my first year at the CMTC called a basic year. After that, you had to do your red, white, and blue years after which you had to take a correspondence course. They called it the old ten series. You had to do those at home then you appeared before a board of officers, and they either said "yes" or "no" you were qualified to be a reserve officer or not. Fortunately, I was able to make the grade.

I finished in 1938 and was finally commissioned in October 1938. From there I went on to active duty with the CCCs as a subaltern [which means] second lieutenant. "Subaltern" is an old British term that we picked up. But I wasn't assigned to the old War Department. I was assigned to the Department of the Interior [with] a rating of GS-4 and $125 a month. Seems like at that time it was considered high money, but it was actually the same pay they were paying the officers in the active duty army.

I stayed on duty with the CCCs as a subaltern officer. I was the executive officer of Camp New Field, outside of Ithaca, New York. After [my wife and I] were married, I had received orders to be transferred down to the Brooklyn army base and was asked by the War Department if I would go down and look it over to see if I wanted the job as a guard officer on duty there. I hopped a train in Syracuse and went down to see them. I came back, and told Jane [my wife] I didn't want that job. So, I called the War Department and said, "No, I didn't want the job." Within a period of two or three weeks, I got an order the from the War Department that I was called to active duty, and I would report to the 1229th reception center at Fort Dix, New Jersey.

In spring of 1942, I [was] assigned to Fort McClellan, Alabama. I was in command of a black company because I was a "Yankee." I was from New York, and we didn't have any prejudice at the time. This was a very special unit that I had commanded for almost six months.

One particular thing that stands out in my mind was one black soldier who once came into my orderly room, said he was going to commit suicide. He didn't like the idea of being in the service; he wanted to commit suicide. So, I said, "If you're going to commit suicide, you might as well do it right here in front of me, the first sergeant, and witnesses so we can testify that you killed yourself here." He said, "I don't have a rifle." So, the sergeant said, "Get the man a rifle." He gave him an M1 rifle. The man said, "I don't have any ammunition." "Reach him this." I got his ammunition. "Now put it in that rifle and shoot yourself." He started crying; he just backed off. I knew that if he was going to do it, if he tried to, we would have stopped him. I mean, we were not going to tolerate that type of behavior in our unit. As it was, I had him shipped back to the medics. I don't know to this day what happened to him.

Thomas Blakeney in front of his CMTC tent, 1937

They were mostly local boys. They weren't educated. They had no training at all. We were supposed to train them and make them ready for fighting, but it was impossible at the time. As a matter of fact, we were on one of our various night marches, and we were going by a cemetery. I turned around and looked behind me, and my troop all broke ranks. They were scared to go by the cemetery. It is just a superstition on the part of the blacks, but we finally got them back under our control.

There was one other incident. I was home at the time, and I heard there was a fight going on at the unit. I went back to the unit with Jane, my wife, and my child with me in a car. I got out to see what's going on. A black sergeant had a black man up against the building, and he was going to stick him with a bayonet. I stopped it, and Jane became frightened. She thought I was going to get hurt, and I said, "No, I won't be hurt." I'm a little fellow, only about five foot six, but I was strong as an ox at the time. But even at that, the fact that I was an officer, a commander of a unit, you know, made a tremendous difference, enough to stop the fight. I got the men separated.

Foster: Was there prejudice that you were aware of either from the GIs complaining or from some of your officers?

Palumbo: Well, I had a white officer and a black first sergeant, who was the biggest and strongest fellow in the unit. I can recall the day I took over the company. I had to stand on a box so I could look over the tops of their heads. They're all big soldiers. I told the first sergeant who I was, where I was from, and that I was going to be their commanding officer. I went back to the orderly tent, and I heard the first sargent tell the assembled company that he was "the biggest and blackest man of the company," and he would "personally beat up any one" who would not do what I told them to do. I kind of laughed to myself, for sure enough he could have done it, too.

Wiltz Segura

Segura left LSU because "the war clouds were gathering," and there was a tremendous need for all kinds of workers for construction at the military camps in Louisiana: Camps Claiborne, Beauregard and Lee as well as at Fort Polk. "The word got out at school that they were hiring people for a dollar a day, which was big wages at that time," says Segura. "About five of us boys from LSU quit school and went to work."

A New Iberia, Louisiana native, Segura reflects on an important aspect of his upbringing: his proficiency in languages. He did not speak English until age six, but his knowledge of French proved valuable to Segura as a World War II fighter pilot surrounded by non-English speaking people.

Segura: I'm half French and half Spanish, but I speak French. My mother never spoke English. She could understand and speak a little in English, but she was educated in French. So, our language at home was French. I learned French at [my mother's] knees, then I studied a little bit in high school and college, but I really learned to speak it at home and in the community.

In the thirties and forties, when I was coming up, at least seventy-five percent of the people around here [in New Iberia] spoke French. I would say that about forty percent didn't speak any English at all. Now, some of these people are still living today, they're very old, and they still speak French. I'd say about twenty-five percent of our people speak French and English, out here, [in New Iberia].

[Knowing French] was a tremendous asset to me after I got in the military and got assigned to foreign countries because if you could speak French, you could communicate with many of the educated people in foreign countries. France, at one time, was the seat of education for foreigners who wanted to educate their children away from their own country. I was in China during World War II, and [it] was very difficult to learn to speak that language. But, most of the educated Chinese could speak French because they had been sent to France to school and had learned the language. So, it was very important, especially in a combat situation where you may be thrown in with some people that you can't understand, and you need to communicate with them.

I graduated from high school in New Iberia and went to LSU in January of 1940. I spent one semester at LSU and one summer school, then I spent one semester at USL, which was SLI in those days. [By then,] the war clouds were looming, and I was going to have to join the service. I left school and worked in military construction camps for about three months.

The military concentrated a lot on [physical fitness]. But you have to understand that they took a whole bunch of us civilians off the street. They had to clean us up, put discipline into us, organize us, and then they had to sort of orient us a little bit. The first thing they did was see if you were physically fit, particularly in flying because you needed to be physically fit. I was very athletic. I was wiry. I came from the country, and I had good legs. But, you know, raised in the country — hunting, walking a lot — prepared me for [military training].

Hebert: Were you drafted?

Segura: I volunteered. This is in December '41, Pearl Harbor. We really got mobilized, and all the guys who belonged to [the] National Guard and [the] reserves were called. So, a lot of my friends left, and I was approaching twenty years old so I was going to have to register for the draft. I wanted to get in the air force then.

There were all sorts of programs to try to get people into the service. I always was interested in flying, but flying was a very remote thing in those days, a very primitive type of situation. But the air force was trying to get a foothold into the military and was having a very difficult time because most of the leaders that were responsible for the air force were ground military army officers who did not understand the value of air power. So, a lot of our farsighted people were having a lot of trouble, such as Billy Mitchell and General Claire Chennault, and these people who then became heroes later on because of their farsightedness of seeing how air power was going to play an important role in the next conflict.

I'll never forget. Several P-40s [fighter planes] flew into Lafayette, Louisiana, at the airport, and I happened to be around there. I saw those airplanes, and [it] really made an impression on me. A P-40 airplane, in those days, was as impressive to me as probably a space shuttle. It really was, especially for a country boy [from an] agricultural society, and so forth. But I never expected that I could ever qualify for [flying a P-40].

You know, you didn't understand it. But, we had a boy from here, who was Leonard Barrow; he'd been in the service since about 1939, and he was in one of those airplanes. That's why those airplanes landed at Lafayette. So, I saw him and knew him, and boy, he was walking around — in those days, they wore riding britches and those boots, and they looked fantastic — and I said, "I've got to figure out a way to get into that outfit."

I'm going to New Orleans on my motorcycle one day and [passed by] Wedell Williams Airport in Patterson, Louisiana. I saw a bunch of airplanes parked out there, little bitty airplanes. So, I pulled in, and I'm looking at the airplanes. This guy comes over and says, "Would you like to learn how to fly?" I said, "Yeah, I sure would." He said, "Well, we'll teach you here." I said, "How much will it cost?" He says, "Eight dollars an hour." "Eight dollars an hour?" That was a lot of money in those days. I was working for twenty-five cents an hour. So, I said, "Well I couldn't afford that." He says, "Well, I tell you what, we got a program that the government is sponsoring."

At one time you had to have four years of college to enter into the air force cadet program. Then, they needed more pilots and not that many guys were eligible because you had to have good eyesight, good ears, and good nose. [Not having] those three things would knock you out. There are not too many guys who don't wear glasses, and so forth, that could pass. If you had an education, probably by that time, you had lost your eyesight. It was hard for the air force to get all the pilot trainees that they wanted because they were starting to really put out airplanes in those days. So, they dropped [the college requirement] to two years of college. Well, I had about a year. And, I still couldn't qualify to get into the air force. But this program was for high school graduates [with] less than two years of college. If you could pass an aptitude test, they would sign you up, and they would give you a private pilot's course free, which is about three months. You would have to agree to join the air force after that. Boy, [I thought] this is right up my alley. So, I signed up.

This is where my ROTC [training] came in. They lined us up there. It was eighteen of us, from all walks of life, and we were anywhere from eighteen years old to twenty-four. We had to buy us a little uniform [with] little khaki pants and shirt, and a little hat. They lined us up: "Any of you fellows had any military training before?" Nobody raised their hand. So, somebody said, "Any ROTC?" I was the only one that had ROTC. So, [they said,] "You're the leader. You march them up and down." All I knew was how to turn them to the right and turn them to the left and how to stop them and how to start them. Fortunately, I had kept my military manual. I started coming back with some sophisticated movements. So, we would march up and down.

One day a month, we would have ground school and would have to march. We were doing this at one of the high schools in Patterson, Louisiana, [which] is a little bitty town, and everybody embraced us there because this is kind of a novelty, you see. So, we started marching down Main Street at night, you know, up and down, up and down. "To the rear. March! Left face." All that. All the people would come out on the street and watch us; and I was the leader. Well, that made me proud. But ROTC did it. It gave you confidence, you see, in a group, how to lead. Wherever I went, I felt I had a little bit of an advantage. I attribute that to my ROTC training.

So, I got in the military and went through all the flying schools that they had in those days. I got in May of 1942, which was about five, six months after Pearl Harbor. I was placed as a private in the reserve waiting for an appointment in the cadet program. And then, August 6, 1942, on my birthday, I got my appointment and left and went to the classification programs. In those days, you would go to a classification program, and they would put you through a battery of tests. They would determine whether you would be a pilot, navigator, or bombardier. Well, I wanted to be a pilot. So they said, "Okay, you have depth perception and all these other physical tests." They would check your ears, and so forth. Then you would have to fill out a bunch of paper. One of them [asked], "What would you like to be, a pilot, a navigator, or bombardier?" And, you know, we had some crazy guys that would put bombardier or navigator instead of pilot, and I never could understand that. But, it was probably better that we got rid of those at the beginning. But, anyway, it was three choices. I put "pilot, pilot, pilot." That's what I got.

So they sent me off to Maxwell Air Force Base [for] pre-flight training. Then we went off to flying school [in Tuscaloosa, Alabama, for] primary flying school in PT-17s. Got sixty hours in that. Took about two months, then went off to basic training.

[During primary flying school,] I was delighted that I had some training in flying, because that PT-17 is a hard airplane to fly. It has [an open cockpit] and narrow landing gear. It's a ground looping airplane that has a lot of lift, so if there's any wind of any kind, it's difficult. A lot of guys, you know, had a lot of trouble with it. In those days I guess they washed out about 50 percent of us. Not at that particular school, but by the time you went through the whole thing, I would say about 50 percent were washed out.

You were assigned an instructor. An instructor had maybe four students. Then you went to ground school half a day and learned your navigation, meteorology, codes, and whatever you needed to know about the military. A half a day, you would fly with that instructor. After so many hours, the check pilot would come up. Parks Air College, a civilian flying school, was running the thing, but the military guys would be the check pilots. I sailed through. Having had a private pilot's license and having flown fifty hours before, that put me ahead of the pack, I felt.

I never had any problems flying. I was very dedicated in following the rules, too, because I really wanted to succeed as a pilot. So, I didn't deviate from anything as far as discipline and so forth. I enjoyed the program. It wasn't an easy program, but it wasn't that difficult.

Went to basic school in BT-13s at Newport, Arkansas, for two months. In [basic] pilot training school, they decide whether you're going to be a bomber pilot, a twin engine pilot, or a single engine pilot. Well, I wanted to be a fighter pilot, so I was agitating for that, and my instructor agreed with me. So, I went to Single Engine School at Selma, Alabama, right near Maxwell [Air Force Base], and we flew North American T-6 trainers, four weeks of that.

By that time, the war was then developing pretty quickly, and they needed pilots in a big way. So, they were pushing us as fast as we could go. Normally, what you do when you get out of flying school, and graduate, you [learn about] whatever airplane you're going to fly. What they did to us is they took about ten or fifteen percent of the class, those of us that they felt could progress a little bit faster, and they brought [in] some P-40 [fighter planes] and let us fly the P-40s [for] ten hours before we graduated. So I got to fly the P-40 while I was still a cadet, which was really an experience. I mean, you know, compared to a T-6, a P-40, in those days, was really something. Big nose, twelve cylinders in front, short stacks, and a lot of power, a lot of torque. I'll never forget. I got on that runway the first time, and you know, they give you a cockpit check and tell you all the things that you had to watch out for. Then, you're trying to remember all that, and of course, you've got a new cockpit and everything else. You're nervous 'cause you're afraid to be washed out. So, man, I lined that airplane up, and you can't see ahead of you, 'cause that nose sticks up. Got on that runway, cleared yourself, and put that thing pointing out towards the south end of the field. I'll never forget when I put the needle to that beast. It just roared. All I could do is hold it up. I think I must have gone ten miles before I pulled my landing gears up, and I didn't stop until I got to ten thousand feet. Then looked down, and I said to myself, if I ever get this thing back on the ground, I'll be surprised.

So, I flew around, and it's like anything else. It's just like meeting a new girlfriend. You just got to spend some time with it, and the first thing you know, it becomes elementary. So, I fooled around up there in the sky and did a few rolls and what not.

So, man, I lined up about six or seven miles out, put that nose towards that runway, and figured, well, I'm going to just go down, down, down, down, slowly, slowly, 'till I get over the runway. I'll just chop the power, you know. Because, I was afraid of over controlling, 'cause that was really a lot of power. Finally, got that thing on the ground, and it was okay.

When I graduated from that, I went to a P-40 transition school for fighter training in Sarasota, Florida. I spent two months there, got sixty hours in a P-40 and learned how to bomb and strafe, and do some combat maneuvers. Then, I got shipped to China.

Dupuy Anderson

The fear that arose as Germany and Japan waged war caused United States citizens to come together for a common cause. Yet during the era of the Second World War in our country, the fear and hatred caused by racism still had to be endured on a daily basis by black Americans. As Anderson makes clear in this excerpt, black American soldiers were not exempt from racial hatred.

Anderson: After we signed up, it was about two or three months before we had army training. We all left and went to Fort Benning, Georgia, for our exam, to be issued clothing, and everything.

The next thing that struck me was, after being examined, we sat out in the bleachers in the hot sun. A colonel got up and made the remark, "Well I'll be damned, here's a bunch of niggers without syphilis or gonorrhea." [That was one] thing [that] stayed on my mind and bothered me.

[During one summer, before he received his medical degree and began his military service, Anderson had been hired to work at Ryan Airfield, Baton Rouge. After a few days of performing manual labor, Anderson was made a supervisor.]

So, I was familiar with Ryan Airport. I was sent to Ryan Army Airfield as a first lieutenant, Medical Administrative Corps. I went in and had my physical. I went over to the hospital [and] every typewriter stopped typing, every head turned toward me. A gray-haired colonel walked out. The captain gave him my papers. He threw them back to me. He said, "They must have made a mistake." I took my papers and came home. Took off my uniform; I felt like burning it. I stayed around here and received my pay until I got orders to move.

When I got orders to move, about a year after, I got a letter from the Air Force surgeon general wanting to know where I had been. Where I had been! I was burning up, furious. I wrote a letter. It has to go through command, and they wouldn't send the letter that I had written. They wrote it over because at that time I was out in the secular world, and I used some bad language telling them the reason why you don't have a record of me at Ryan Army Airfield is they denied me signing-in because I was black.

I went out to Fort Huachuca [in Arizona]. That was a base we often said that Talmidge, Bilbo, and all these senators passed over and said, "This is going to be where we put niggers." It was out in the desert. Well, they had a white group out there at one time, and the bases were known as the old and the new base. We were put on the new base. Hardly any facilities, recreation facilities. No swimming pools, nothing. Up on the main base they had a nice club, swimming pool, and everything. We weren't allowed up there. So, a group of us decided we were going up there. And we went up there. So, those things changed out there.

I was at Tuskegee Airfield [in Alabama] most of my time. I spent my career at the hospital. I cried a lot when I was in the army. I didn't want to go overseas [because of] the humiliation that I had seen, and I griped and complained. I said, "If you send me overseas you may as well send a brick overseas. You'll send a dead weight." A young lady told me [that my] papers came in to go overseas. I was supposed to go overseas.

We had a softball game. Our commanding officer said the first one to hit a home run will get a forty-eight hour [pass]. I hit it inside the park and stretched it into a home run, and then I laid out in the field. I had a bad knee. I went to the hospital. It did hurt, but I complained and complained. They sent a boy by the name of Wells [overseas] in my place. So, I got out of that duty [and was sent to Tuskegee Airfield.]

[When] we got into Atlanta, I didn't know blacks went in the bottom of the train station. They had a basement, [but] I went through the front door to synchronize my time. A policeman walked behind me and hit me on the head. Well, we almost had a race riot there with those soldiers and everything, but we calmed them down. I took it, got back on the train and told [the others I was with] the time and when we were leaving out.

Crump: You just got back on the train and told them what time it was and forgot about it?

Anderson: Well, at that time it was hardly anything we could do. Hardly anything that you could do.

Crump: How did it make you feel when the police officer hit you just for checking the time?

Anderson: How would you feel if you wore a uniform? This wasn't the first time I had been humiliated. I saw things happen in Phenix City, Alabama, and Atlanta, Georgia. It brings tears to my eyes even now. I saw a black soldier killed in cold blooded murder. We went over to

Atlanta and a black soldier was backing up to park in a space. A policeman drove up and started questioning him. And the soldier spoke back to him and said he was "just going to park here." He had seen this space and was pulling in. The officer said, "Oh, you're a smart nigger," and shot him.

Crump: Did anything happen to the officer?

Dupuy Anderson

Anderson: No. No. No, nothing happened. He's just another dead person. The army wouldn't take up your cause hardly at all.

Crump: This was a soldier, and the army did nothing?

Anderson: Will do nothing. You rode on the back of the buses in

Atlanta. [In] Phenix City, a black person couldn't be seen with a black gal after dark, [if] she's nice looking. Things you did, you had to hide and do, and you were scared most of the time.

[In] Montgomery, [Alabama,] I had an incident with my wife [who's light skinned]. I got off at the train station in Montgomery on my way to Tuskegee Army Airfield. I knew we had to wait on the outside and go to the back to get a cab. I had my bags and things, and I called a cab over to get it. The cab driver came over and attempted to get my bags. A policeman came up and cocked his gun and beat that fellow across the head and told him, "You don't pick up a nigger here." I had to walk across the street and get a cab.

I knew the young lady that worked at the USO [in Montgomery]. She went to Southern University. I went in, and about two seconds after I had gone in, they had about fifteen or twenty policemen marching up and down looking in. So, [my friend at the USO] told me, she said, "Look, I'm going to take your wife home with me, and you stay here with my husband." [The policemen] must have come in and questioned him and everything. And they stayed there. Finally, I left and went over to his house. Left word that if anyone would come in town — I was expecting some of my friends to be in town — [they should] come by and pick me up, and I'd motor to Tuskegee, which was about forty miles away. So, they did. Don't you know, we had to break all laws in traveling and almost turned over because the group was behind us. We don't know whether it was Ku Klux Klan or policemen or not. So we got to Tuskegee.

Crump: You didn't know if they were policemen or Klansmen

Anderson: No, I didn't know what they were, and we didn't try to find out.

Crump: Why were they chasing you?

Anderson: Because they thought probably my wife was white. That's why.

I had so many things happen, and not only to me, to a lot of us, a lot of us. [In] everything that we did, we had to fight our way, and we had to prove our value. The [black] men in the air force flew the old airplanes, while the white boys flew the new airplanes. [Senators] Bilbo and Eastland and them said that Negroes weren't capable of flying a plane. That's [in the] *Congressional Record*. It has taken a long time for us to get recognition. We are just beginning to get recognition in the aviation field.

Blacks did fly. At that time they took the cream of the crop of blacks. Guys with their Masters, Ph. D.s went into the air force. They volunteered, to [prove it was] a lie [that blacks couldn't fly]. One of the fellows that was at Tuskegee was ferrying planes from Canada to England because he could not ferry them from the States to England because he was black.

These are the things that motivated me more and more to do what I can to try and improve conditions. At one time, I thought, foolishly, I could make a change. But as I grew older, I say, "You can only do so much." But it took me a long time to realize that.

I used to fight about everything. I used to be angry in my fight. I hated what was done to me and others. To say I hate a person, no. I had to realize it because I was beginning to hate myself. I couldn't do justice even to my people. I would hate so. So, I had to make a change. I say well, do what you can, work with them, work within the system, and see if you can't make a change.

Johnnie Jones

Jones was majoring in industrial education at Southern University when he was drafted into the United States Army in 1942. Working to organize supply warehouses in Louisiana, Jones' good work was recognized by the U.S. Army's inspector general who promoted him to sergeant. Jones was eventually promoted to warrant officer.

I was not discriminated [against] as a warrant officer until I got to Charleston. That's the only place, during the time of my being a warrant officer, that I ever experienced any segregation. When I got to Charleston, the army did not segregate me. I was placed in the same quarters with the other officers of my battalion. But the people who kept the barracks clean, they were non-military. In some parts of the army, they had enlisted men to do that, but in Charleston, South Carolina, that was a civilian job. Every officer at that time had an orderly who kept his stuff clean and everything. They don't have that now I understand. I had my orderly just like everybody else. When I got there, my orderly saw that all my stuff was placed just like it had always been placed everywhere else — in Harahan and in Chalmette down in New Orleans, all those places. I went on to work, back on over to my job. Then, the civilian took my stuff and set it out in the company street. When I came off duty to go to dress to go to bed, I didn't have a place to sleep.

Hebert: He put everything out into the street?

Jones: The civilian, non-military personnel, at the post at Charleston, South Carolina, put all of my stuff in the street. That's where it was. I didn't have any place to go. So, I talked to my commanding officer, and he says, "I didn't do that. I didn't have anything to do with that." I says, "I know Colonel, you didn't have anything to do with that, but why didn't you tell them that they couldn't do it when you found out it was being done?" He said, "I just didn't have any authority to do that. Didn't know what to say." I say, "Colonel, you could have told them this man got to sleep somewhere tonight."

He could have called them and told them. He knew it was done. I say, "Now, it look like to me, Colonel, you should have just told them that you have to put it back in there." But really it wasn't in his heart. He didn't want blood shed. That's really what he didn't want. He didn't want blood shed. He says, "That would be just a matter of creating insurrection." I says, "Colonel, this is the army." I said, "I'm a soldier in the army. We are headed overseas." Our next stop was in New York, at Staten Island, and then from Staten Island, we was facing Hitler, the Germans. So, I said, "Colonel, you should have told him something. What did you say?" He said, "I didn't say anything." So, I said, "Well, I don't know what to do." I couldn't stay there — wasn't no place for me to stay. They were, you know the civilians, waiting to see what I was going to do. So, I just got in my jeep because I had my car assigned to me — my military vehicle was a jeep. My driver was named Jackson. So, I say, "Jackson, go get my jeep and let's go to Charleston." So, I went on to Charleston and stayed in the YMCA that night. I say, "Jackson, tomorrow morning, you come pick me up."

So, that next morning Jackson came and picked me up. I came back to the post and had breakfast with the colonel. Then, the colonel says, "What you going to do?" I say, "I'm not going to do anything Colonel." So, I went on back, and I checked with the noncoms who worked under me. I told them to keep on doing their work. I'll be back to sign all the papers and what not. I say, "Jackson, take me to the general's office, up to the post headquarters." So, Jackson just took me to post headquarters.

Now, I had met General Duke. General Duke was a small fellow, about an inch or so shorter than me. A small man. When we first came to Charleston, he met the colonel, me, and the adjutant. When he came, we saluted, then he started talking. I happened to be the first black warrant officer that he had seen so he shook my hand and spoke to me. He started talking to me, you know, exceptional. I knew he was making a difference because he started asking me where I was from and what school did I go to and all of that. He didn't have to ask all that, but he wanted to know so I told him where I was from. Then, when he got through doing that, I says, "You know, General, I have always thought that to be a general you had to be six feet tall and broad shoulders." I said, "But now I see that a general can come smaller than me." I say, "You give me hope." My commanding officer didn't like that.

Hebert: How did the general take that?

Jones: Oh, he loved it. He forgot about all of them. After we finished talking with him, he came back to my office, and he spent almost a half an hour or better, just with me, just sitting down talking. "Be at ease," he had told me. We just talked.

Frankly, the officers in my company didn't like the way that the general and I picked up right away. So, [the general] says, "You have any trouble just call on me. Just call on me. Come by to see me any time you want to." I didn't know I was going to have any trouble that soon. And [then] they put me out of the barracks.

So, I just told [Jackson] to drive me to see the general. When I got up there that morning to see the general, his aide came out. I had to salute him, and so, I says, "I want to see General Duke." He said, "Do you have an appointment with him?" I said, "No, I don't, but I want to see him." And he says, "Well, you got to have an appointment with him." I said, "I'm here to see him because he told me to come whenever I wanted, or if I find myself having any trouble to come see him. Now I'm doing that." So he left and went back [and] told the general that I was out there and who I was. And the general said, "Oh yes, tell him to come on in." He said, "Bring him on in." When I got in, I saluted. He didn't hardly want me to salute him. I saluted. [He said], "Oh sit down, sit down, have a seat." So, I sat down.

I had a seat, and then I started talking with him. First, we just had a general conversation, just played around a little bit talking about each other, patting each other on the back you know. And then he finally asked me, "What's your problem?" I told him what the problem was. I says, "I can't travel this post because all the white soldiers, and everything, resenting my being on this post. They curse at me. They use derogatory statements at me, and everything. I can't stay on the post. They put me off the post. I don't have a place to sleep. I don't have a place in the barracks, anywhere." He says, "What?" I said, "No. They threw all my stuff out in the street, the civilians did." So, he says, "Well, I don't know what to do about that. That's rather unusual." He says, "But see if you can rent a place in the town. The army is going to have to pay for it. If you can't stay here, we're going to have to find a place out there you can rent."

So, I just went on out of town, and he says, "I'm going to solve all these problems." So he rented a place, and [the] military paid for it. I didn't pay for it. I stayed on at 22 Johns Street in Charleston, South Carolina. I think the family name was Green, who I rented with, a lovely home — blacks. So, I stayed there with them.

Then, [the general] asked me did I like it? I said, "Yeah, but I would rather stay on the post because I'm military. But I got to stay out of town." I say, "General that's awful." And so he says, "It is, but we got to settle it. We're going to get that straight." So I didn't bother too much about it. He then says, "How are the enlisted people treating you?" Everywhere I go and every office that I go in and had to do business for the army, they were white civilians. Everything was most manned by the white civilians. They resented the fact that I had to negotiate certain contracts and things like that for the military with certain people.

Hebert: Was this everywhere or just in Charleston?

Jones: Just in Charleston, South Carolina. Just in Charleston. And so [the general] says, "What does the military [personnel do]?" I say, "They won't salute me. The white military won't salute me." He say, "I'll put a stop to that." He says, "I'm going to take your jeep from you. I'm going to give you my command car." Now really, he did that. So, he gave me his command car.

The command car has the general's stars on it, and when they see that car coming, they don't have to see who's in it, they got to start saluting because its supposed to be the general in there. So, he gave me that command car. And we drove, and they would salute the command car. When we came up to points, where they had guards, you couldn't pass the sentry. Sometimes they have two sentries, one on one side and one on the other. One would salute and the other one wouldn't. "That's that nigger in that car." The other say, "I don't care who he is I'm going to salute." Then one be fussing at the other one because the other one didn't salute. Some of them wouldn't salute after they found out I was using the car. They made sure to look and see whether or not the general was in there, you see.

Hebert: Were most of these people from South Carolina?

Jones: I don't know where they was from. All I know is that they were military. They wouldn't salute so therefore that's what happened. Most of them must have been southerners, I guess. But you had them from places like Indiana, which is not a southern state. It's just as bad. You had some places in New York that were just as bad, and Chicago. Mostly you find very little difference in Indiana than the ranks in the South, members of the Ku Klux Klan. It wasn't much different than some of them. So, then, we left and went to Staten Island. From Staten Island we went overseas and landed in Glasgow, [Scotland].

Carlos Spaht

When LSU alumnus Spaht was called to active duty in July of 1941 he was ranked as a captain. Spaht's first assignment was as the executive officer at Jackson Barracks in New Orleans. By the time he left New Orleans, he was a lieutenant colonel.

Hebert: Describe New Orleans during wartime.

Spaht: Well, of course New Orleans at that time was a tourist center as it is today. It was free of crime though, pretty much. It was really a lovely old city to visit and to live in. We lived in the French Quarter. We rented an apartment, and we lived there in French Quarter for a few months. Then since I was assigned to Jackson Barracks, I was directed to move there and [I] lived on the post.

Hebert: Was there a fear in New Orleans about a German attack?

Spaht: It became a very dangerous area. The German subs came right to the mouth of the [Mississippi] river, and they were sinking our ships right and left. As a matter of fact, for a while they even quit shipping because of the danger. Oh yes, there was a number of our vessels that were sunk there in the Gulf.

I remember, particularly as executive officer, one of my jobs was to select officers to go with the ships as they went overseas. And, there was a good friend of mine who came, and I gave him a job of commander of troops on a vessel to go to [the] Canal Zone. As his vessel hit the Gulf it was attacked. The [German] subs attacked and sunk the vessel. Of course, fortunately, all of the personnel pretty much were saved. When he came back, he said, "You're a good friend of mine. Give me something else the next time."

1. Quoted in Mark S. Watson, *Chief of Staff: Prewar Plans and*

Preparations (Washington, D.C., 1950), p. 26.

2. Eric Larrabee, *Commander in Chief: Franklin Delano Roosevelt, His Lieutenants & Their War* (New York, 1987), p. 114.

3. George C. Marshall to Col. Hjalmar Erickson, 6 Oct. 1941, Larry I. Bland, ed., *The Papers of George C. Marshall* (vols., Baltimore, 19), II, 630-631. The standard work on Marshall's pre-Pearl Harbor activities is Forrest C. Pogue, *George C. Marshall: Ordeal and Hope, 1939-1942* (New York, 1966).

4. Quoted in Lee Kennett, *GI: The American Soldier in World War II* (New York, 1987), p. 70.

5. Quoted in Geoffrey Perret, *There's a War to be Won: The United States Army in World War II* (New York, 1991), pp. 71-72.

Chapter Five

European Theater

The Japanese air raid on Pearl Harbor and Hitler's subsequent declaration of war on the United States forced a reexamination of American national strategy — and the result was a reaffirmation of the Germany-first commitment. Washington's Soviet and British allies understandably hailed FDR's attitude, but there was no consensus among the Big Three as to how best to go about defeating the Reich. Roosevelt and his top military advisors believed that the way to win the war was to send armies into Western Europe and fight a decisive engagement with Hitler's forces. To that end, the army dispatched General Dwight D. Eisenhower to England in 1942 to oversee the gradual build-up of men and materiel. That strategy coincided with Soviet needs. By the time the United States entered the conflict, German divisions had conquered one-third of the USSR and were threatening Leningrad and Moscow; a second front in the West seemed the only way to relieve that pressure and perhaps save the Soviet Union.

The stumbling block was the British. The government of Winston Churchill, fearful of mass casualties and wanting to protect Britain's lines of communication to the Middle East, opposed an immediate direct assault on Fortress Europe. Instead, London advocated a peripheral strategy designed to weaken Germany by blockade, by strategic bombardment, and by clearing Axis forces from the Mediterranean. Because a cross-Channel invasion of the continent in

1942 would necessitate the use of Great Britain as a trampoline, and because British troops of necessity would play a dominant role in such an undertaking, Churchill had significant bargaining chips. Roosevelt's desire to get American forces into action in Europe as quickly as possible, in part to deflect pressures for a strategic focus on the Pacific and in part for domestic political reasons, strengthened the British hand even further. Churchill, as a result, was able to persuade FDR to overrule his military advisors and acquiesce in an invasion of French North Africa in order to relieve German pressure on Egypt and the Suez Canal. The stage thus was set for Operation TORCH, which, under the overall command of Eisenhower, was intended to squeeze General Erwin Rommel and his Afrika Korps between Anglo-American forces in the West and British forces moving out from Egypt.

In November 1942, three Allied convoys, one sailing from the United States and two from Great Britain, reached their main assault points in French Morocco and Algeria: Casablanca, Algiers, and Oran. Some 300 warships, nearly 400 merchant vessels, and 107,000 troops made up what was, up to that time, the largest amphibious assault force ever formed. Efforts to secure the cooperation of local French forces were not entirely successful, and they offered often fierce resistance, especially the French navy. Overall, the amphibious landings, launched on November 8, went well: within four days the objectives had been secured and the Allies were in possession of 1,300 miles of Africa's Mediterranean coast. Casualties had been relatively light — the heaviest fighting had occurred at Casablanca, where General George S. Patton had seen 500 of his men killed in action and 700 wounded. In the following weeks, British forces from Egypt, after winning a decisive battle (El Alamein) that blunted Rommel's drive toward the Suez Canal a few days before the Anglo-American landings, pushed the Afrika Korps and its Italian allies westward, while TORCH forces pressed eastward, eventually corralling the Axis armies in Tunisia. The German high command rushed reinforcements to Tunisia, which were insufficient to permit any sustained offensive action. The only significant German thrust westward came in February 1943, and green American troops suffered heavy losses in two engagements, the more famous at Kasserine Pass, where, despite 2,000 casualties, they ultimately held a defensive line, absorbing Rommel's blows and forcing him to pull back. His successor in Tunisia managed to hold out until May 1943, when Allied forces crushed the last pockets of resistance.

What should be the next step after the anticipated victory in North Africa? That was the question that guided discussions between Roosevelt and Churchill at the Casablanca Conference in January 1943. Disgruntled American military strategists had hoped to resume the build-up in the British Isles for an invasion of Western Europe later that year, but FDR once more succumbed to British arguments: the Allies would next invade Sicily and use it as a springboard for an invasion of Italy. The only consolation for American military strategists was that the British did make a firm commitment to mount the cross-Channel attack in the spring of 1944. In the meantime, said Churchill and his advisors, knocking Italy out of the war in a quick campaign would be a severe blow to the Reich. The two sides also agreed at Casablanca to intensify the strategic bombing campaign against Occupied Europe.

Operation HUSKY, the amphibious assault on Sicily, began on July 10, 1943. The armada that transported the invasion force dwarfed its TORCH predecessor: a total of 1,400 ships bearing 160,000 American and British troops took up positions off the southern tip of Sicily. Favored by terrain, the German and Italian enemy forces in Sicily numbered approximately 230,000 and included what were considered to be crack units. Of the two German divisions, for example, one was the Hermann Goering Division. Furthermore, once the battle started, Hitler sent in two more divisions as reinforcement. Nonetheless, the campaign lasted less than six weeks, which is not to say that it was easy or that the

Allies did not make mistakes. They suffered 20,000 casualties; friendly fire killed or wounded 300 American paratroopers; the worsening rivalry between the two army commanders, Bernard Montgomery and George S. Patton, both of whom had made their reputations in North Africa, hindered cooperation; Patton, because of the famous incident in which he slapped a soldier who had suffered a nervous breakdown, would end up losing his command; and the Allies failed to prevent the escape to Italy of the four German divisions. As Geoffrey Perret has noted, "When the Sicilian campaign drew to a close, Hitler had four intact first-class divisions in southern Italy with an abundance of materiel."[1] But the Germans fled from Sicily to avoid being annihilated or taken prisoner. They had met an adversary they might be able to delay but could not defeat.

The immediate political result of the Sicilian campaign was the overthrow of Benito Mussolini; the military result was the campaign up the boot of Italy, launched with the crossing of the Strait of Messina by Montgomery's Eighth Army on September 3 and the landing at Salerno of joint forces commanded by General Mark Clark days later. The new government in Rome announced Italy's withdrawal from the war, so the protracted, bloody conflict that now ensued saw Allied forces pitted against the Wehrmacht. The campaign did not develop as the Allied high command had envisioned it. The terrain in Italy was admirably suited for defense, and the Allied forces found themselves slugging their way up the peninsula step by step against a tenacious foe. To the chagrin and anger of the Churchill government, which had spoken glowingly of a quick campaign, it took Allied forces nine long months to liberate Rome, that is, to reach the middle of the country.

In the meantime, however, the Americans finally had imposed on the British serious preparations for the long-desired invasion of Western Europe. In military terminology, "d-day" represents simply the first day of an offensive operation, but the Allied landings on the beaches of

Normandy in the late spring of 1944 so stirred public emotion throughout the Western world that the event forever transformed June 6, 1944 into D-Day. On the eastern front, where most of the slaughter of the Second World War occurred, the Soviets could point to the Battle of Stalingrad (1942-43) as the great symbol of resistance to Nazi tyranny and a moment at which the nation rallied together to wage an epic struggle that signaled, for them, the beginning of the end. For the Western world, that moment was D-Day. What came after the landings was not, in a military sense, anticlimactic; indeed, the following weeks would be filled with drama and sacrifice — the Battle of the Bulge, the crossing of the Rhine, Hitler's suicide, and the final German surrender- but the moment of doubt, and hence perhaps the moment of greatest emotional triumph, came with Normandy. The fact that the 1944 landings signified the beginning of the end of Nazi occupation of a humiliated and long-suffering France added to the psychological impact of D-Day.[2]

The organizational effort behind D-Day, which represented the largest amphibious invasion ever undertaken, was stupendous. A million and a half American troops crowded into Great Britain, along with so much matériel that a popular saying was that the only thing keeping the island afloat was the barrage balloons. The planning and training for OVERLORD, the code name for the cross-Channel attack, accelerated in the spring of 1944 under the direction of General Eisenhower, now supreme commander of Allied Forces in Europe. An integral part of the preparations was a deception plan, the most ambitious ever devised, to convince the Germans that the main Allied landings would occur at the Pas de Calais, opposite the narrowest part of the Channel. British and American planners also mobilized the support of the French underground, which would play a key role in isolating the invasion area and disrupting German communications. The Allied high command, furthermore, intensified the air war from bases in Great Britain and

North Africa, attacking not only the German homeland, but tactical targets in France and Belgium on an increasing scale in the weeks preceding D-Day.

The armada that supported the Normandy operations on June 6 was the largest ever assembled: more than 5,000 ships of various kinds. The air armada was just as impressive: a total of 12,000 aircraft, including 5,000 fighters that would face 169 German fighters. Overall, the landings went well, and although the Allied battlefield deaths approached 3,000, the number was considered slight in view of the dimensions of the undertaking. American forces at "Omaha" Beach and the paratroopers of the 82nd and 101st Airborne Divisions, who were the first to go in and who landed behind the invasion area on the Allied right, suffered the heaviest casualties. At the end of D-Day the Allies had put more than 100,000 men ashore. Ten days later the total was 500,000 and counting. Before a month was out there were a million Allied soldiers in northern France, and the days of the Third Reich were numbered.

The breakout from Normandy took longer than expected as the British forces commanded by the cautious and unimaginative Montgomery bogged down on the Allied left and the American forces faced hard-sledding in the bocage country. But late in July the Third Army, led by a resurrected, fire-breathing George Patton, smashed through the German left flank and raced toward the Rhine. The liberation of Paris in August; the Battle of the Bulge, the Wehrmacht's last offensive gasp on the Western front, in December; the seizure of the Ludendorff Bridge at Remagen and crossing of the Rhine into Germany in March 1945; the shocking discovery of the concentration camps; the linking up of American and Soviet troops on the banks of the Elbe on April 25; and Hitler's suicide five days later were the dramatic moments of the process that began on the beaches of Normandy and culminated with Germany's unconditional surrender on May 8, 1945.[3]

In the capitals of the Western world, people poured into the streets to celebrate when the news of the German collapse reached them. Some of the GIs in Europe, those with enough points to be eligible for transport home and discharge,[4] could share that euphoria. But others, those without the requisite points and not slated for occupation duty, could take less comfort from victory over the Nazis. They would have to stay in Europe, marking time, waiting to be shipped out again. Their destination would be the Pacific, where another and very different war still had to be won.

Cyril Guidry

August 1942, Guidry embarked from New York City for North Africa with the Ninth Infantry Division. At this time, Guidry was a private paid fifty dollars a month.

Guidry: [We] boarded ship [in Scotland] and stayed on ship until we [left]. We didn't know where we were going. They didn't tell us anything. We thought we were going to Madagascar until just before we entered the Strait of Gibraltar [then] they briefed us on landing near Algiers, North Africa. Some of our troops were going to land in French Morocco, at Port-Lyautey and other locations.

That was November the 8th [1942, when] we landed in North Africa. They had a big concern from the beach. One of our ships was hit by a torpedo, and fortunately, we weren't. We disembarked at about five o'clock in the morning in little one-squad boats and had to climb down rope nets into these little boats. They had a beacon shining from the beach, and as soon as we started disembarking, the French forts started firing cannons over us at the ships out at sea in the Mediterranean. But, we landed without too much opposition. They beached [the] one boat [that] was torpedoed, and all the men were saved. We lost approximately six men that missed the boat and fell with their equipment and drowned. But, other than that we got off the boat safe.

We captured the Maison Blanche airport [outside Algiers] at

approximately 8:30 a.m. and proceeded down the highway and secured a bridge. Came back to the airport, guarded the airport for a few days, and were bombed by German planes — one night for sure.

In late November, [we] were sent to Bougie, North Africa, [on the coast of Algeria] and attached to the British to guard the port where supplies were coming in. We were stationed at a French stadium the first night. The second night we were bombed by German airplanes and the attendant, a Frenchman, was killed. We were moved out of town, and we'd send details in to guard the port at Bougie. We drew English rations, British supplies, everything British. [We] got tired of tea and crackers. No coffee, nothing. Eating mutton stew.

Foster: Did you have heavy casualties during this incident?

Guidry: Very few casualties there. Very few up to that point. We stayed at Bougie, North Africa, attached to the British, until March of 1942 after the Battle of Kasserine Pass where my outfit lost quite a few men. We were sent up to Kasserine Pass to prevent the Germans from advancing further. We were pretty much in a holding position at Kasserine Pass until we were moved up to the edge of the Sahara Desert.

We moved up toward the town of El Guettar — what they call El Guettar Pass [in Tunisia] — where some of the hardest fighting of the African campaign was. We lost quite a few men the first day of attack at El Guettar Pass. We lost — had wounded and killed — about 90 men the first day. Then we pulled back and maneuvered around and finally the position was taken.

I had wondered for a long time what my feeling would be at being shot at. And afterwards, I found I had no feelings whatsoever. I took it for granted. I was going to be shot at and had to try to survive. We had very little water, very little experience in semi-desert fighting. It was not easy.

Foster: At night did you sleep in tents?

Guidry: No. On a battlefield if you were in a holding position, you dug a hole and you stayed there.

Foster: And how long a period are we talking about?

Guidry: Well, it could be for a day or two. You might move in the middle of the night. And we got lost a few times in the mountains. The officers would read the maps wrong, and we'd get lost. Almost all the hills had a number. It was always trying to capture a hill. The Germans always had the high ground, and we had to climb to try to capture it.

Men that were wounded in the mountains in that region, they had to crawl out [of the desert]. No ambulance could get to them. You had to take details out to get rations. We rented donkeys from the Arabs, and you would haul rations with donkeys up into the position we were occupying and fighting.

I remember particularly one case when I took men to get rations. Going back, the wounded were crawling back, some holding up those that couldn't walk. There was sweat and mud running down their face, and it was not a good picture. It was just a picture of survival.

Foster: What was morale like?

Guidry: Well, morale was fairly good considering the conditions. We all accepted our lot in life, I'd say.

Foster: How was your relationship with your officers?

Guidry: I had a good relationship with my officers. I still correspond with the officer that was wounded with me. We fought in North Africa together. We fought in all the campaigns of what they call the Sedjenane Valley campaign in Africa and [in] the Sicilian campaign. We fought together until we were wounded, September the twenty-seventh, 1944.

Foster: Were you able to maintain your sense of humor?

Guidry: We always joked about the war. Fighting in North Africa, while pinned down by machine gun fire, there was a soldier [that] crawled by me. I was piling rocks up in front of me to get behind. A soldier about fifteen feet ahead was in a little depression, and this fellow crawled up to him and caught him by the heel. He shook his heel and said, "Fellow, you dead? I need that hole." I had to laugh. The fellow didn't raise his head and said, "Hell no! I'm not dead." That is the thing that you see in combat.

Foster: Well, you had to remain sane.

Guidry: Had to remain sane. In another combat incident, we were under machine gun fire, and the machine gun was clipping twigs. Hand grenades [were] even being thrown. A fellow by the name of Oswell [was] a few feet below me. He rolled over and grabbed his self. I said, "What's the matter, Oswell? You hit?" He says, "No, I done messed on myself." [Those things] actually happened. Oswell deserted right after that. He was given thirty years, and I don't know what happened to him.

Foster: You had been in the mountains. Were you taking ground hill by hill?

Guidry: Yes. That's right. When we entered [the] Sedjenane Valley campaign, it was sort of a different landscape. It was green. We weren't far from the Mediterranean coast as we advanced. It was rocky terrain, and the Germans contested almost every inch. When we'd get on high ground, we could see the British advancing along the Mediterranean coast. We continued until we got to the town of Mateur, a French town around Lake Bizerte. We were in the capture of Bizerte, and I entered the town. After that, we moved out of town. When the Germans surrendered, it was a sight to see. Thousands of German soldiers being moved into POW camps there.

Foster: Were these the [prisoners] who were sent to the States very early on in the war?

Guidry: Yes. They were sent to the United States.

Foster: Weren't there some in Louisiana?

Guidry: Yes. When I came home, they still had German soldiers [in Louisiana POW camps]. I [saw] some on the Cinclare Plantation after I got home. [Also,] there was a big camp in Port Allen.

Foster: That's what I thought. That must have been so strange to think that there were Germans here. You were there, and they were here.

Guidry: Yes. After the African campaign, we were sent near a town they call Magenta. We stayed there and trained. It was called a "fly" area because the flies were so bad you couldn't hardly eat your food. Hot. Not very far from the desert. We went on past to Sidi-bel-Abbes, the home of the French Foreign Legion and got a chance to visit their headquarters. Then, we were taken by trucks on a parade for King George VI and President Roosevelt at Oran, North Africa, along the coast [of Algeria].

We went back to Magenta and stayed there and trained a while. One interesting incident that was never put in the papers, a bunch of people from the US — I'd say politicians, maybe, or diplomats — they were going to put on a demonstration to show how troops advance under what is called a "rolling barrage of artillery." So, they lined us up by two lines of white tape. They gave the order for the artillery to fire. When the artillery would fire, we would get up and advance. The range was incorrect, and the first barrage killed and wounded twenty-one men. Killed the third man in the line where I was. Part of the head was left, in his helmet. One man was hit in the throat and [there was] blood gushing out. Oh, I'm about to sweat, but anyhow, I'll go [on]. We had no ambulance out there. I don't know if he lived or died. But after they picked up the wounded and the dead, we was ordered to line up again and go through it. And we went. We didn't like it, but we went.

We were sent near Bizerte, North Africa, to gather for the invasion of Sicily. We were stationed in a large, bowl-like thing that could have been created by a meteorite or something, but when we moved in there the first night, German bombers, big six-engine bombers, bombed us with napalm bombs. Some of the men got up and ran, and hey, I don't know how many men were killed, but it was a bad night. We survived it. You could see the bombers. One was caught in the searchlights with the anti-aircraft firing at it, and you could see the bomb being released and coming down on us. It took a while to gather everybody together again. Then later, we boarded ship. We landed at Licata, Sicily.

We were in the first wave there too, at Licata. My regiment was separated from our regular division and attached to the First Infantry Division. We started up the coast of Sicily. Very little opposition from the Sicilians; the Italian army did not give us too much trouble, and [we had] very little loss.

We went down the coast toward the town of Syracuse. Advancing along the coast it was very interesting to see some of the medieval castles on top of high hill outcroppings. Further along, one evening late, the commanding officer of two batteries of artillery offered to surrender them to me. I just turned them over to the officers in the rear because that's how easy it was.

Cyril Guidry in tank with Jack Forsythe

To remark on some things that happen during war, while we were boiling some corn we took out of an Italian field, we received a notice that we were going to move up into an attack further back going up the coast. A fellow by the name of Sergeant Morgan said, "Well, I want to tell you fellows, the next battle is going to be mine. I'm going to get it." And strange as it seems, he was killed in the next battle. That's what I find funny about war: how you can understand these things. We went on.

We advanced past Mount Etna and fought hard battles in the hills and dry sections of Sicily. Sometimes we would dig in where they had dry grass. The Germans would shoot phosphorous shells and try to burn us out. But we advanced, bypassed Mount Etna — we could see Mt. Etna smoking — and got [as] far as the Strait of Messina.

When the Sicilian campaign was over, we came back into bivouac and stayed in an olive grove and trained a little, right on the

Mediterranean. We were swimming in the Mediterranean. We stayed there until early September of 1943. While there, I went on a trip to Palermo, Sicily, and enjoyed just looking at the old churches and sights. Then we went to Palermo to embark for England. Went back through the Strait of Gibraltar [and] landed in England in September of 1943.

Ida Turcan

Ida Turcan became a nurse in 1939 and joined the army in 1941. While stationed at Fort Benning, [Georgia] one of Turcan's roommates suggested that they go overseas. Turcan remembers, "She came and told me the next day that she had signed my name to go overseas. So we went. We went to Fort Dix and to North Africa."

Turcan: [Before the U.S. entered the war,] we didn't get too much of the news. I remembered little things, bits and pieces. When Hitler had invaded Poland, I think, was one of the things that hit me. But, I have to truly say that wasn't why I went in the army, not to get Hitler. I would be far removed from that. My brothers may have had that feeling, but mine was more of doing what I did when I got there: taking care of the wounded.

We were in a staging area [in North Africa] for about two weeks, and then, we set up our own hospital. We received wounded from the battles in North Africa then. At one time, we had to move our hospital, you know, "bug out" because they were getting too close to us. They knew that the front lines were coming a little too close for comfort. But we didn't bug out very long because it was during the time we began to get the advantage [over] Rommel's army. We got [to North Africa] just before winter, and we left in the spring. At that time, I was working in the station hospital. We had field, evacuation and station hospitals. Station was supposed to be kind of permanent, but it wasn't. In North Africa, you didn't know what was going to happen. They weren't too sure of how the Arab community felt towards us, but fortunately they must have been on our side. They didn't kill any of us.

A hospital in North Africa was set up right next to an Arab cemetery. I thought it was interesting. On one side was a cemetery, and on the other side was a wheat field. We did have one casualty who was an African native who got run over by a jeep and put in our hospital. We had him in our tent, and [the Arabs] had some belief that they had to have their head covered, which we didn't know about. So when he woke up, he took off all his pajamas and wrapped them around his head. We thought he was, you know, maybe a little not all there, but it was custom that made him do that. He smelled to high heaven and didn't want a bath. Anyway, we nicknamed him Sweet Pea.

About this time was when Bob Hope visited North Africa. I have a picture in Life magazine of me and Bob Hope. He was entertaining troops in the compound, and the boys on my ward wanted to see him. They couldn't leave to go because they were all bed-ridden. And I said, "Listen, we'll get him over here." So, I sent my sergeant over to ask him to come over because these boys wanted to see him.

Foster: And how many boys were in your [ward]?

Turcan: Twenty-four. There were huge tents set up. And he did come over and was most amiable. He talked to each one. Went up and down the corridor and just was very nice. I asked him for a piece of gum. I think he was giving up smoking at the time; he gave me a piece of gum. Should have kept it instead of chewing it. From time to time, they sent [other] entertainment troops over. Marlene Dietrich came, and she used our latrine. We wrote around the hole, "Marlene Dietrich Sat Here." The enlisted men, when we moved from one place to the other, swapped holes on us, you know, took the big piece of wood with the holes on it and put it in their latrine. I thought it was a kind of cute joke.

Foster: What was it like the first time you saw casualties?

Turcan: Rather nauseating and shocking, you know, to see young people mangled. We also had German patients, you know, casualties.

Foster: Was that common?

Turcan: Yes. Somebody had to take care of them. For a short time, we had a couple of German doctors and German nurses. We let them take care of their own, under supervision. Their army techniques were not up to ours. I had always thought before that Germany was up here, and maybe we were down here because we bought instruments and things from Germany.

Foster: They were more primitive?

Turcan: Well, dirty is what I'd call it. Their techniques were just not as good as ours. We didn't think so. Very shortly, [the German doctors] had arguments with the [American] doctors, and they decided that they would no longer let this continue because, after all, we were responsible. [A wounded German soldier] was a patient just like an American was a patient. Nobody had any bad feelings about them like "you dirty German" or anything. He was another young fellow that was in the army. He couldn't help it. And that was about all.

Foster: Was serving in North Africa traumatic for you?

Turcan: Oh, the lack of water was a big problem. In the day, we had one helmet of water to take care of our personal needs with. So, you used that to brush your teeth, wash your face and what other bathing. And don't throw it away because you had to wash your underwear in it.

It was kind of sloppy living, you know. Like camping. Later they got showers put in, but our first couple of weeks there, we lived with that helmet of water. It was because they were in such a hurry to get a lot of people over there that they got more people than they had water. Africa was a country that didn't have too much water anyway. So, they used it, I guess, to irrigate their fields, and whatever they had to do with it.

Foster: What about eating?

Turcan: Eating. [Laughs] We ate rations like the soldiers did for a while. I don't even remember what was in them. They weren't labeled. You just opened up a can, and you got this funny stuff. One of the big things I can't eat till this day is Spam. Ick! [laughs] We had a lot of Spam, and we got dried eggs. When they got the kitchen set up we had those things, but we ate canned rations for at least two weeks before we got anything.

Foster: What about R and R?

Turcan: Yes, we did have R and R. We had a place set up in Oran in Algeria. We were in Algiers first, and then we were moved to Oran, where we set up a hospital. They had a beautiful Mediterranean beach, and we had a week of R and R before we went to Sicily. We didn't have a bathing suit, so we had to improvise. Some girls did [have suits]. I never thought of packing a bathing suit. So I wrote my sister right away, but I didn't get the suit for a long time. I made one out of camouflage material. It was a funny looking thing, but it was a swimming suit, and I wore it — with a top like a bra and the panties. I didn't know how to make pants, so they were kind of funny-looking too. Took my elastic out of my regular underwear to hold the top up. And that didn't work too good, so I think I put a string or something, you know, a piece of rope and tied it. They were funny looking.

Foster: Who lived in your camp, just girls? Were the boys with you too?

Turcan: It was just the girls at one camp, and they had another one not too far [away] for enlisted men and one for army officers. The army was like it is now, you weren't allowed to associate with enlisted men. That went astray sometimes.

Foster: That wasn't enforced?

Turcan: Well, it really was, but you know people, if they're attracted to one another . . . It was like a girl who married a sergeant was looked down upon, almost. Put the girls and boys together, you're going to have problems. But for the most part, we got used to it.

Foster: Did you ever have the chance to get to know any of the GIs, or was it move them in and move them out?

Turcan: With the patients, mostly, it was move them in, move them out. The idea was, if they were all right, to get them back to duty. In the army, you either had to be ready to go on duty or stay in the hospital. Of course, many of them were able to walk around, shower themselves, but mostly, we'd move them [from the] station hospital to a general hospital. Then, they either went home or went on duty.

Foster: Did you see any shell shock?

Turcan: Yes. Most of those were transferred to psychiatric units. Pretty early in the war, they started having psychiatric hospitals that they went to, and [then they would] send them home. They were small units — I don't even know where they were located — I know they'd say, "We have to send him to psych," and off he'd go.

Foster: How did you feel about General Patton?

Turcan: General   Patton?   I
didn't know about that right away.
General Patton was in North Africa,
of course, as you know. He was also
at Fort Benning. I rode his horses.

[General Patton] had polo
ponies at Fort Benning, and he wanted
them rode. So the nurses had first
choice to go out and ride the ponies
when they weren't having polo games.
He was a great horseman, but he was
also a hard hombre. And I guess he
would be considered a kind of sick
man. You know, he had arthritis. He
was my husband's commander when
he was at Fort Benning, when he first
went in. When [my husband] was
introduced to [Patton], the first thing
he did was go to his home, and
[Patton] handed [him] a glass to chug-

Ida Turcan & coworkers

a-lug. If you were able to do it, you were a good guy. But I saw the movie about Patton, and I did hear of the time he slapped the boy in the hospital. I didn't know him; I saw him when we were at Fort Benning, but I was just a little nurse and he was God Almighty [laughs]. I don't understand his reasoning that way, but I didn't have to.

Foster: In North Africa, were you handling amputations?

Turcan: We didn't have that many amputations in North Africa. Where we really got them was in Italy because they had set up land mines where they would hit them. Some of them were set up in trees, where they would hit them here [in the upper torso], hoping they would kill them. A lot of them were arm amputations for that reason. Of course, a lot of them they killed, too. In North Africa, I would say, we got as many jeep accidents as we got casualties, bullet fragments, and so forth.

Foster: Why was that? Carelessness?

Turcan: Carelessness or the roads. The roads weren't too good. The terrain wasn't too good, either. We were on desert, part desert. Then, there were mountains. Speed, I guess. And young people.

Foster: Did you date?

Turcan: We dated a lot. We had dances and, from time to time, marriages. Let's see, three of my roommates married officers that they dated overseas. They got back earlier than I did because if you were pregnant, you couldn't stay overseas. I remember Millie saying she wanted to wait to get married, she said, "But I want to go home worse than I want to wait." She got married overseas.

[After North Africa], we went to Sicily, and we weren't there very long. We got our hospital set up, and a storm blew in and blew it down. Then, they decided we didn't need to be in Sicily anyway because the invasion was not coming to Sicily. They thought it was, but it came to Italy. So we were in Italy, and we set up our hospital in the place that would have been the 1945 World's Fair. It was beautiful grounds and buildings. They had a swimming pool. They set up two or three hospitals in there because it was so much space. Then, they transferred me to an evacuation hospital. They broke up our unit.

Thomas Blakeney

Prior to shipping out for Africa, Thomas Blakeney trained in Texas, with what he calls "the tankless tank battalion." At first there were no tanks at the camp, and when tanks finally arrived, Blakeney says, "We got a few small ones that were left over from World War I. They were called Mae West because they had two turrets, something like a brassiere, you know." Despite the initial meager training conditions, Blakeney became astute at tank operation, eventually naming his tank for the young lady who became his wife, Girlie.

Blakeney: The ship that we rode on [to the invasion of Casablanca] was the sea train Texas. It had been a ship that had sailed from Florida to Cuba and carried railway cars in the hull, and so it was ideal for tanks. We would drive the tanks right into the hull of it. The only danger was that it had no compartmentation, like most sea vessels did, and had we received one torpedo, we'd have gone down like a rock.

We sailed in convoy for Casablanca in October of 1942 for the invasion there. We had one interesting thing happen while we were in the middle of the ocean; we lost our power. They blew a gasket in the engine of the sea train Texas. So we fell about eight hours behind the convoy, and again, we were in considerable danger from torpedoes. But I can remember hearing them start the engine. They had to start it with a charge, like a shot gun charge, and it was a little loud explosive noise. It started up, and we fired up. And we started in toward Casablanca.

When we got to Casablanca, the fighting was just about over. It only lasted a couple of days, initially, and we disembarked in the harbor of Casablanca over the decks of the French battleship Jean Bart. The Jean Bart had been one of the biggest battleships in the world, and the French had scuttled it, along with the rest of the French navy. So we disembarked there across the decks of the Jean Bart and went back to a place behind Casablanca where we built our battalion living area. We stayed there for several months.

We moved up to Rabat, which was just north of Casablanca, and bivouacked in a cork forest. The cork oak is what they made the corks out of for wine bottles and various other things. We stayed there several months, and I got a chance to go to Tunisia, where the fighting was still going on. I went up to Tunisia with several other officers to find out what it was like.

We were in Tunisia maybe three or four months before we finally captured Rommel's Afrika Corps in Tunis. We captured several hundred thousand Germans there. They'd been driven in to us by the British and our own American forces. They [had] just started off as far away as Egypt and had [been] driven back into Tunis.

Carville: So your first taste of actual combat was quite a significant event, wasn't it?

Blakeney: Well, yes it was. It made me wonder if I was smart because it was pretty scary. It was pretty scary. You see, we were supposed to have air superiority in North Africa, but every time a plane came over and started shooting at us it was a German plane. It was usually a Ju-88. I learned real fast that they not only had machine guns that fired out the front, but they had some machine guns that fired out of the tail, too.

When the six or eight officers that had gone up there came back from Tunis to [the] cork forest, to join the Seven-Sixtieth again, the Seven-Sixtieth had orders to move. We moved up to a place called Oran, in Algeria, to get ready for the invasion of Italy, or Sicily. Nobody really knew where they were going to go. But the invasion of Sicily started about that time, and they didn't call us because they had enough tanks.

They didn't need anymore tanks. We were diverted and went into the invasion of Italy.

We landed south of Naples and went into Italy. We got into the fight almost immediately, moving towards Naples. [It] was a pretty grisly place then. The Germans were still bombing it. They were using the fires of Mount Vesuvius as a guide to come in, and there was a lot of bombing and artillery going on around there. From Naples we moved north and got involved in the fight at [Monte] Cassino.

Cassino was well known then because it had a big abbey, full of monks, and it was sitting right on the high hill. You could see everything that was coming, and it was pretty damn dangerous. I know that the pope was reported to have said that there were no Germans in the abbey. Well, if there weren't any Germans in the abbey, the monks were shooting because I could see tracers coming out of that big abbey every night.

Anthony Palumbo

From Fort McClellan in Anniston, Alabama, Palumbo was sent as an officer to Africa in 1943.

Palumbo: Africa was kind of a dull place for me. We went into Casablanca after the fighting started. They had already captured the city Casablanca from the French. We didn't know what was going on; we were just fighting. If they would ask us to fight, we would fight. We didn't have any reason not to fight. We were just so far down the totem pole, we didn't know the reasons for any of the fighting — other than the fact that we were fighting there so that we could get that licked and go over and fight the Japs as soon as we could.

Foster: How did you feel about fighting Italians?

Palumbo: Being of Italian extraction? The Italians were not big fighters anyway. The Italians that I had contact with were mostly prisoners of war, and they were anti-Mussolini as much as they could be without getting themselves caught.

I had an uncle who was pro-Mussolini for a long time. As a matter of fact, he was killed by the partisans after World War II. This is my father's only brother, younger brother. [The Italians] sided with us during World War I. We didn't know much about World War I, ourselves, but this time they were following Mussolini's dictate. Mussolini was a fascist from the word go. Those Italians that actually opposed him were just put out of the way in a hurry. So, it was easier to go along with him, than not to go along with him.

Foster: During the war when you were in Africa did they use you for special purposes because of the fact that you were fluent in Italian?

Palumbo: Yes. They did. They used me at the headquarters in the T-2 section because I could talk to the Italian prisoners of war and see if they had any problems. I was able to help somewhat on that score, but it wasn't what I had been trained to do.

Foster: Can you describe a typical day [in Africa]?

Palumbo: A typical day in Africa? In the town of Bizerte for instance, we were being bombed by the Germans almost daily. We had one particular phase where we were hit by Germans. They had come over from Sicily. This is before we invaded Sicily. But a typical day for me in Africa was trying to dodge bombs. I do recall one incident where the bombs had hit the unit's medical station, and all of our medics were either killed in action or wounded in action. We had to call in for more support.

Foster: What was morale like?

Palumbo: [It] was real down when the bombs hit. [We] wanted to get out there and fight, if we could.

I recall one instance that occurred in Casablanca. I was walking down the street in Casablanca when I saw this jeep come by with "U.S. Military" on it. It was a navy jeep. The driver in the jeep was the Lieutenant Z. Carey, who lived about five doors from me in Rochester, New York. So we stopped, and he said to me, "Tony, how you doing?" I said, "How are you doing fellow?" We both embraced each other, both coming from the same neighborhood. He asked me if I had seen my brother, Albert. Albert was in the navy. I said, "No." He said, "He has been trying to contact you." Last he heard, he was somewhere in the Port of Oran. Oran is about maybe 150 or 200 klicks [kilometers] north of Casablanca, right on the sea. In any event, Albert had been to Oran, and I had missed him, although we had been trying for years to get together somewhere.

Charles Titkemeyer

After training in aviation navigation at Monroe, Louisiana, Titkemeyer became a second lieutenant in U.S. Army Air Corps in January 1943. Titkemeyer was sent to Tucson, Arizona, where he began training as a crew member of a B-24 Liberator Bomber. He recalls that the bomber "looked like a bumble-bee and like a bumble-bee, it defied aerodynamics." After spending time in Newfoundland, Ireland, and Scotland, Titkemeyer and the other crew were assigned to work with the 44th Bomb Group at Shipdom Air Force Base in Norwich, England.

Titkemeyer: [In England] we were issued another B-24 [Bomber].

Now there, again, we practiced a lot of shakedown cruises to make sure we knew what we were doing. Then one day, they sent us to Banghazi, [Libya,] on the north coast of Africa. They said to us, "We're sending you down there for a special mission." We had not flown any combat missions in England, although we had been there for several weeks.

The base [in Banghazi] was nothing more than just a leveled off place in the desert, and we had tents to live in. That's where we were for a few weeks. They had us practicing low level [flying]. Now that's unusual because we were in a plane that was designated to fly up to 20,000 feet, but they made us practice low level.

Finally on August 1, 1943, we were sent on a low level raid on the Ploesti oil fields in Romania. We were briefed the night before and told, "If you are lucky, and they don't find out you're coming, a third of you will get back. If you are unlucky, and they find out," he says, "none of you are going to get back." And they said, "The following men will volunteer." They had it posted on the board. The first name I saw was a great big long "Charles William Titkemeyer" will volunteer. So I volunteered!

Besch: Was this your first combat mission?

Titkemeyer: That was our first combat mission. And, believe me, it was one that matured you and made a seasoned veteran out of you.

Well, this raid [was vital for the war effort] because of the oil. Germany depended on oil to keep their tanks and their planes going. In Romania, they had a huge oil field, and a lot of that oil field was actually run by Americans: Shell and Texaco. They were the ones who were exploring and bringing out this oil. The object was to destroy this oil field and the cracking plants around it so that we would deny Hitler the source of oil. We had excellent intelligence on it because the American companies that owned it showed us exactly where each building was. So we knew where we were going.

On the way over there we had a little mishap. We were flying B-24's, Eighth Air Force, but there also was the Fourteenth Air Force from the desert who were also flying on that mission. Now, on the way over there, we run into a big bank of clouds. In England, we were trained if you come to a bank of clouds, you circle and slowly climb until you get above the clouds, and then you go over the clouds. The Fourteenth Air Force was trained [that] when you hit clouds, you separate a little bit but hold your position and go straight threw those clouds without changing heading. Well, as a result of our making that big circle to get above the clouds, they got about fifteen minutes ahead of us. When we got to the target, they [had been] there fifteen minutes ahead of us. They, of course, alerted the [enemy] gunners to the fact that we were doing this low-level [bombing mission]. They came across that target and didn't have a loss.

Along we came and not only did we have the gunnery aiming at the right height to get us, but we also had their exploding bombs, all the fire, and the exploding oil tanks to go through. So, we literally flew through hell in order to get across that target. But it was exciting. I'll say that. It was exciting. Things happened so fast that it was difficult to remember it until you talked it over later. I looked out the window and saw a plane going right straight at a big smoke stack, but the smoke was so thick ahead of him he didn't see it. He hit that smoke stack, and down went the stack and the plane and all. Also, at that low level, if a small caliber weapon hit one of the engines, then that engine [would] shut out before the pilot could stabilize it. That wing would hit the ground and she'd roll.

Besch: How high were you?

Titkemeyer: We were on the ground. So help me, there were planes that came back that, when they closed their bomb bay doors, picked up stalks of corn. We were on the ground. We had to be because the gunnery platforms were up high, and we were trying to fly under them. But we were as low as you could possibly be over a city and over an oil refinery.

aug. 1, 1943   Ploesti oil fields

A B-24 Gropes Its Way Through
the Smoke and Fire of Ploesti

Besch: Where did you go after you hit the oil fields?

Titkemeyer: Well, then we went back to Banghazi.

Besch: You turned around and flew back across the continent?

Titkemeyer: We flew back. Now, this was the longest raid that had ever been pulled up to that date, so we just barely had enough gasoline to get back to Banghazi, which we did. We had [a] 50 percent loss that day. We were lucky. We were among the 50 percent who got back.

Besch: How many losses did the fourteenth suffer?

Titkemeyer: I'm not sure of their losses, but they had very few losses.

Besch: Was this after Rommel's defeat?

Titkemeyer: Yes. It was after Rommel was defeated. The desert was full of tanks that were burned out and full of old jeeps and that sort of thing. It also was full of land mines. You had to be careful walking away from the beaten path, or you'd step on a land mine. I will say this for Rommel, he was probably the greatest general in the entire war. It took all of Montgomery's forces to capture the famous "Desert Fox." The only reason they finally caught up with him was because Hitler had given up and quit sending him supplies. He ran out of fuel.

Besch: Where'd you go from Banghazi?

Titkemeyer: We took our beat-up airplanes and went back to our original base in England. We made a few more raids [from England,] which [were] not particularly important. And then they sent us back down to Africa because of our boys at Palermo Beach, [Sicily].
    [The U.S. military forces] were attacking at Palermo, and our boys were about to be pushed off of that beach. Suddenly they said, "We want somebody to give them some quick help and the quickest help we got are the bombers." So they sent us back down there. This time we were based in Tunis, and our job was to bomb ahead of our troops at Palermo. Well, by the time we got down there, they had already taken [Palermo]. They didn't need us for that. So somebody got the idea,

"Well, now let's go up and bomb out the airplane factory at Wiener Neustadt, in Austria."

[Wiener Neustadt] was a city not far from Vienna, actually. When we got up there, we discovered that the Germans, in their flair for parades and that sort of thing, were having a big day for flying their airplanes. They had all of their planes lined up in a row ready to take off to go show how great they were. We did not bomb the factory. We went right down that line of airplanes dropping our bombs and wiped out almost every one of them. We never got a shot fired at us. They didn't know we weren't German! I don't know why they didn't recognize that those old B-24s weren't German. We got through that one very easily.

A little later somebody got the idea, "Let's go now and get the factory." They were waiting for us. Goering and his Hornets were up there, and that's the day they really wiped us out. Out of our squadron of eight planes, we got the only one back home. I immediately became squadron navigator with a captain's rating because we were the only crew left in our squadron.

Out of twenty-eight planes, we got seven back. We did have two crews that crash-landed in Italy, and we did get the crews back. So then again we went back to England. After that, we stayed in England until we finished our tour of duty.

Erbon Wise

Wise was one of the earliest American officers to arrive in England in World War II. "As Finance Disbursing Officer, I suddenly found myself paying most of the American military there," says Wise.

Wise: When I arrived in England in 1942, our military was seemingly highly disorganized, as it generally is at the beginning of all its wars. My unit had few supplies. For help, I went by train to London, trying to find American headquarters that had been recently set up there somewhere. This was at the beginning of the American arrivals. I walked the streets of London asking for American headquarters, and people thought I was a spy.

To spend the night there, another young officer and I went to the only hotel of which we had heard — the Savoy, one of the grand old hotels of London, down on the Strand in the theater district. I guess because we were the first American soldiers they'd seen, they gave to us two second lieutenants a royal suite. I had never seen such luxurious quarters.

That evening as we came down to the dining room, there were these reserved English people having dinner. An orchestra was playing. As we walked in, everyone rose and clapped. Here were the Americans to enter the war and the orchestra struck up their version of "Dixie." My friend, who came from the mountains of Tennessee, couldn't bear this high drama, so he let out the loudest rebel yell that I guess has been heard since Bull Run. I have never seen such shocked people.

The English warmly welcomed us, as they were really on their last legs. Their shipping, which they desperately depended on for food import, had been largely sunk by enemy submarines. Much of their military was down in North Africa fighting the war there.

American troops were paid considerably more than British soldiers, with an American private earning more than an English lieutenant.

We brought in thousands of young men, and here were thousands of lonesome girls whose men were somewhere else. There was an awful lot of romance and many marriages. Visit any town in America today, and you will find English girls who married American soldiers. At that time, some English complained of the Americans as "Over paid, over sexed, and over here."

For our soldiers there were social activities such as dances on military posts, dance halls in London, USO clubs, and English families who invited Americans into their homes. Through the hospitality of these families I met many fine people who, through the following years, I have corresponded with and visited again.

The English are a great people of true grit who fought hard and sacrificed greatly in this war.

Although in the Army Air Corps, I was not a flyer. In 1942, I was a ground officer in the headquarters of the Ninety-first Bomb Group, the second heavy-bomber B-17 to be sent to England. I spent two years in England where at first we had only three B-17 groups. We were trying to develop precision daylight bombing of the enemy. The three groups could launch only fifty to sixty planes for a mission and invariably fifteen or more of them would be shot down. We were having about 100 percent turnover of flying personnel in 1942, and it was a very stressful time for the Army Air Corps in England.

Air crews were promised that if any ever finished twenty-five missions, they would be sent home. But the planes were always shot down before they finished twenty-five. This was mainly because we did not have long range fighter planes to protect the bombers. At that time, the labor leader, John L. Lewis, had all the fighter producing plants in America shut down on strike. When our fifty or sixty bombers flew over France or Germany, they'd be hit by five hundred German fighter planes.

At our airbase at Bassingbourn, near Cambridge, in the fall of 1942, I saw a miracle occur. The *Memphis Belle*, one of our B-17 bombers, returned completing twenty-five missions. Everyone else there felt they truly saw the same miracle that day. William Wilder, the movie director, saw it and later produced an excellent movie documentary called the *Memphis Belle*. The movie of the same name, produced about 1996 by another director, was a farce. Later in 1943, 1944, and 1945, we had thousands of planes over there. But in the early part of the war in England, we had only three groups, and they suffered grievous losses.

Oscar Richard

Richard was the bombardier of the 384th Bomber Group stationed at Grafton Underwood Air Base in England. Richard and the crew of the B-17 flew two missions into Germany, first, to bomb a synthetic fuel plant and then, an aircraft assembly plant. On their third mission, six months prior to the D-Day invasion, the crew of the B-17 had successfully destroyed its target, a launching site for German V-1 and V-2 rockets on the coast of France, when its bomber was hit. All of the crew members, except one, were captured by Germans.

Richard: I was shot down over France and came down in a parachute right into a flak battery and picked up right away. In fact, the other planes were coming over, still dropping bombs when I was on the ground. I had to spend a half hour or so in a foxhole with a German GI. The only one of us that wasn't captured was the navigator, Ernie Lindell. He was the only one of us wounded. I remember him tapping me on the shoulder. I looked around, and he was all bloody. He had gotten his arm shot up from flak. I never saw [him] again until last September, and we had a nice get-together.

Ernie told me about his experiences. He got help from the French Underground and holed up in a farm house near Amiens [close to] the Normandy coast for about three months before they could move him out of there. They got him down a little bit at a time, all the way down through France into Spain — through Spain and over the Pyrenees, down to Gibraltar. He got to Gibraltar on June 6th, D-Day, six months after we were shot down. They sent him home.

Besch: Where'd they hold you?

Richard: It was in Stalag Luft 1, which is right on the Baltic Sea, directly north of Berlin, in Barth, Germany. We were there until the Russian Army came in and liberated [the camp] in May of 1945.

When I got there the enrollment was about eight or nine

hundred, mostly RAF [British Royal Air Force] because it was one of the oldest camps in Germany. Some of the RAF fellows had been there for years, since the outset of the war, some of them even before war was declared. And by the end of the war, I think, there were at least ten thousand [prisoners of war, almost] all airmen.

"Photo of our bomber crew taken at Grand Island, Nebraska, Army Air Base shortly before we flew to England, October 1943. Top. L to r: Clarence Wolfe, tail gunner; Morton Harris, radio operator; Morton Mason, waist gunner; Donald Tucker, engineer; Conway Nichols, wist gunner; (unidentified--replaced by Bill Argenbright), Ball turret gunner. Bottom, l to r: Neil Britt, pilot; Oscar Richard bombardier; Ray Haley, co-pilot; Ernie Lindel, navigator."

There were few, very few, infantry people that had been captured during the Battle of the Bulge who had been shuttled around to different camps [that] wound up in our camp, most of them really suffering from frostbite and pneumonia. They were in bad shape.

They had all the airmen together [at Stalag Luft 1], and I found out later that there was a big battle between Hermann Goering, who was head of the Luftwaffe [the German Air Force] and Himmler. Himmler tried to convince Hitler that he ought to be in charge of all the POWs as a matter of state security, but Goering, I guess, had the close ear to Hitler, [and] convinced him that "I ought to be in charge of all the airmen," which was a good thing because he had the strange notion that all airmen were knights of the sky, fellow flyers, that type of thing. As far as treatment was concerned, we were a lot better off than a lot of POWs until the attempt to assassinate Hitler. Then, [the] Wehrmacht took over, and it got real tough.

Besch: In the German prison, what was your most impressionable experience?

Richard: My most impressionable experience was when we got out of [Stalag Luft 1]. It was toward the end of the war. The German transportation railroads were all tied up, and they claimed they couldn't get the Red Cross food packages in. We didn't have much to eat there for about two or three months; this would be from February to mid-April, '45. It got to the point where we figured we couldn't last much longer on the caloric intake that we had, just a bare amount to get by. Finally, it was sometime in April, the Red Cross made arrangements with the German people to have American trucks come in [with] the parcels. They finally got them in shortly before Easter of 1945. I would say that period toward the end of the war was the worst. We didn't know what the heck was going to happen to us.

Besch: After you were rescued, what happened?

Richard: We were there for about two weeks after the Russians came. No, less than that. I would say a little over a week we remained [at the POW camp] At first the Russians said they were going to move us out of there through Russia, through Vladivostok or one or the other ports, I don't know which. And then Hubert Zemke, who was our ranking officer — he was a young fighter pilot, he could speak Russian — convinced the Russians, "Hell, we don't want any part of going through all of that crap." So he had contacted the American officials who were coming in from the West, and they made arrangements to have the Eighth Air Force come in with planes to pick us up. But first they had to clear an airfield. The Germans had left, and they had mined the airfield, which was adjacent to our prison camp. They had to spend several days clearing the runways and removing booby traps and all that stuff. Finally on, I think it was on May 8th or 9th , I forget which, they came in; it was a Sunday, Mothers' Day. I remember that. They sent in about three or four-hundred B-17s. They just came in one after the other. They didn't even stop. They'd just taxi, and we'd pile in and take off and fly into France. We were sent to the big tent city there on the Normandy coast called Camp Lucky Strike. They had several named after cigarettes for some reason. And we were there, seemed like, another two weeks. In fact, I didn't even wait; a pilot that I knew came in from our base, and I flew back with him.

Besch: Back to the U.S.?

Richard: No, back to England, back to our old base.

Ralph Sims

As the program manager of Baton Rouge radio station WJBO, Sims had followed closely the events leading up to the bombing of Pearl Harbor. Once the Japanese attacked, he decided to enlist in the Army Air Corps and after training, joined a B-17 bomber group flying missions from England into Europe. Sims' first mission was

Berlin, "the most heavily defended target in Europe." "How we survived that day,"
Sims still wonders, "I don't know."

Sims: As I mentioned earlier, I was stationed near Attleborough, which is near Norwich, an old cathedral town in East Anglia. There were times when we couldn't fly, when the weather was too bad and when Europe was just clouded over, and we couldn't see the targets. So occasionally we'd get a pass for a couple of days. We could go wherever we wanted to. I headed to London. It so happened that Charles Manship, Sr.— who owned the radio station WJBO and both newspapers, the *States-Item* and the *Morning Advocate* — was in London and was head of the Office of Censorship. He had a suite at the Dorchester Hotel, one of the finest hotels in London, overlooking Hyde Park. As soon as I got to London, I got in touch with him. He was very nice to me, took me to lunch at the Savoy Hotel, and we walked along the Thames.

I had called earlier to the Dorchester Hotel saying, "This is Sergeant Sims calling from our base in England, and I'd like to book a room for such and such a date." They were very polite and said, "We're sorry, but we don't take enlisted men." I asked if they could recommend another hotel in the same area, and they said, "How about the Mayfair?" I said, "I'll try the Mayfair," and the Mayfair turned out to be fine. I happened to meet Dinah Shore and Robert Preston and a few other people [there].

At any rate, Mr. Manship had a stroke while he was over there and had to be sent up to the country somewhere up away from London to recuperate. But he left word at the Dorchester that whenever I came to London, I could have his suite. From then on, whenever I came to London, I took advantage of that, but they always referred to me as "Lieutenant." They upgraded me. They never called me "Sergeant." They said, "Lieutenant Sims, good morning. So nice to see you again."

I never went anywhere else [in England], generally. I just went down to London, enjoyed the theater. I met people who had friends in the theater, and they would introduce me to actors and actresses. So, I enjoyed it as much as I could, although I found that many Americans did not enjoy England because it wasn't like home. I can still hear: "These damn Limeys! They have to stop every afternoon for tea!" which was probably true; that's just the custom. I made the most of it and enjoyed everything I could, even though London was blacked out at night, and there were buzz bombs coming over.

[I was in London during the Blitz.] You'd go to the theater, and they didn't sound any alarm. But there was a sign that would flash below the stage: "Bomb Alert. Bomb Alert." So if you wanted to leave and go to a bomb shelter, you could. I found most people, including me, just stayed there to watch the show and took our chances. But there were a lot of people bombed out. At night, there were a lot of people who slept down [in the] Underground, which is what they call the subway in London, because they had nowhere else to go.

What impressed me about the English as opposed to the Americans during war — there I was in a luxurious hotel, I could press a button, I could get somebody to come and ask me what I would like to have. They might not have much to offer. It might be powdered eggs and sausage or whatever for breakfast, but they would roll it in on a trolley with nice silver and beautiful napkins and everything. The waiter dressed properly. There was a spirit of service; whereas, back in this country, when I was in a hotel, [and] I called for room service, the answer was, "Don't you know there's a war on? Room service!" And they [the English] carried on with the theater. That was the spirit of the English people that impressed me so much. They said, "Life has to go on; you just can't cower in bomb shelters all the time."

Foster: Did you experience any close calls during the Blitz?

Sims: Oh, yes, I remember, my brother-in-law happened to be in the airborne infantry and was stationed up in the Midlands near Leicester in England. Through the Red Cross, we were able to establish contact with each other, and he came down to visit me one weekend. One morning we heard this bomb coming over. You could hear them coming. But when it stopped, you knew it was coming down. It sounded like it was right on top on us. I happened to be shaving [in] a bathroom with lots of glass around me, mirrors and windows and things, so I immediately left the bathroom and jumped under the bed, expecting that maybe it would hit us. As it turned out, it hit near Barkley Square, which was maybe two or three blocks away, but [it] gave us a good shaking. It let you know that those things were still around.

Foster: Can you tell me more about the B-17 bomber?

Sims: Well the B-17 was one of two heavy bombers in the U.S. Army Air Corps. The other was the B-24, called the Liberator. The B-17 was called Flying Fortress. It was a sleeker looking ship as compared to the 24, which we called the Flying Boxcar. Nevertheless, they both had their place in the strategic bombing of Germany and other Nazi targets in Europe.

   The B-17 had a crew of ten. I was the tail gunner. We had a pilot, a co-pilot, a navigator, a bombardier. Those were all of the officers; the rest were enlisted men, and we were all either tech sergeants or staff sergeants. The flight engineer was a tech sergeant. He was also the top turret gunner. The armorer occupied the ball beneath the ship in the belly. They both had twin guns — these were fifty caliber machine guns. Then, there was the radio man, who was not a gunner. He was strictly the radio man. The two waist gunners had guns on each side of the plane with open windows, so they had to endure a lot of cold. I was back in the tail all by myself. To get back there, I had to actually crawl, and I sat or knelt on a sort of motorcycle seat. We were connected by intercom. We all had throat mikes so the pilot, every fifty minutes during flight, would ask us to check in, starting with the nose and going around to the tail, so he would know that we were okay.

We flew at fairly high altitude — twenty-five, twenty-six thousand feet as a rule. That required us to use oxygen masks because the plane itself was not pressurized as planes are today. That was sort of an irritating factor because the oxygen masks would sometimes freeze up, pretty cold up there. We had electrified underwear, you might say. They were like electric blankets, except that this was underwear. All those had to be plugged in. If the equipment went out, we might have frozen to death. On top of that, we had fleece-lined jackets, pants, boots, and helmets as well as lots of wires going in and out both for the intercom and for the heating and also for the oxygen. All of that had to be connected. It was sort of cumbersome, but we got used to it. So, back there in my tail, I always saw the plane going away and what was behind us. That was called "six o'clock." "Twelve o'clock" was the nose of the plane; "three o'clock" on one side; "six o'clock" back in the tail; "nine o'clock" the other waist gunner. That's the way we identified enemy planes coming in. For example, "Enemy planes spotted six o'clock high" means I better get ready for action. So, I had my twin fifty-caliber machine guns that I could maneuver sideways, up and down, and so on.

There was one moment — I can't remember the particular flight or mission — but one of my guns jammed. I had to try to get behind an armor plate that was in front of me, as a protective measure, to try to un-jam the gun. To do that, I had to undo the cord that plugged in for the heating apparatus. Also, I had a harness on me for a parachute, which attached to a chest chute in case we had to bail out. In getting behind this armor plate, my parachute got caught somehow, and there I was stuck in the tail. I had taken off my throat mike; I could not communicate with the rest of the crew, and I felt like I couldn't get out. I was just stuck. Somehow sometimes you have superhuman strength under those circumstances, so something let me get free. I pulled and tugged and finally tore the harness apart but, nevertheless, got out after I'd finished fixing the machine guns. That was kind of scary, but as it turned out, things worked out okay. I got hooked up again with the microphone and with the heating equipment.

Foster: Why didn't you get a milk run for your first mission?

Sims: I guess whoever planned these things decided that Berlin needed to be hit again. It had been hit before — I'm sure many times — by those who preceded us. We didn't start flying until the early part of April, [1944]. When I went in for briefing and they said, "Berlin, Big B," I thought, this is the most heavily defended target that we would ever have to try to hit. I wasn't too happy about that, but orders are orders. We all got briefed and got in our plane. The ground crew got us all equipped with our ammunition and everything we needed for the flight.

Incidentally, we carried rations with us in case we were shot down so we could subsist for maybe a day or two. We also had what we called "escape kits" with fake passports, maps of Germany and adjacent countries: Belgium, France, maybe even Switzerland. [We] also [had] money in various denominations — Germany money, Belgian money, French money — in case we were shot down and managed to escape. We never had to use that except when we took that mission to the Ukraine, to Poltava, when our plane was destroyed on the ground.

Foster: What was the briefing like for the D-Day invasion? You had gone for so long not knowing where the invasion was going to take place.

Sims: Yes. There were hints and rumors that D-Day was not too far off, but I remember this well because [of] the daylight. They had what they called "British double-summer war time," so it was like double daylight time. It didn't get dark until midnight or later, and it didn't stay dark very long. So, I was down at the NCO, the non-commissioned officers' pub, having a few beers with the guys. Somebody came around and said, "This is it. Report for breakfast," at such and such an hour, like two o'clock in the morning, "for a briefing at three, and then you'll get the rest of your orders." I wished then that I hadn't had too many beers because I didn't go to sleep that night.

We reported to the flight line, got in our ship, and then, I discovered that just about every plane that could fly was in the air that day. We took off in darkness, but when I could see, the whole sky was almost black with planes. I suppose that almost everyone involved wanted to be part of the D-Day invasion. At any rate, we had two flights that day, two missions. [Both] were relatively short, flying across the channel, dropping bombs on targets that were strategic and that we hoped would hinder the Nazi effort.

I don't remember specifically [what the targets were]. They were behind the lines to some degree, but not too far inland. Then, we went back and reloaded and came back and did the same thing again. After the successful landing by the troops on Omaha Beach and the other beaches, when they began to push the Nazis back, we had the unfortunate experience of bombing our own troops. They were moving so fast — this was at Saint Lô, in Normandy — and there was some mistake in signals. We later learned that we had bombed our own troops. Whether we killed many of them, I don't know, but there must have been some casualties. We were pushing back the enemy fast, but we were not able to communicate exactly where our troops were. So, instead of hitting the enemy, we hit our own people.

Foster: Were there landmarks big enough to be able to see from the plane?

Sims: Well, they had a lead bombardier, and he was the key to finding the target. Even though we had a bombardier [in our plane] who was trained to do this and read the maps and look at the ground and see where there were rivers and other landmarks, it was up to the lead bombardier to decide to drop his bombs, and that was the signal for everybody else to do the same thing. Well, we know we hit targets, many times. But sometimes we may have missed them too. According to today's technology, it was pretty crude.

The weather was terrible [on D-Day]. Eisenhower really hesitated about deciding on that particular day, June 6th, 1944. They felt that by that time the Germans knew what was going on so the decision was made, "Let's go," regardless. The channel was choppy. I could see through the clouds the navy ships with their guns belching fire and smoke as they were pounding the coast too. It was a joint effort of infantry, navy, air corps, all doing their thing to make it possible for these guys who were landing on the beach to reach the objectives. It certainly wasn't easy for them, and as history has told us, many of them didn't make it and a lot of equipment was lost. The weather was rough. It was just a terrible day for this kind of thing. The decision was made, and we went ahead and did it.

Foster: Do you remember any announcements that evening or the next day that [D-Day] had been a success?

Sims: Well, we had the *Stars and Stripes* newspaper. Incidentally, Andy Rooney, the commentator and columnist who's on "Sixty Minutes" every Sunday, was writing for *Stars and Stripes* back in those days, and he took a particular interest in the air corps and airmen, subsequently even wrote a book about it. But I remember every day, I'd go back and take a look at the *Stars and Stripes,* and they gave our account of what happened. Sometimes who knows whether it was completely accurate or not, but that was our source of information. Occasionally, we'd see English papers that would give accounts. But I think *Stars and Stripes* was probably more accurate because after every mission we were interrogated [by the reporters], these days sometimes called "debriefing." But we would tell them what we saw.

I might say that when we got back from almost every mission, we were welcomed by Red Cross workers who handed us a double scotch to steady our nerves. We had sandwiches and coffee, then we would go in for interrogation to tell what we'd seen on that particular mission: what happened; whether we saw the planes go down; whether we hit the target; what we saw; almost anything.

If a plane didn't come back, sometimes they were not lost, as in our case when we had to land at another base. Most of the time we knew that if they didn't come back, they had gone down. In some cases, some of the crew might have been able to bail out and parachute down, some might have been able to escape, or some were attacked by farmers with pitchforks. I don't know how accurate it was. I still have, today, accounts of all of our missions, just about all, that appeared in the *Stars and Stripes* and other papers.

Foster: Where did D-Day fall in your order of thirty-two missions?

Sims: I don't know. I probably have a record somewhere, but since we started in April and ended in August, somewhere in the middle. And [the D-Day flights were] relatively easy missions compared to the others that we'd gone on. [The Germans] were being hit from all sides. The Luftwaffe didn't come up that day. I don't know why. Maybe they had run out of fuel by that time because we'd been pounding away at oil refineries and oil storage dumps and tanks and things of that sort.

Foster: You remained with the same crew the whole time?

Sims: Yes. Except for the one mission when I went to London to do a broadcast, I was with them the whole time. We came from various parts of the country. It was an interesting group. I was the only one from the Deep South; I was the rebel.

Erbon Wise

Wise: In the Normandy Invasion of France, the crossing of the English Channel was a memorable experience to me. I boarded the ship at Southampton and felt, "Well, this is certainly a fine way to go to war." On this ship overnight I had a fair place to sleep and food. But at daylight next morning, I had to climb down sixty feet of rope netting strung over the side of the ship to get into an assault landing craft. I had broken a finger a day or two before that and had it in splints. So, I found it difficult climbing down that sixty feet of netting on a swaying ship, holding on with only two fingers of one hand and carrying a heavy pack on my back.

        Off Utah Beach there were hundreds of ships, some shelling the enemy and they shooting back. Dozens of assault landing craft were ferrying troops to shore. The beach was heavily mined, but engineers had gone ahead and marked with flags little walking paths on which to stay clear of the mine fields. I remember it began raining heavily, and I was miserable under that heavy backpack.

Steve Chappuis
On completing LSU and ROTC, Chappuis was commissioned as a second lieutenant

in the U.S. Army and eventually trained for airborne missions. During training, he remembers that in addition to all of the physical exercises, "the theory was that you were required to pack your own parachute that you were going to jump with. So, that was an incentive to do it right."

Chappuis: The division I was in, the 101st, jumped or landed, some by glider, in Normandy at about midnight on D-Day. That would be like between twelve and one o'clock, nighttime, on the sixth of June, 1944. The landing [on Utah Beach] came ashore about daylight.

[The 101st Airborne Division] took a lot of losses because we had a tremendous spread on the ground. Some of the airplanes were shot down; some of the airplanes landed in the water in the North Sea before they got to land; and then, there were some pretty good battles. But, probably the infantry, which landed at Omaha Beach, had a harder time than we did. We weren't that concentrated. The situation at Omaha Beach was touch and go.

Hebert: What was your mission?

Chappuis: We had a bunch of missions. One was to secure certain roads which led to the beach, in order to expedite the landing of the troops coming ashore. Other missions were to prevent the destruction of some dikes, which could have caused some serious flooding, and to neutralize certain objectives such as heavy gun emplacements.

Hebert: Were you dropped off target?

Chappuis: My unit — I was commanding the battalion at the time — was pretty well spread, and we were as much as maybe three or four miles from our drop zone. When we got to our objective, we were almost on the water's edge and saw the landing of the U.S. Fourth Infantry Division. They were almost unopposed initially on Utah Beach, much different from Omaha Beach, or further up [on Juno and Gold beaches] where the British and Canadians were.

Cyril Guidry

At twenty-nine, Cyril Guidry was one of the more experienced soldiers in the Normandy Invasion. His division, the Ninth Infantry, had fought in the Battles of Kasserine Pass and El Guettar Pass, as well as the Sedjenane Valley campaign and the Sicilian campaign in North Africa and the Mediterranean. Now, the Ninth trained in England for its most important mission on the beaches of France.

Guidry: The [Ninth Infantry Division] had to be reviewed by General Montgomery, General Alexander, General Patton, Eisenhower, and most of the famous generals of World War II. We were considered the seasoned, older divisions. So, we were naturally being groomed for the [D-Day] invasion.

Foster: What was the attitude toward Montgomery?

Guidry: We had a lot of respect for General Montgomery because he was a sort of cocky general, we would say. He would walk in front of you and give you that look, you know, up and down. We knew we were being trained for something big. We knew what was ahead of us. Never knew whether we would be in the first wave or the second, but in the spring of 1944, things were beginning to get to where we knew.

They moved us a few days before the invasion to Southampton, England. It was what they call a staging area. They moved us into a fenced enclosure with barbed wire and electric wiring to where we couldn't communicate with anyone. We were fenced in until our turn to board ship. Fortunately, we were not the first to land in the invasion of France. We were not going to be in the first wave. That was good news for people like us.

They told us we were going to land in Normandy. They gave us a prep talk and said it wouldn't be easy. We knew. They told us what it would be. When it came our turn, we boarded ship. The English Channel was full of ships.

At D-[Day plus] three [days], we disembarked, and they were still shelling the beach. We landed, and when we advanced up the beach, General Collins — was the general in charge of us then for the landing, one of the supreme commanders — he met us on the beach. We moved in a little and relieved a part of the 82nd Airborne Division at Ste. Mère Église. [We] then moved back along the beach to the town of Quinéville to clear up some pillboxes, still occupied by Germans, that the main invasion force has bypassed.

While going through a Catholic church, with all the walls shot out — parts of it were still burning — one of the men in my section stepped on a mine and blew part of his foot off. By the way, he is from Gramercy, Louisiana. And so that ended the war for him.

We advanced and just had to clear some pill boxes. From [Quinéville], we moved inland, and it was like different things — small armed fire. Going into the Cherbourg Peninsula, when a small town was liberated, they would ring the bells. But, combat is not a thing that has any glory to it. It was just drudgery. It's just mud, sweat, moving slow, and that is all. You live from a day to day existence.

You had to support one another. You had to be very close. One thing about combat: to survive you can be friends, but never get too attached to anyone, because if they were killed, it affects you too much. So you survived by not ever being attached too close to anyone. I tried to have that philosophy and always have a sense of humor, to joke about any incident small or large.

Johnnie Jones

After seeing "the first and second wave almost completely annihilated," Johnnie Jones landed on Omaha Beach. Jones was one of the first black warrant officers in the army and served with the Fifth Engineering Division, General Omar Bradley's First Army,.

Jones:　　　　I was attached to the Fifth Engineering [Division]. My basic unit was the 494th Port Battalion Squadron which unloaded the ships and the supplies as they would come in. They were something like the quartermasters, you see, unload[ing] the supplies, the ammunition, the guns [that] came from the ships [for] the front line. Those were dangerous outfits. But I didn't do that. You see, as a warrant officer, my job was purely administration.

Hebert:　　　　But you had to go in with them?

Jones:　　　　I had to go in and keep records on all of that stuff. I had to keep records on the shipments and everything. I was still exposed, you know. It was still the same thing. That's the irony of the army. That's the irony about the whole thing. People think that this [work] is non-combat. There's no such thing as non-combat in the military.

All blacks are in service units. Don't let that fool you. [The difference is] they have more to do than the man on the front line, [who is] being shot at and got to shoot back. We had to get the supplies out. The man on the front line don't have to do nothing but only two things: duck from being shot at and make others duck from him shooting at them. But, they changed that during that time. During World War II, during '43 and '44, they put blacks into what they call combat units.

We went in at the Omaha Point on D-Day in the third wave on Dog Red [Assembly Area]. That's the worst part of the Normandy invasion. Utah was bad, but Utah was flat. [Omaha] was mountainous. It was hilly. The Germans were on top and in — they had excavations there. They had those pillboxes, where you didn't have that at Utah.

That's where we went in. I went in right there, D-Day. I went in.

My ship that I crossed the channel on [the] *Francis C. Harrington* was hit. Approximately twenty-five or more killed. My driver, Jackson, was knocked across the rail of the ship, but he wasn't hurt. I thought he was dead. I went up in the air, and I don't know how I came back down. I remember going up, and I came back down in the midst of that twenty-five dead.

I didn't get a scratch. I don't know how it happened. And then, I took a rifle from one of the dead. That's the only way I would have had a weapon. When the landing craft came for us and took us ashore, I had to hold that rifle up like this [over my head], because we had to wade in water after we got off the landing craft.

At that time a seventy-five mile an hour gale was coming on. The ship right next to us, I think it was the *Missouri*, was totally, completely annihilated, destroyed. Just went up in splendor. All you could see was soldiers floating in the channel. That whole German front that was set up on an army hill where they had the pillboxes, they just went down through there. They just shot all back up under the ground and set that hill on fire.

But, there was somebody in one of those pillboxes up there. Some German in that pillbox who was doing a lot of damage. There was an American solider, and I don't know where in the devil he came from. I don't know what state or what he came from. I don't know whether he ever survived or not. That rascal got in that bulldozer and just drove that bulldozer right straight into that pillbox and just tore that pillbox up. If that hadn't of happened, we wouldn't have gotten in. Now, the reason why that was risky, he was going in on the enemy while we were shooting at that same enemy. You know, by both ways. If he died, you don't know whether he was killed from our shooting or theirs, you see.

Hebert: The Germans in the pillbox were shooting down at . . .

Jones: . . . the ships. They were shooting at us until we got off the ship, you see. [Also] the Germans were sending over a few planes, but we took care of them pretty good. Once we got ashore our ack-ack, that's our anti-aircraft [guns], were very effective.

We had a fellow in the ack-ack unit adjacent to us, name was Hill. His last name was Hill — black. He came from Missouri. I think St. Louis. But anyway, Hill was an ack-ack gun expert. He could shoot real fast, and you know, you had to switch barrels. They call them boze in the army. He had to switch barrels after [he] fired so many rounds. It [would] get too hot for him to continue because it [the barrel] would get so hot it would melt and bend. He was knocking them out real fast. Night after night.

Now, Hill shot down a lot of planes, a lot of German planes. When he would hit them, they would go right down, go right into the English Channel nose down. Hill would wait until that plane would get into a certain limit, then he'd hit. He had that thing down perfectly almost. He would shoot, shoot fast, fast, fast.

I was in the Normandy Invasion a hundred-fifty days, you see. That's written up in there, in the *Stars and Stripes*. And I guess in some other paper too, but the *Stars and Stripes* was the military paper. It's called "One Hundred Fifty Days of Hell." It's dedicated to the outfit which I was in.

Erbon Wise

Wise: A most memorable experience of mine on the Normandy beachhead was our so-called "Gas Attack." Our commanding officer, a "re-tread" from World War I, was a character like Captain Queeg in the *Caine Mutiny* movie. He completely went to pieces in emergencies, a very dangerous situation in war. He was full colonel and I, then, was a lowly captain. One midnight, he ordered us to retreat because the Germans were breaking through the lines. Well, we could almost see the English Channel behind us — there wasn't any place to retreat. He was out of his mind with fear.

As finance officer I carried $600,000, American money, that, in an emergency, I was supposed to burn, rather than let fall into the hands of the enemy. I decided, "No, I am not going to burn it. I'll spend the rest of my life trying to explain to the U.S. Treasury, for whom I disbursed, what happened to it." Soon some sensible senior officer [said] to our colonel that there wasn't any place to retreat — "Stay in your foxholes."

But, the story I started to tell was about when everyone thought we were under gas attack and our commanding officer again went berserk. He called all our officers together, and as I was officer-of-the-day, that day, he decried that I was responsible for the gas attack. He shouted that he was going to shoot me. He screamed and cursed me for about fifteen minutes, slapping his gun holster like he was going to draw his .45.

He was out of his mind. Our chemical warfare officer was in great turmoil — all his training had been in preparation for this kind of emergency. He kept interrupting the colonel with, "We have got to do this; we have got to do this." The colonel shouted to him to shut-up or he would be shot next.

None of us had our gas masks because you usually didn't walk around with them. The enlisted men did not know what to do. The colonel would not dismiss the officers to prepare for the gas attack; his only immediate thought was to shoot me. Well, I knew that I was not going to just stand there and be shot down; and so, like Gary Cooper in his *High Noon* movie, I stood facing him awaiting his action. If he went for his pistol, I was going to go for mine. I took an awful lot of his verbal abuse.

Here was a case where some of the other senior officers there should have done something. Nobody did. Eventually, exhausted from his hysterics, the colonel collapsed to the ground, crying. Everyone else hurriedly tiptoed away to prepare as best they could for the gas attack. I was the last to leave, backing away slowly as to not risk a shot in the back.

In stressful situations, even high military officers sometimes go completely out of control. I saw it happen a few times. This is scary when officers are commanding troops. This colonel would have caused all of us to be killed that night, had we had a true gas attack. He was a sadly incompetent officer who could not meet this emergency.

This widely remembered "gas attack," a false alarm caused by falling smoke bombs, frightened thousands of troops on the beachhead. We had been cautioned that if ever the Germans were to use poison gas again after World War I, it would be on this congested troop area.

Robert LeBlanc

Like other LSU graduates, Robert LeBlanc was commissioned as a second lieutenant and called to active duty. Because of training he received in censorship and because of his knowledge of French, LeBlanc soon was recruited by the Office of Strategic Services [OSS] as an intelligence officer. During the Normandy Invasion, LeBlanc went into France where he coordinated the activities of agents who had previously parachuted into the country.

LeBlanc: A lot of propaganda went into France. Leaflets and also BBC broadcasts. A lot of our communications for D-Day were based on BBC broadcasts. In other words, "The cow jumped over the moon" meant something to an underground team somewhere. Or "Aunt Esther" probably meant that one of the teams was going to receive an agent coordinator, or "There's going to be a delivery for Aunt Jane" meant that the airplane was coming over to drop supplies that night.

It was all coded. Even the D-Day activities were coded. What railroad cuts to make. There were about five thousand railroad cuts made on D-Day [which] prevented the German Army divisions from moving up to the front in the area where the Americans had landed.

We were trained as agents, but when they decided that they would put OSS people in the armies after the invasion, they selected eight of us, and we ended up with the army instead of dropping in. And, those agents that we dropped in did the activities which we coordinated.

What [our] mission was going to be [was] sabotage and whatever havoc we could do behind the lines to deter the Germans [including blowing up bridges]. The Germans had taken down all the road signs, and you didn't know in which direction the next town was. But we could provide guides who knew the areas and who knew the woods where the Germans were.

What we did before we landed, we took the area that we were going to land in, and we learned who the agents were in that area. Besides that, we learned what their call signs were. We learned what their code names were. We learned how to contact them. Then, as we moved forward, we'd get a new list of those agents. But, it was strictly an area of about fifty miles in front of the front in order not to compromise the other agents further back.

For instance, you might go into a certain bar or a certain restaurant and ask for so and so, you see, which was a code. You'd ask for a certain type of food or a certain type of drink and that was your key word to start the conversation on a legitimate basis. From then on, you'd use the code name.

When we were behind the lines with the OSS groups, we would radio London. We utilized "one time pad, " [which] scrambles the letters of your message and gives you another word. It's only used one time. They have a copy of it on the other end, and you have a copy so it's pretty hard to break. We used the one time pads to [send] our request.

We did this to OSS London directly. They'd fly in with supplies, and they'd drop them in canisters.

One of the airbases in England had pre-packaged so much ammunition, so much food, so much medical supplies, and that type of thing. You'd radio in, and they'd drop you so many packets. What you'd do, you'd go in a field [where] you wanted them to drop [the supplies]. For instance, if they were going to do it in that back pasture down there, you would put a flashlight on one end of the field, another one on the other end of the field, to signal the plane. Well, then he'd line up on the two flashlights, he'd circle around and drop them between the two flashlights. They primarily used British Lysander aircraft. You hoped one of the canisters didn't fall on your head.

Erbon Wise

Wise: Our P-47 planes gave close dive-bombing to the front lines, later following General Patton's Third Army troops in their rapid race across western France.

I had a rather interesting event happen at our primitive airfield. I was out on the strip one day when a small English plane accompanied by two Spitfire fighter planes landed. It was unusual for English planes to come onto our strip.

You may remember in reading war history that Great Britain's Prime Minister Winston Churchill, an old veteran of the Boer War and World War I, had been determined to go in with the "D-Day" invasion forces. It was King George and General Eisenhower who persuaded him otherwise. However, about a week or ten days later, he did "slip off" to Normandy and to our strip in this small plane.

I was about the only one on the strip at that moment, saw the planes come in and went out to challenge this unusual landing. As I opened the small plane door, out stepped Mr. Churchill with a big cigar.

He wanted to see the war, and the only transportation I had was a bicycle. I quickly commandeered a passing jeep and sent him out to view what he could see of our narrow beachhead. I suppose his impulsive and unplanned visit with me caused some concern in London.

John J. Doles, Jr.

After training at Ft. Sill, Oklahoma, Doles was assigned to the 501st AFA Branch of the 14th Armed Division as a forward observer and sent to France.

We sailed for Europe in September, 1944, on a converted Liberty ship, the *Sea Eagle*. We zig-zagged for fifteen days crossing the Atlantic dodging German U-boats. The ship was very crowded, and many of us were seasick. When a man in the top bunk got seasick everyone below suffered the effects. I wasn't seasick until we were in a terrible storm in the Mediterranean. Then everybody aboard got sick. Fortunately we landed in Marseilles soon after, on the first of October.

Christmas Eve, 1944, we were in Alsace-Lorraine close to the Rhine River. It was very, very cold. We were staying in a house with a German couple. Every month we were given a bottle of scotch and cigarettes. Well, I'd wrapped my scotch in a blanket and saved it. On Christmas, I sent my driver out to get the scotch from the tank. We were watching him when he held it up for us to see, but his hands were so cold he dropped it, and it crashed on the tank. But we celebrated with a drink anyway. The German couple gave us all a drink of potato schnapps!

Our division became known as the Liberator division. This is how we got that name. As the German army retreated, they kept herding all the prisoners (POWs) toward Nuremberg, Germany, and this was their final POW camp. In April, 1945, our division overran the camp and released all of the prisoners. The prisoners were from all the allied countries, and they lined the streets when we went through. As we marched through the town we gave them our food packs, cigarettes, candy, extra clothing — everything we had. I didn't know it at the time, but one of the prisoners was a good friend of mine, Milton Pittman. I had played football with him at Plain Dealing High School.

Jack Gremillion

Jack Gremillion was detached from the 106th Infantry Division, while it was still on U.S. soil, in order to take an assignment as a replacement officer for the war in Europe. From England, Gremillion went to France, landing on Omaha beach shortly after D-Day, where he was assigned to the Fifth Infantry Division.

Gremillion: The Fifth Infantry Division had relieved the First Infantry Division, the Big Red, which was on the American left flank. I was assigned to the Fifth Infantry Division as a platoon leader in the weapons section. Then, we started combat. I don't remember the exact date, but I do know it was in the middle of July, or thereabouts.

On July the thirtieth, 1944, I got wounded in a skirmish with some snipers right in front of our company in the hedgerows. [Hedgerows looked] exactly like you'd taken a lot and fenced it off. But, these hedgerows were dirt. The hedgerows come back from almost biblical times because in those days they didn't have enough lumber [for fences]. What [the farmers] would do is let the trees grow on the property line and the sediment, like leaves and everything, would build, and the first thing you know, you had a row. They called it a hedgerow. That's a perfect place for snipers. Or, [the sniper] would dig a foxhole and cover it up with dirt. After you passed over, they'd jump out and shoot you in the back.

My company was right outside of Saint Lô. I never did see the town of Saint Lô. I have no idea what it looked like, but on Sunday evening, six o'clock, I got hit by a 88 mm shell. It was a sniper [that] caught us. My platoon sergeant was with me at the time, and we were probing to see the extent that the Germans were [there] because we were getting ready to launch an attack in the morning. This sounds fantastic, but it's absolutely true. This 88 mm shell came in and broke quite close to us, and I got hit in about four or five places. One of them was my leg. It was very bad. I was wounded eleven times.

I still have shrapnel, a little shrapnel, in my shoulder and a little in my leg, but the doctor said there was no need to take it out; it doesn't bother me. But, I got shot twice in the leg. I got shot in the thigh. I got shot in the shoulder. I landed on my side . . . it was in the corner of a hedgerow. We threw hand grenades over and fought back a little bit, but they killed my poor sergeant. Burp gun just rattled him right up the center of his body. I was bleeding pretty profusely. I tried to put a tourniquet on my leg because that was where I was really hurting, really bleeding.

The grass was pretty high, and I knew I had to get out of there. So I start crawling. And every time I'd crawl, [the sniper] would shoot where I had been. One time he caught me from the back, and if he'd just hit me one inch higher, he'd of split me. I wasn't unconscious; I knew what was going on, and I kept tightening that tourniquet but I couldn't put the tourniquet around my belly. I was bleeding pretty bad there and was holding the tourniquet in one hand and [in the other hand] my jewels — let's call it that, my manly jewels — which were pretty well shot up, damn shot up. I jumped over this hedgerow. When I jumped over this hedgerow, he shot me through the foot. A lot of boys were getting out the army by shooting themselves in the foot, but that was from the front. I got shot from the back of my foot. Anyway, as I told you, when I jumped over the hedgerow, [the sniper] shot me through the foot, my left foot. I was picked up in a litter and taken to a field hospital right outside of St. Lô.

[The bombardment was] just like you see in the pictures. That's the way it was. Definitely. There's a lot of shooting back and forth. There was a lieutenant pretty close to me. He got shot and killed, dropped down at my feet. It was just as real as it could be. I can't describe it more pictorial than to tell you it was horrible. It didn't make any difference who they were shooting at; they were killing everybody. We weren't involved in tanks at that time except that the Allies and the Americans had to combat with these hedgerows. They had devised a system like a caterpillar tractor pushing it. They'd take a big old blade, like a tractor blade — a big huge thing — and they'd weld it on the front of a tank. Then, they'd go through these hedgerows and bust a hole through them, but I didn't have the joy of any of that because that was started after I was injured.

Of course, I was picked up by litter. Picked up . . . I wasn't picked up. Hell, one of the medics came by, and I hollered at him. He came over and looked at me and saw how I was bleeding at the shoulder; I was bleeding at the foot; I was bleeding at the leg; I was bleeding all in my innards and all. And you know how you take a rifle to signal to a dead man? You put the rifle down and the butt up. He stuck that thing right by my body, and he said, "I can't do nothing for you." And he didn't. He stuck that thing up. I looked up, and I saw that rifle sticking up by me, and I said, "Oh, no, this is not for me. I'll be damned if I'm going to die here." I still tried. Still holding onto that tourniquet and still holding on to where I got shot in the middle, I started inching. I could hear my company, oh I suppose, about a hundred yards away, and they knew where I was. I wanted them to come get me, but they didn't want to come get me because they were dropping shells in there.

So, finally, I crawled. I don't know how far. It seemed like eternity to me. I crawled until two of the men from my company jumped over the hedgerow and picked me up and brought me on the other side to apparent safety. From there I got on a litter. They brought me to a hospital in a jeep, and I was operated on right away. And they patched me all up. I stayed in the hospital about three days.

I was transported from that army hospital which was right there outside of St. Lô. They flew us by Dakota airplane — a bunch of litters, about eighteen to twenty patients — to England, and I was in a hospital between Ipswich and Norwich in England. There was a big army hospital there, and I stayed there. The doctor who operated on me turned out to be a good friend of mine. I stayed in touch with him after the war was over with. He came to Louisiana and visited us, and we went to Boston. He was from Providence, Rhode Island. Anyhow, I suppose I was operated on about seven or eight times.

Of course, my wife got the usual telegram [that] her "husband has been wounded in combat. He's in a hospital, and we'll keep you advised." But in the meantime, I had run into a lady, a nurse, an army nurse, who was from Louisiana. God knows, I don't remember her name and I tried to remember, tried to make a record of it. She found out I was from Louisiana, and I dictated a letter to her. She wrote it in her handwriting, and then, she took it back to her quarters and mailed it via V-mail. My wife got that letter before the Army ever notified [her] and, of course, I had described what I had been through and everything to the nurse and so forth.

The Purple Heart was all I got, and that was enough. Of course, I had the European Theater Service and all those combat infantry badges and all those others. But that was the story, more or less, of my military career. My story is the story of many a boy who went into service and was lucky as hell to come back. Oh, you just don't know how I thank the Good Lord on many day — on many, many a day — 'cause I was given up two or three times out there on that field.

Cyril Guidry

Guidry: The hedgerow fighting was slow and hard. We cut the Cherbourg Peninsula off and advanced toward [the town of] Cherbourg, very slow advance, and I remember almost to Cherbourg, one of the men in my section was mortally wounded. While laid out, he asked me for a drink of water. And having soldiered long, [I knew] a man hit in the stomach, you don't give him water. But he knew he was dying. His name was Harlow. He said, "Guidry, it don't make no difference now." So, I gave him the water. He lived a little while. The other man with him was killed instantly. Those are very, very hard things.

Fortunately, I always had the attitude I would survive. That was my attitude throughout the entire war. When anyone spoke to me about it, I said, "No, I figure on surviving." Who was it, the American that said he "only had one life"? I said "I'm not giving this one. They got to take it." That was my attitude.

I realized we had a cause. Having known before the war the brutal expansion of Hitlerism and the conquests of Poland and the Low Countries and how the Germans killed people and the crimes they committed, I figured we had a good cause.

After the capture of Cherbourg, we moved back and started our advance through the hedgerows in the direction of St. Lô. During this part of the campaign through France, I have to mention, we were under command of a regimental commander by the name of Colonel Patty Flint. He put our emblem on our helmets: "Anytime, Anywhere, Anything." He was a wonderful commander, a man up in age who was eligible to be retired from combat command, but he wanted to command combat troops. So, advancing in the direction of St. Lô, Colonel Flint got in a tank and stood up, trying to force the tank through the German lines, and a German sniper shot him through the head. We had to take him in the back. After he was killed, a few days later, [we] had a memorial service. I had the honor to be chosen as one of the men that would go in the flying squad for a memorial service for him, and I was proud to be chosen for that honor because it was an honor to serve under him, because he was a very good commander. He led.

In that same engagement is where my friend, Ellison, who advanced ahead of me was killed. Like I said, I remember that incident very good. I wrote his mother as soon as I could to tell her about his death.

[Ellison] was a good soldier, too. He was a soldier that never believed in digging foxholes and all, thought it was a waste of time. The hedgerows in France were approximately four feet high, and he was back of a hedgerow. A German had dug out the back side of it, and a mortar shell hit the opposite side. There was only a thin layer of dirt. They'd hit him a piece in the heart. And his only words was "B.B. they got me." That was his only words to the fellow was with him — fellow by the name of Bartley, Bernard Bartley, called him B.B. "B.B. they got me."

So, those are things that happened in combat and one other thing to mention — a strange thing about men in combat. Sometime a man mortally wounded don't even sound human anymore. The way he scream and holler, it's pathetic . . . heart wrenching . . . hard to understand . . . never forget it.

In preparation for the breakthrough at St. Lô, they got together three thousand airplane bombers, large bombers, light bombers, fighter planes, and on July the twenty-fourth, they notified us to dig in. They were coming over to soften up the Germans so we could move. They started the bombing at approximately eleven o'clock in the morning. The planes started coming over, and when they started to drop the bombs, we had ringside seating watching the dogfights and the bombers releasing their bombs. Then the dust clouds, instead of going away from us, came toward us, and during the bombing approximately six hundred American soldiers of the 120th Infantry and the 9th Infantry Division, my division, were wounded and killed.

While the bombing was going on, the noise was so bad you couldn't hardly stand it. You'd get in your foxhole; you'd get out, hold your ears. We survived it — some of us. After it was over, we started to move. It was like looking at a picture of the moon, the craters. And the Germans, a lot of the Germans were killed. Some were blown literally to pieces. Their arms were missing, their legs, their heads were gone. Nothing but the torso of the body. We moved on.

Despite all this bombing, we met a few pockets of German resistance. So we continued to advance, and after that breakthrough [at St. Lô], we moved fast. We were put on tanks and half-tracks, tank destroyers, or anything we could ride on in the move toward Belgium. We moved into Belgium, and with the exception of a few German planes strafing us, when we'd have to jump off the tanks and get in the ditch, we continued to move on into Belgium. We were on the line for four months. We had only five days off the front line in four months, my division did. We captured approximately 28,300 prisoners.

Robert LeBlanc

LeBlanc: [I was selected for OSS because I could] speak, read, and write French. I was along the Loire River where most of the people spoke the same type of French I did. To give you a little amusing tale, we were sitting one day eating with a family, and I used the word *asteur* [now], and the Frenchmen started laughing. The old lady's sitting there asked me, she says, "Where did you get that word?" I said, "That's the word I use for *maintenant* [now]. And she says, "You know, when I was a child that's what we said, too." It was that type of old, old French that was utilized [by Cajuns]. But the main thing that we had to learn more than anything else was the methods of eating and things that would give us away while we were behind the lines. For instance, Americans eat their soup this way [with the bowl on the table and spoon the soup toward themselves]. The French lift the plate close to them, and they go the other way. [The spoon] goes away from them. These are the types of things that you had to learn. [We] studied a lot of the French mores and different types of things like that. Smoking. A Frenchman smokes to a very little tip and doesn't waste any [of the cigarette].

Ralph Sims

Sims: Stalin split with Hitler, [and] the Soviet Union had become our ally. So, as a diplomatic mission, as a demonstration of goodwill, a group of us went over to drop bombs on Germany, and instead of coming back to England, [we] continued on through Russia to the Ukraine, where we would load up again with bombs [then] come back and bomb Italy.

Well, the first part worked fine. The first night we were [in the Ukraine, however,] the Luftwaffe came over. And, apparently, the Russians didn't have adequate defenses, and [the Germans] destroyed all of our planes on the ground. So we were stuck with no way to get out [of the Ukraine]. We wondered, "Are we stuck here for the duration? What's going to happen?" Each day we would ask [the Russians], and they would say, "Uncle Joe say no," meaning Joe Stalin. Finally, the Russians we were with did their best to entertain us. They somehow had vodka, despite the devastation of the land, and they had caviar. Some of them had a balalaika, a mandolin or something, a stringed instrument to play, and they did dance and try to entertain us. Eventually, the U.S. Air Transport Command came and flew us out by way of Tehran, Cairo, and Casablanca, stopping off a little while in each place, then eventually back to Prestwick, Scotland.

We made our way back to our home base, which had given up on us. They thought we were all gone. My wife did too because she had not heard from me for a couple of weeks, where she was accustomed to getting a letter almost every day. I wrote her every day. She wasn't notified that I was lost or missing in action. But we found that people had gone through our tents and taken some of our private stuff, thinking that we were gone and what difference did it make?

Erbon Wise

Wise: The liberation of Paris was an interesting experience to me. After the St. Lô breakout in Normandy our unit was moving very fast and often.

One night we came into le Mans, about one hundred miles out of Paris, and began setting up camp when word came over the radio that General Patton was moving rapidly forward. My colonel called me and said, "Take this convoy and go into Orly Airdrome in Paris." He added, "By the time you get there it will be liberated." So I took a convoy of trucks and troops, and leading in my jeep, I headed across unknown territory for Orly. When we later arrived, it was not quite "liberated."

Rather than fight through the city of Paris, our combat forces had mostly gone around the city, as was their plan. But the French irregulars, called the FFI, had come out openly and were having running battles with the departing Germans. When I led my convoy into Orly Airdrome, these two forces were having quite a firefight in the local buildings. So I led the trucks over to the far side of the airfield and circled them up, like the early western pioneers arranged their wagons to face Indian attacks.

Late in the evening, after military action calmed down, I drove my jeep into the center of Paris, and at five p.m. found myself on its main boulevard, the Champs Elysees, just as citizens were going home from work. Unlike London, where about half the city was bombed and burned, Paris was not destroyed in the war. Life was going on as usual, it appeared to me. I was quite shocked at the amount of food and merchandise displayed in the stores.

When I parked on the Champs Elysees, I guess about ten thousand people crowded around honoring me for "liberating Paris." I didn't "liberate" it; but, I still think I was the first American officer to get into downtown Paris. This was August 1944. Thousands, it seemed, kissed me and poured wine down me. It was quite an event.

One individual invited me to his home for dinner three nights later. In those three days, we became quite settled in our tents at Orly Airdrome. For the dinner, I thought I had better get out of field clothes and dress up a bit. In my barracks bag I found a pair of dress trousers, but my military blouse, wadded up for months, was impossible to wear. So, I just put on a leather jacket and found a tie.

The custom in food-short England, when invited out to eat, was to always carry some tins of food with you to help out with the meal. Here in Paris, with some cans of food from the mess hall, I eventually found my way into a rich neighborhood near the Arc de Triomphe. At the door of the home, the lady hostess graciously accepted my sack of canned food and ushered me into a dinner party of twelve formally dressed couples, all gathered to honor me for "liberating Paris."

My host, I learned, was a top executive of Ford Motor Company in Paris. Others there included leading Parisian business executives and two prominent French movie actresses. All were fashionably dressed and, as a courtesy to me, they all spoke English for the evening.

I was seated at the head of a beautiful table displaying French and American flags. Waiters stood behind every guest, constantly refilling the wine glasses. It was a great meal. I never saw the cans of food I had brought with me.

Here in my leather jacket, a captain at age twenty-four, I was honored for "liberating Paris." Of course, I had not rescued the city; I had merely blundered into it before I should have.

Before moving on to the military front, our unit spent two weeks in Paris, one full night of which I again was an officer-of the-day and had to stay awake in a headquarters tent. The movie star Fred Astaire, and his USO group that night gave a nearby show to the soldiers. Afterwards, having nothing to do, Fred wandered into my tent carrying a bottle of scotch. We two passed the long night "celebrating in Paris."

Paris is probably the most beautiful city in the world, and I saw it at one of its greatest moments — its liberation.

Robert LeBlanc

Hebert: Do you think that the OSS agents who went with the Third Army were at least partly responsible for its rapid movement through France?

LeBlanc: We assisted. We can't take credit for that. The man who can take the most [claim of] success for the rapid movement of the Third Army through France is Patton. Patton was the type of individual who could select people such as him for commanders. There was some discussion at the initial phase of the breakout that General Troy Middleton was too slow. [He was an infantryman,] and was too deliberate. Woods was his armored division commander and was a cavalry man. He's the one who headed straight south and really busted that thing wide open. By getting these types of individuals, who were armored people, he was able to use the pursuit-type activity: break out and pursuit. He did it, continuously, all the way through.

Now, we did help a lot in securing bridge heads. I know in the Twelfth Corps, the major thing that we were able to do for the Fourth Armored Division was to get the French underground to keep the Germans from blowing up the bridges. Bridges are key in armored combat. If you don't have a bridge, you have to stop, you have to develop a line, you have to make a bridge head, and you have to rebuild a bridge. So, that kept the thing going real well.

Hebert: Would you also disrupt German communications?

LeBlanc: You'd disrupt German communications in the rear, and you could also cut the wires. You could take sand and put it in the grease boxes of the trains, and maybe a hundred miles down the road they'd freeze up an axle. You put a cup of sugar in the gas tank and about six hours later you got a ruined engine. These type of activities that you could do. Also, if you could get enough refugees on the road, you'd clog the roads.

The Frenchmen were very much interested in volunteering after the lines were crossed. As a matter of fact, when we got to the Thionville area, we organized a battalion of Frenchmen, and we equipped them with captured German rifles. They took a position as guards in the line, in the static area there to help the American linemen where we were short of personnel between divisions. They helped in a lot of ways that way; they helped to guard our pipeline and our supply lines. They helped guard the trains coming up to the front. There was a lot of things that you could get them to do. I think that the bitter battle between [Charles] de Gaulle, Eisenhower, Churchill, and Roosevelt detracted a lot from what the Frenchmen did for the American army in France.

Naturally, when history is written, [it] is written by the leaders, or the aides who had nothing to do but keep the diaries all through the war, you see. But, the front line people's history is the interest that develops after everything is gone.

One of the things that the Third Army was always short of was fuel. When we got near Thionville there was a methane plant, or some type of fuel that could be utilized for fuel in the vehicles. We found I don't know how many thousand gallons of fuel, which we reported to the division, and the division was able to use some of this fuel for their jeeps and re-con vehicles.

Hebert: I'm sure Patton was very happy about that.

LeBlanc: Very happy because Montgomery was getting all the supplies. There again, the political battles that were going on.

We were at the Troyes, and the French Underground told me that there was a supply of liquor in the warehouse just to the north of us about fifteen or twenty miles. So, I was telling this to the S-3, Colonel Clark's combat command, and he says, "Where is it?" And I told him. He said, "Can you lead us there?" I say, "Yes, I have a Frenchman here who knows exactly where it's at." So, we got a tank platoon and a truck company, and we went up there. It was warehouses of Cointreau, champagne and cognac. All of this was stacked up in these warehouses, and we drove right up there; we had a few German encounters along the way, but they were nothing serious. When we got to the warehouse, there was a Frenchman working in there. I asked him where the cognac was. I said, "You've got better than this Hennessy Three Star?" He said, "No." So, I told my driver, I said, "Go get a carton of cigarettes." I then told him, "I know you've got better than Hennessy Three Star," and he says, "Well, come with me." We went to a big storage area. There was a lock on it, and he says, "It's locked." So, we shot off the lock, and it was full of Napoleonic brandy. We loaded up the jeep with that, and we brought it back. We loaded up all of the two and a half ton trucks, and they gave [the liquor] to the men, whenever they had their breaks, you see. They'd pull them out of the line, let them rest for a day, and they'd give it to them. I still have a few empty bottles around here from that escapade.

Another time, it could have been July the fourth, I had gone back for some instructions, and my colonel, Colonel Powell, who was head of the OSS group, said, "All we've been having is canned rations." He said, "Can't we have something good for this festival?" I said, "Well, would you like some geese?" He says, "Yes, if we could get them." He says to the mess cook, "Can we cook some geese?" "Sure," he says. So, I went to the French village, and they had geese a-running all over. I wanted to know whose they were. Nobody owned them, and I said, "Well, in that case, I'll just start picking up some geese." One guy came over he said, "No, they're mine." I said, "You want to sell them?" He said, "No, I don't want to sell them." So, I pulled out a carton of cigarettes. I [again] said, "You want to trade them?" He says, "Oh yes, I want to trade them!" So, that's what we exchanged, the cigarettes for the geese, and we had baked goose for the fourth of July.

Cigarettes were a very, very important means [for] transaction of business in France. Frenchmen are heavy smokers. Cigarettes were fifty-five cents a carton in the PX when you could get them, and they were a good means of exchange. That and soap.

Before we crossed over from England, they were closing the PX in England that supported us, and they were going to re-open in France. I asked one of the agents who had just come back from France, I says, "What is the best bargaining material?" He says, "Cigarettes and soap." So, I had bought a case of Lux soap.

Anthony Palumbo

Prior to the invasion of Normandy, Palumbo spent a year in North Africa. Soon after D-Day, he went into France as a replacement officer where he was assigned to the Sixth Armored Division. The Sixth was one of General Patton's Armored Divisions in the Third Army.

Palumbo: We took a train down in the heart of England, just south of London, and we were there maybe two or three weeks. We were just up there and waiting our turn in the so-called pipeline. We were all replacement officers or enlisted men that were waiting to be sent to various units where we were needed. We crossed over at Normandy, went into France to St. Lô. From there we went directly across to Nancy. Then, I joined the Sixth Armored Division outside of Nancy, France.

I'll never forget my unit sergeant telling me, "Sir, you're the fourth officer we've had in this unit. We've already killed three of them." I said, "Well sir, I may be the fourth, but I have a pregnant wife at home, and we're expecting our third child. I don't know if it is going to be a boy or a girl, and I'm not going to be a casualty." I said, "I have had about a year's experience in Africa fighting the Germans and the Italians, and I certainly am not going to be a casualty here in the Sixth Armored Division." I was just being a little bit, I don't know what you call it, fresh.

I joined the Sixth in Nancy, and, at the time, I didn't know what the Super-6 was. It was just one of Patton's [divisions]. I met Patton once. I can still see him as we were crossing the Rhine River. He was standing on the banks of the Rhine, flagging us, "Go ahead boys, go ahead, fight the Germans the best you can. I'll be back here backing you up." He had his pearl handle pistols on his side.

I had heard about Patton earlier, too, when I was in Africa. When they had that incident in Sicily when he slapped the G.I., at that time, I thought it was actually blown out of proportion. I think that he just tried to slap some sense into the young fellow without really hurting him. As it was, I had one man in an argument, matter of fact it was an officer. He was commander of one of our platoons when we were involved in very heavy fire fighting. He broke ranks and ran back. I finally caught up with him. He was down in a cellar some place. He had just flipped his lid, and I tried to slap some sense into him, but it wasn't doing any good. I sent him back to the rear echelon, and I haven't heard from him since. That happened just once for me. It was an officer, a brand new second lieutenant. His first time in combat. He just didn't have it.

Foster: Were you given special instructions about how to handle that?

Palumbo: No, we weren't given any special instruction. We just handled them any way we could. We were just told to do what we could do for the man, but your first priority is your so-called mission, that was our number one goal, our mission. And our mission at that particular time was to hold the line, and he didn't hold the line. He just flipped the line.

I had another officer named Lieutenant Rollins. "Rough and Ready Rollins" we used to call him. He was just the opposite. He would go anywhere and do anything anytime you wanted him to. I don't know what happened to him, but last I saw him, he was on his way home, was on his way out of the battle. He was shot in the foot, shot in the leg, and he had a million dollar wound. He said, he's getting out of that S.O.B. place, but he was rough and ready all the time.

We were able to fight our way across France and go into the town of Sarreguemines. Sarreguemines is the town in the Alsace-Lorraine area where the people were either loyal to the Germans or to the French depending on where they were at the time. Alsace-Lorraine is a part of France right now, but it had been a part of Germany for a long time. It goes back and forth depending on who is in command.

Sarreguemines has a special meaning for me because there is where we lost our battalion XO [executive officer]. Major Johnson was killed going into Sarreguemines. He was riding his jeep, and he got a direct hit with a Kraut 88. A Kraut 88 is a big weapon that just blew him to pieces, and he was dead before he even knew what hit him.

In the town of Sarreguemines, I also was able to make friends with a local family. We had house-to-house fighting in Sarreguemines, and we were trying to clear out all the German soldiers that were still fighting us in the town. Now, this particular family had a daughter who was engaged to a German soldier, who of course at that time was fighting our forces. We didn't know that he was engaged to this French girl. By being in [the Alsace] area, [the German soldiers] had the tendency to enter into marriage without any problems. And we didn't know about this [engagement] at the time, but I was able to capture him along with several others.

I spoke French at the time, and the [young] woman told her mother that if her friend would surrender to me, I would save him because I was going to church every morning, a local mass in a local church. She'd say [to her fiancé], "He seems like a fine young officer, fine young lieutenant. He won't kill you on the spot like most of them would." I had members in my company, Sergeant Hunt for instance, who would. I didn't know this at the time, but I had asked him to take two or three POWs back to the rear. He took them back about a hundred yards and killed all three of them. This was contrary to our way of thinking and also contrary to the war principles and war rules. He had seen his own buddy get killed by a German so he was just the type that you couldn't trust with a German POW. Had I known, I would not have turned over the POWs to him.

I don't know [the German soldier's] name; I know her name was Jung. Her father and mother's name was Jung. In any event, I did capture her fiancé, and I sent him back to the POW encampment in England. Apparently, he was able to survive, and he learned to speak English.

I was there again, about five or six years later, in '51 or '52, with my family, and I stopped to see the people in the town of Sarreguemines. This woman came to the door, and she invited us in. They had a brand new home they had just built on the site. They asked us to stay and spend the night, and I didn't want to spend the night because we had been camping, but she insisted. So we did spend the night. Her daughter said her husband, [back then] her fiancé, was the POW that I had sent back to England. At the time, he was at the local movie house. So we waited. About a couple of hours later, he came storming in and said, "I want to shake the hand of the American who saved my life." And he came in, and I didn't recognize him; he was grown up, but he was very, very happy. It made me feel real good that I had done something worthwhile.

Because I was commanding the unit, I had to be rational in all of our approaches. I had members in my unit that were very, very hard and bitter against the Germans. Even after the war ended, and we were in Germany, the Germans were asked [by some soldiers] if they were Nazis. Some said they were, and others would say no they weren't. I could care less if they were Nazis because the war had ended, and they had been beaten. We were just happy that all of us were safe.

We had an incident [in France] where the Germans had been there before we were and had thrown hand grenades into this group of people, mostly French women and children, civilians. They were huddled downstairs in the cellar. The Germans, prior to leaving, had thrown their so-called hand grenades down there and killed, oh, a good number of them. They were civilians. We had an opportunity to follow up later on, and they were so happy to see the Americans because we didn't treat them like they had been treated by the Germans.

The Germans as a whole — I don't know what to say about them — but all of those that we had met on the battlefield, they were either S.S. Troopers or they were Volksman [Volkssturn or "People's Militia"], the old man's army or a young man's army. They had used just about all of their manpower when we finally were able to contact the Germans themselves. I remember one incident where a young man, young German must have been fourteen, fifteen years of age, had to go to potty, and he squatted down, and I came upon him. He was so terrified; he thought I was going to kill him. I just told him, "No, go on back to the troops." Just a baby, fourteen, fifteen years old.

One incident in France, too, where I was involved in a firefight in the towns of Michamp and Oubourcy. The sergeant in my company, we used to call him Sergeant No-Neck, because he had no neck — his head sat right on his shoulders — he was armed with a BAR, Browning Automatic Rifle. I had just gone around the corner of a hay stack and had come face-to-face with a German, who had his rifle right at my head, level with my head, and he was going to pull the trigger. Whereas Sergeant No-Neck came around the other side and caught him, opened up with the BAR, cut the man in half. I still say if it wasn't for Sergeant No-Neck, I would not be here today. That was the closest call I've ever had. That was in the Battle of the Bulge.

Foster: Tell me about the Battle of the Bulge.

Palumbo: We had joined the 101ˢᵗ Airborne that had been surrounded by the Germans in Bastogne. We, in turn, had made a forced march going up into the town of Luxembourg, through Luxembourg and into Bastogne. A forced march is [when] we were told to get up there as soon as we possibly could, without any breaks, overnight breaks and stuff like that. We waited outside of Bastogne. Whereas, the Fourth Armored Division, our sister division, was actually there a half a day before our units got there, and they fought their way through the German lines into Bastogne. We followed the Fourth Division in. We fought night and day against the Germans that were trying to get through.

The towns of Michamp and Oubourcy were outside of Bastogne, and my particular unit was ordered to take these two towns, and we did. We were the only unit in the entire Sixth Armored Division that had accomplished its mission that day. While we were out in these two towns, we were counter-attacked by the Germans in their tanks, tank destroyers, and other weapons, heavy weapons. So, I got on the horn and called back to Colonel Ward and asked if I could pull back to my original position [that we started from] in the morning because we were being subjected to enemy fire, and I couldn't call for air support because we didn't have the clear weather for air. So, he said, "Sure, shoot yes, come on back, Tony." So, I started on back, and on the way back from Oubourcy or Michamp, one or the other, I had a half-track that was hit by a direct round of a German 88 tank. It landed right in the back of this half-track. It was commanded by Sergeant Walker from Paducah, Kentucky. I'll never forget Sergeant Walker. He stopped by me with his tank. He had about seven or eight men in the back of that half-track that were completely wiped out. They were KIA [killed in action] on the spot. He didn't know what to do. I just told him to go on back to the first aid station.

Meanwhile, I had Sergeant Tom, who had been killed by a sniper fire in the town of Oubourcy. I had him on my front bumper of my half-track. "Curb service," I called it. In any event, I told Tom, "Hang on!" Because if he was to fall off that bumper, we would have had to leave him because we were being hit by Krauts. I just rested him on the bumper; I thought he'd hang on one way or another, but he bounced around. The front of one of those half tracks has got a big wide bumper, and there's room to put a body on it without any problem. I found that out the hard way.

We finally got back to our starting position where we had started from that morning, and I had taken over A Company; they had lost all their officers that day. [That is,] I had taken over what was left of A Company and formed one task force they called, Task Force Palumbo. We used that task force for a long time after that. But getting back to Tom, Tom was able to hang on to that front bumper. [At the time,]I didn't know if he hung on. [He did.] He bounced back and forth, up and down, all the way back, but I finally got him back to the aid station. I wasn't going to leave him behind to have his body taken care of by the Germans.

[This was] in December '44 and January of '45, and we had a bad winter, bad cold winter. I remember scooping off the snow and putting down my old sleeping bag on the ground and sleeping inside of that. And I was sure glad to get that sleep. Wake up five a.m. in the morning, and you're covered with snow, but you still were sleeping. I had a lot of casualties with frostbite feet. They had these shoe packs that they were supposed to put on their feet. Inside the shoe pack, they had a felt liner that they were supposed to keep next to their body to keep them dry. When they change in the morning they put these other ones in the shoes, the fresh ones, and the old ones they put next to the body.

Ralph Sims

Sims: Except for the one [mission] we flew to the Ukraine, the rest were bombing various targets in Germany and France and in one case, Czechoslovakia. A total of thirty-two. I remember the last one [in August of 1944], which indeed was a simple one. The war was kind of winding down, the Nazis were being pushed back, [and] the Luftwaffe had pretty much been destroyed. We had destroyed all the oil refineries, all their supplies, [and] they couldn't fly. The last [mission I flew] was to drop supplies to the Maquis, the French resistance fighters, who were at the time in that area of France called Lons le Saunier, near Switzerland, with the Alps in the distance. A beautiful day, clear skies and each of the chutes we dropped were different colors, some for medical supplies, some for food, some for ammunition, some for other things. Dropping these colored chutes made a beautiful sight, the Alps in the background, blue skies up above Lake Geneva in the distance. [Because] we were at a fairly low altitude [we could see] the French resistance fighters [make] the V sign for Victory. [There was] no resistance, and that was the end. When I got back to our base, like the pope does, I leaned and kissed the ground because it was my last mission.

Cyril Guidry

Guidry: We advanced out of Belgium, entered Germany and advanced in the direction of the Siegfried Line. We had quite a bit of resistance off and on, but we continued to advance. We passed through the tank traps that were along the Siegfried Line. [It was well] into September. The weather's beginning to get rainy and cold. On the morning of September twenty-seventh, Lieutenant Downs and myself had spent the night under a half of a pup tent. In the morning, he got me up to make a reconnaissance in preparation for an attack. While we were looking over the terrain in the forest, he tripped on a mine. He turned to tell me he did not think he had tripped it off, then everything blew up. He was wounded through the leg, and I was hit through the leg, in the left thigh, and in the side. Had I not been carrying a blanket, I would have been killed, I know. Why I picked the blanket up, I don't know. But this blanket saved my life.

He was bleeding as I started to bandage his leg, and I began to pass out and blew my whistle and called for help. The company commander and another soldier came and assisted us out to a fire break where we could be evacuated out to a first aid station.

When I was wounded, the only thing saved me from being wounded bad in the thigh [was] a pocket full of coins I'd picked up out of houses, a large coin that I picked up that said, "I will never sail on a German ship. Remember the Lusitania." And I transferred the coins, after my pocket was all torn up, to another pocket and saved all the coins. That was the end of that.

When I was wounded, my leg only took two stitches, but my side, it took twelve stitches to sew the wound. It went all the way through except in the last thin veil that protected my internal organs. I was not fed anything for a period of time until they could remove the shrapnel and everything and stuff me with gauze.

I was transferred from the field hospital on an ambulance to an airport and flown on a hospital plane from Belgium to England and put in the 107th hospital. I was in the hospital and well cared for and received a Purple Heart while in the hospital.

Stayed in the hospital until the Battle of the Bulge started on December the sixteenth of 1944. On December 24, a colonel called me in his office and interviewed me. He said, "Sergeant, I see by your record here, you've fought through Africa and Sicily, and they are badly in need of experienced men on the front lines at the Battle of the Bulge. Do you think you feel well enough to go back and help out?" I said, "Well, put it that way, I'm ready. I'll go back." I ate Christmas dinner at the convalescent hospital and headed back to France and landed at le Havre, France on New Year's Day.

Ate dinner at le Havre. Went into an old medieval horse stable along the coast at le Havre. Boarded a train in Paris and headed back up toward the front line in the dead of the winter with the snow waist deep, the snow ploughs clearing the way. We went up by a truck after we disembarked from the train. We went by truck into Belgium and to what they call replacement depots where soldiers would gather and disembark to the division they were with before. Or you could request another division, but I had no desire to go in any other divisions. I requested my own. I envied a soldier with a size fourteen foot that they could not give him overshoes, so he stayed by the nice warm heater while we shipped out to our regular divisions.

My division was some distance from Liège, Belgium. They were kicked back out of Germany, so it was almost back where we started from. So, I went back, and they were dug in, in dug outs in the snow around Liège in a holding position. We would have patrols, and the Germans would shell. We stayed there up until January and it was real cold — snow deep. In January we started to move into the forest again and attack.

During the winter, they issued us capes to wear, made out of sheets with a hood. You'd put [them] over your head so it was camouflage with the snow. Now, an amusing thing, during the day, you was moving and the sheet you were covered with was pliable, but by nightfall it would begin to freeze. They issued us in the morning, two sticks of TNT and two short fuses. At night, when you stopped advancing or fighting, you would take your TNT and pick a hole into the snow and light the fuse and blow your place to get below the snow line. If you wanted a hole for two men, you would put two sticks of TNT and blow a larger hole. Big chunks of ice would fly up in the air, and you had to duck sometimes.

We would spend a miserable night in these blown out holes. It wasn't much sleep. You would survive, I'd say. Sometimes, if we found a trench, we would spend the night in a German trench that was lined with ice, and we'd continue to advance.

[Once] while advancing in the forest, we were mistaken by some of our own men for Germans. They shelled us, and in my company, we had eleven men wounded and killed. Four in my section were wounded, and I patched them up. Those that could walk assisted those [who couldn't] back to the rear.

When we would get in a blow hole or get in a trench, we would protect ourselves by not letting a soldier go to sleep long. We would keep waking one another up to keep from freezing to death. That way, we survived. The next morning, we were up and at it again.

In our advance, after fighting so long, I had learned that the only way a soldier could survive is to travel as light as you possibly could. I carried one blanket, a half of a shelter tent, a pup tent with the end cut off, and some chocolate bars, and maybe one can of ration. All my men, I advised them to do the same because in traveling light, you could move fast, and it helped you to survive.

I had no desire to stay in the rear. I wanted to do my part. I went back as willingly as you could. Went back to the front line.

O. B. Johnson

O. B.. Johnson trained night fighters in Orlando before he was assigned to the first squadron of P-61 fighters going to Europe. As a pilot trainer, he recalled, "I picked out the [pilots] that I thought were best, and I kind of put them in storage, so they'd be assigned to my squadron whenever I got one. And, I had a fine bunch of pilots."

Johnson: It was while [we were] at Florence that the Battle of the Bulge occurred. We were flying, the weather was bad, and the Germans came right up to the river that was twelve miles from the base we were flying out of. People didn't know whether they were going to come across that river or not, but they had blown up all the bridges on it. We put dynamite under the runway so that the runway wouldn't be usable if they did continue to come, and we were flying off a runway with dynamite under it.

Lt. Col O. B. Johnson, CO of 422nd NFS, France , August 1944

General [Anthony C.] McAuliffe, who was commander at Bastogne, gave us a citation, and we ended up getting the Presidential Unit Citation for the flying that we did during that time of bad weather. [It] said we drove off the German tanks several times, and [they] were very appreciative of our effort of flying at night.

Basically, we learned how to fly instruments. We were much more capable of flying instruments than the day fighters were, because they hadn't had the practice and hadn't been trained that way. The weather was so bad, the day fighters just couldn't get off the ground in the daytime, and my boss, General [Elwood R. "Pete"] Crossada asked, "Can you fly?" I said, "Yeah, we can fly, but I don't know what we can do." He said, "Well, they need some help out there." So, we flew some day missions which didn't do much good, but at least we were out there annoying the Germans somewhat in the daytime. Basically, our effort was at night. During the Battle of the Bulge, I think we shot down probably fifteen German airplanes. We had the best record of any night fighter unit squadron.

Ida Turcan

Ida Turcan's reasons for serving as an Army nurse had less to do with defeating Hitler and more to do with "taking care of the wounded." Turcan worked in Army hospitals in North Africa and in Italy before being stationed in Marseille, France, during the Battle of the Bulge.

Turcan: [During the Battle of the Bulge] all the leaves were canceled and so forth. Casualties were the big problem, and keeping people alive. The war was getting more organized. The United States really, at the beginning, didn't know how to supply us. By that time, they knew how. There were more airplanes bringing things in. Before, everything was sent by boat.

Our hospital was bombed at the end of [the Battle of the Bulge]. No one got killed in the bombing, because it just hit one place, and it was where the laundry was. The only bad thing that I thought happened, we had German patients at the time, and we had a sergeant — I think he got court-martialed for it — but [the sergeant] went around and he told the German patients — you know he could hear the bombs falling — that if they bombed us, that he was going to cut them off first. And, the nurses who were taking care of the patients, we didn't think much of that, so we reported him. I thought he needed to be [reported] because he was taking advantage of his privilege. I don't know what they did with him. I would imagine he got court-martialed. He disappeared, anyway. That's the only really close thing that we came to.

Celine Ganel

Soon after graduating from high school in Donaldsonville, Louisiana, Celine Ganel took jobs as a legal stenographer and as court reporter. Hearing of the need for women in the military during the war, Ganel applied to the Women's Army Corps (WAC) and soon found herself working at the Pentagon. After the D-Day invasion, Ganel requested overseas service and, in February of 1945, was transferred to a U.S. Army office in Paris.

Ganel: I was a personnel clerk, in effect, and I did the same thing I did in the Pentagon. I took dictation from the officers in the office. Now [in Paris we had] a larger office, right within sight of the Arc de Triomphe at l'Etoile. It was unbelievable. We lived in hotels in Paris. My first assignment for living space was at the Hotel California on the Rue Du Berri which was just two blocks off the Champs Elysees, so we were right downtown. Most of the time, I lived within very easy walking distance of the Champs Elysees. In fact, the Hotel California was right across the street from the *Stars and Stripes*, the army newspaper. The *Stars and Stripes* was housed in what was the *Herald Tribune* building.

There was another thing about that location. There was a staging area right off the Champs Elysees where they brought people from the concentration camps and the labor camps. They brought them there in trucks, in these stake-body trucks, and they were still in their prison uniforms. That was another exposure to how horrible the war was because they were the most emaciated — they didn't have an ounce of extra flesh on them.

You saw them right from the camps. They were bringing them in at the end of the war. I don't remember seeing them while the war was still on, but there might have been [some] in the last months or so of the war, and it continued for a while after the war. For months after the war, there was so much work just getting people back to their homes, military people as well as former prisoners.

Joseph Dale

Joe Dale went into France several months after the D-Day landings as an artillery battery commander attached initially to the First Army and then to the Third Army.

Dale: They pulled us out of the First Army and moved us south to the Third Army as a support artillery unit again. We were facing the Siegfried Line. The Siegfried Line was like the national line. It was solid concrete with dragon teeth in front of it. And the infantry were heavy into battle getting through there. So the tank commander had asked if one of the barrack commanders would volunteer to take one of the 155 mm Howitzers up under cover of darkness to a position where we could direct fire on the bunker that was holding up the advancing infantry. Well, "Volunteer" is my middle name, so I volunteered. I took one of our [Howitzer] guns up with a gun crew and sighted [the bunker] at night time, and at dawn, we started firing. Strangely enough, there were some German soldiers down at the base of the bunker, and when we started firing, they started running up toward the bunker for protection. I chased one of them with 155 mm shells up the hill to the bunker. I never hit him. But, anyway, we got on through, and the infantry went on through. I took my driver, my radio operator, and a couple of men who went to this bunker. I thought, "Well, we'll see what we have in here."

We fired a couple of shots in the bunker and had nothing in return, so we cautiously went in. Well, the bunker was blacked out, and we just had a flashlight with us. Next thing I know, there was a tremendous explosion from below and just a ball of fire, flame came up the stairwell, engulfed my driver, and he was immediately killed, and it blew me out of the bunker. I ended up with burns at the top of my head and my hands and was subsequently evacuated. I returned to the unit before we crossed the Elbe River, though. But that's how I was blown out of a bunker.

In the wintertime, you can see only on my hands, if I don't have gloves on, you can see the difference in the skin between my wrists down to my hands. Of course, the hair on the back of my neck was completely burned to the top of my head. I was fortunate, but my driver, I lost him.

[For that operation I earned] the Bronze Star and the Purple Heart. That was Patton's Third Army. Now, after I was wounded and we crossed the Rhine, our unit was then detached and sent up to the Ruhr Pocket, and it was in the Ruhr Pocket that we were subsequently attached to the British Second Army and went across through the north to the Netherlands. Then we were reattached to the 82nd Airborne Division to cross the Elbe River. I got up there before we crossed the Elbe and rejoined my unit. So the Third Army was directed toward Austria, but we left them after we crossed the Rhine.

Cyril Guidry

Guidry: We pushed on into Germany around the Ruhr section. Moved on and ran into a few pill boxes [then] continued to move on into Germany. We had to cross some cold rivers and moved [on until we] captured [a] village and continued on into Germany.

Sometimes, we'd advance fast. Other times we would hit stiff resistance, and we were getting to find where the Germans were surrendering more because [they] were running out of the fanatic Germans, and they were beginning to draft the World War I veterans, [who] would surrender fairly easily.

We captured men — I mean boys — as young as twelve or thirteen. We captured men as old as thirty-five and forty. The people in the villages [of Germany] did not give us any trouble. If they stayed in town, they would go in the cellars. One thing about the Germans, they were good at storing food for the winter. We would enter the cellar, and it was usually full of potatoes and salami. They had a way of preserving eggs. We would eat well when we captured a town.

The bridge at Remagen was captured by the Ninth Engineers on March the seventh [1945]. We were notified to start a forced march to the bridge, so my regiment reached the town of Remagen, which is on the west side of the Rhine River. [We] went through town and crossed the Remagen bridge. We all gathered at the entrance of the bridge where they had a tunnel. You would wait your turn to dash across the bridge because the German artillery was constantly shelling it.

When our turn came to dash across, the shrapnel was hitting the bridge. Just on the east side an American jeep carrier was waiting their turn. An artillery shell had hit and burned the entire crew, killed them in the jeep. We got across the bridge and advanced up a hill and got into a position where we had some protection. For the first three days, we had very little but light equipment to help to defend us against the Germans. After the bridge was captured, we were in a little sheltered spot. It was with great joy that we noticed after so many days that tanks began to cross the bridge, and we had heavy support.

Anthony Palumbo

Palumbo: We — I say we, myself and my troopers, and my other people — had no idea that they were trying to kill all the Jews off in

Germany, or Europe too, if they could. But I can tell from my personal experience that when I went into Buchenwald, I saw, personally, these bodies stacked high. I went into the barracks, and there were these wooden beds with no mattresses, people sleeping on them. They were just skin and bones. Those that were strong enough to survive were just barely able to stand on their own feet. They were so happy to see us, as Americans and as so-called liberators of the concentration camp.

We didn't know about this at all. We just stumbled upon it with our two combat patrols that had gone out earlier in the day. It was the ninth or tenth of April [1945], I think. It was just before the war ended; the war ended within a month of that. The German guards had all taken off and had left the camp, just left the camp period. I don't think there was any play by the Germans to try to cover it up, personally. It was a terrible thing to see these bodies stacked high and most of them were naked bodies.

I saw bodies that had been dead for weeks at that time, others that had just died. It was a terrible, terrible sight to see these bodies stacked up one on top of another. We didn't stay in [Buchenwald] long. We were there perhaps two, three nights at the most. We left on the twelfth or thirteenth of April. It's something that's going to be ingrained in my memory forever, and, hopefully, I'll never see it again — not in our lifetime or our children's lifetime.

Just before we hit Buchenwald, we hit another camp. I don't know exactly where it was now, not too far from Buchenwald. We were told by the people that in that camp there were all young girls; they were all prostitutes. They were made prostitutes by the Germans. I don't know if they were Jewish. I imagine most of them were Jewish girls. We stopped, and they came out. I'll never forget. One put a kerchief around my neck and wanting me to stay. I called back on the horn and asked if we could spend the night, and they said, "No, nothing doing." We had to move on out. [The girls in the camp] were well taken care of, well-fed, and well nourished.

Foster: The night that you found Buchenwald, when you first liberated the camp, did you talk about what you had seen?

Palumbo: We didn't do much talking among ourselves. I think we were more shocked than we were anything else. Looking back on it now, we were wondering at the time why we even found a camp like that. This was just one of many camps in the area under the command of the Nazis. Hitler must have been such a crazy individual then. [In Buchenwald] all we saw were just men; we didn't see any children there at all.

Foster: Can you describe it?

Palumbo: No, all I know [is that] there were many, many barracks lined up — temporary buildings, probably fifteen or twenty of them, maybe more or less. I don't know.

Foster: Did you speak to any of the survivors?

Palumbo: I don't remember speaking to anybody there, because the stench was so bad you didn't want to get too close to . . . people . . . . We crossed the Siegfried Line, and we got into Germany after which we were pulled out and asked to go south. We went back into Germany by Frankfurt and ended up at the Elbe River. The Elbe River is where we made contact with our allies, the Russian forces. They were the most rag-tag army I had ever seen in my life. They had been through so much. They carried all their women with them, their wives and children. They had horse-drawn equipment. They were so antiquated. I wondered how they were able to fight as well as they did. They had lost millions of men in battle. They lost many, many men in battle. But they were happy-go-lucky individuals, mostly peasants, whereas our forces were a mixture of Americans, Italians, Irish, Jewish.

[When] we crossed the Elbe River, and we made contact with the first Russian unit that we had ever seen, we were told that if we wanted to eat chow with the Russian forces, we could. So we did. For their lunch, they had cold fat back, suet and bread, and wine and that was their lunch. I couldn't tolerate that. So we, in turn, asked them if they wanted to come to our officers' mess. They did, and we gave them everything we could possibly give them. I think we had chicken from the old number ten cans, chicken, and that was a treat to them.

Once we were in Germany, we used to go to the German peasants and farmers; we'd speak in German, a little German that you pick up, and ask, "Haben sie eier?" "Do you have any eggs?" They'd say, "No, next time." And we'd point a rifle at them and go, "Ja, ja, ja, ja, ja!" They'd come out with a handful of eggs, and then we'd take the eggs and we'd boil them and eat boiled eggs. That would supplement our own rations.

Foster: Do you think they believed that you would really hurt them?

Palumbo: I don't think so, but we were threatening. "Haben sie eier?" I'll never forget that. "Haben sie eier?" "Have any eggs?" It was quite an honor for us to get the eggs because we had powdered eggs all the time and Spam. We'd get so tired and sick of Spam and powdered eggs. Let's get some fresh eggs. Boil them ourselves.

Also, I remember one little incident. It was somewhere in Germany on a railroad trestle painted in big block letters: "You'll Get Berlin Now; Moscow Will Get You Later." It was an omen. I didn't realize it at the time, but my commanding general, the Third Army Commander, General Patton, had wanted to go all the way to Moscow at the time because he had that vision that most of us didn't have at the time. "You'll Get Berlin Now; Moscow Will Get You Later," and I'll never forget that as long as I live. This was before we had even talked about the Cold War. General Patton was able to see far in advance. He seemed to have a psychic ability. I don't know; it was a shame he had to die when he did, but the Lord has his reasons.

Cyril Guidry

We were informed by radio when President Roosevelt died. We also heard when Hitler died, and we continued our advance. My company would capture three hundred prisoners a day. One day, we had so many prisoners in an enclosure — and I had charge of holding them — we had to get some of our men to drive the trucks to haul them to the rear. I had been frisking German prisoners and had two saddle bags of pocket knives and different things. Had a little river near and brought [the knives and things I had collected] and dropped them over a bridge. I kept half a dozen to put in my pocket and dropped the pocket knives in the river.

Most of the German prisoners were glad [the war] was over. They weren't any trouble, except for a few SS prisoners. One of them in particular, a blond, they had to hold him down and restrict him because he was belligerent. But there was nothing he could do.

Well, we advanced through Germany, and our goal was to advance to the Elbe River. So we were capturing prisoners by the hundreds. We reached the Elbe River and waited thirteen days for the Russians to come to us.

We could have easily advanced into Berlin. We were forty miles out of Berlin when we stopped fighting at the Elbe. [But instead,] we just waited for the Russians. I was not disappointed because I was glad to wait for them.

The Russian soldiers' equipment was rather crude because they mass produced everything. They had a machine gun, a pistol — we called it a grease gun. It was a very crude thing. I had German machine pistols when the war ended and a Luger and different guns I'd give away. I had to get rid of the machine pistol since we were coming home by airplane. That was V-E day on May the fifth, 1945.

We were very glad, I'd say, that the war was over. Almost three years of fighting from one front to the other.

Foster: What did you do to celebrate?

Guidry: We couldn't do much of anything. We hadn't anything. We was at a little farming town, and we were friendly with the people there. We had plenty to eat and stayed in a home owned by a woman we called Mrs. Klaus, and she had a teenage daughter. I'd say, we treated them with respect, and they cooked for us, kept house.

We stayed there until the first of June. We were put on trucks and sent down to southern Germany on the autobahn. We went across the Danube river and went through Augsburg, and about thirty miles out of Munich, we were stationed in the army of occupation [camp].

[I had] 124 points [which was] considered a lot of points. We stayed there a few days, were put on [a] train, [an] electric train, and sent back through Germany, into southern Germany, and to Marseille, France.

On the way, we could see the destruction of Germany and France. At Marseille, we stayed a few days and [then were] put on a ship. I don't remember the name of the ship. We went back through the Strait of Gibraltar and then we continued on our way back to the United States.

Joseph Dale

Fiser: Where were you when the war ended?

Dale: We were in a little town about sixty miles north of Berlin, and we had met up with the Russians at that point. Of course, this is not [the] noted meeting up of the Russians and the Americans. That was down south. But this was just another part of the meeting at the end of the war. We stayed there, I guess in this town, about ten days or two weeks. The only recollection that we have of the Russians we met up with was that they apparently liked [and] got a hold of some German schnapps. It was not too infrequent that around midnight they'd come roaring through the town in their little jeeps with their vodka and also firing off their weapons. That was almost a nightly event, firing their weapons in the air, just in celebration.

I can see it today, the church we all went to on V-E Day when we got word that the documents had been signed. That was the Italian commander who said we all had to go to church. We were overtired, and with the exception of those who were on duty, we all went to church in this little German town.

1. Geoffrey Perret, *There's a War to Be Won* (New York, 1991), p. 193.

2. Studies of the Normandy invasion are numerous. The most useful and thorough analysis, and also the most recent, is Stephen Ambrose, *D-Day, June 6, 1944: The Climactic Battle of World War II* (New York, 1994).

3. On the period between D-Day and V-E Day, see Martin Blumenson, *Breakout and Pursuit* (Washington, D.C., 1961), and Stephen Ambrose, *Citizen Soldier* (New York, 1997).

4. The army's point system for discharge was simple: "A soldier got one point for every month in the service, one point for every month of service overseas, five points for each campaign star or combat decoration (including the Purple Heart), and twelve points for each child (up to three children). To qualify for discharge, a man had to amass eighty-five points." Lee Kennett, *G.I.: The American Soldier in World War II* (New York, 1987), p. 223.

Chapter Six

The War Against Japan

The American fighting man in the Pacific Theater of Operations (PTO) encountered conditions markedly different from those faced by his counterpart in Europe. The most obvious difference was geography. Contrasting with the relatively compact European land mass were the island chains of the Pacific area — the Solomons, Marshalls, Carolines, Gilberts, Marianas, Philippines, and others. The distances between bases or target areas in the Pacific were enormous compared to those in the European Theater of Operations (ETO). From Pearl Harbor to Tarawa, in the Gilberts, for example, it is more than 2,000 miles; and when the Army Air Force began strategic bombing of Japan from new bases in the Marianas in the fall of 1944, the aircraft had to fly a round-trip of nearly 3,000 miles. The climate of the central and southwestern parts of the Pacific and of Southeast Asia was similar to that of Louisiana on a particularly hot and humid summer day. While American soldiers, sailors, and marines fighting the Japanese experienced the hazards and discomfort of disease-laden tropical jungles — malaria would inflict more casualties on American troops than the Japanese — the GIs in the ETO found a climate and terrain more similar to the northern latitudes of the United States. Geography also imposed different weapons systems. In the ETO, the war was primarily a land-air conflict in which armored divisions, for example, found room for maneuver and played a critical role on the battlefields. The war against Japan, on the other hand, was one in which naval and air power predominated and had to be projected over vast distances. The aircraft carrier, the submarine, and the B-29, the largest bomber the U.S. employed, were of vital importance — along with the Marine Corps, which had taken the lead in the inter-war period in developing the doctrine and techniques of amphibious landings and island warfare.

The conduct and character of the enemy was markedly different in the Pacific. The German army on the Western front basically waged war in accordance with rules accepted by both sides. Determined, resilient, tenacious, yes, but Wehrmacht troops in the West would surrender when the odds were hopeless and by and large they treated Allied prisoners reasonably well. Atrocities did occur, such as that at Malmédy during the Battle of the Bulge, but they were few and usually involved SS units. Battlefield atrocity on a grand, even daily, scale the Germans reserved for the "racially inferior' enemy troops they faced on the Eastern front. The Japanese soldier, on the other hand, fought with extraordinary fanaticism everywhere, frequently preferring death to surrender, which he regarded as dishonorable. As a consequence, in part, of that attitude, Japanese losses in the Pacific typically were horrendous. And that was a pattern from the outset. On Guadalcanal, where the American counter-offensive began in 1942, the Japanese suffered 25,000 killed in action during a six-month period, while American fatal casualties were under 1,500. On Okinawa (1945), total American deaths were just over 12,000, but the Japanese exceeded 107,000, a figure that does not include the thousands of Japanese civilians who killed themselves.

The war in the PTO had a racial dimension missing from the conflict in Western Europe, and that fact, coupled with Japanese fanaticism, led to barbarous treatment of Allied prisoners of war. Indeed, atrocity seemingly became the norm for Japanese troops from the very beginning of Japan's efforts to conquer the Asian mainland. "Their atrocities frequently were so grotesque, and flaunted in such a macabre manner," one historian has written, "that it is not surprising they were interpreted [in the West] as being an expression of deliberate policy . . . "[1] One striking consequence of the battlefield environment in the PTO, in addition to the conduct of the enemy, was the fact that neuropsychological casualties were much higher among American troops there than among the GIs in Europe.

From an industrial and technological standpoint, Japan was at an enormous disadvantage vis-a-vis the United States — and therein lay another contrast of sorts with the European conflict. The Allies enjoyed overall logistical superiority over Nazi Germany, but the Wehrmacht possessed artillery and armor superior to that fielded by the Allies. Indeed, one of the main reasons American forces suffered a higher casualty rate in Europe than in the Pacific was the effectiveness of German artillery. The Reich, furthermore, took the lead in developing jet aircraft and put a jet fighter into service before V-E Day. But Japan enjoyed a technological lead only in restricted areas — the Zero fighter plane and certain kinds of torpedoes — and only at the outset of its war against the United States. Japan lacked the industrial base, the skilled labor, and the engineering skills to field a truly modern army. It was with little option, therefore, that Japanese military leaders found themselves emphasizing the superiority of "spiritual" factors over material ones. Japanese troops, of course, learned the hard way that their limited technology and logistical poverty did not win battles.

For the first six months of the war, however, the Japanese appeared to enjoy all the advantages. Simultaneously with the attack on

Pearl Harbor, they launched air raids on the Philippines, Guam, Wake, and British bases in Hong Kong and Malaya. Troop landings and conquest soon followed, so that by mid-1942 Tokyo's limited war strategy seemed to have worked with precision. But reality now set in. First, in the Battle of the Coral Sea in May, the American navy stopped the Japanese drive toward Australia and then, the next month, inflicted a catastrophic defeat on the Japanese fleet at Midway. The clash at Midway proved to be the turning point in the Pacific War: from that point on the Japanese found themselves on the defensive, facing an inexorable American advance.

The war against Japan was basically an American undertaking, so it was the United States that dictated strategy, except in Southeast Asia, where the British had control. Unlike the unified command that supervised the war against Germany, Washington established a bifurcated or dual structure in the Pacific. In the Southwest, General Douglas MacArthur served as supreme commander. His counterpart in the South, Central, and Northern Pacific was Admiral Chester Nimitz. The high command took its first step toward rolling back the Japanese tide in August 1942, when American forces landed on Guadalcanal. With victory achieved there, the basic strategy became that of a two-pronged thrust toward Japan, "island-hopping" and, in some cases, "leap-frogging" over Japanese strongholds so long as they were isolated and not in a position to do significant damage to American forces. The navy preferred to head directly for the Japanese home islands. MacArthur, however, because of his extraordinary prestige, was able to secure approval from the Joint Chiefs for a convergence of the two drives, his in the Southwest and the navy's in the Central Pacific, on the Philippines, where he had been in command when the Japanese struck in December 1941, and to which he had promised, "I shall return!"

But before reaching the Philippines there would be hard fighting by brave men on both sides. While MacArthur's forces conquered or neutralized remaining Japanese strongholds in the Solomons, such as Bougainville, and then moved along the northern coast of New Guinea, the war waged by Nimitz took American troops to the Gilberts, the Marshalls, and in mid-1944 the Marianas. The navy-directed campaign left names such as Tarawa and Saipan permanently etched in the memories of the men who fought it. The capture of the Marianas set the stage for the showdown in the Philippines beginning in the fall of 1944. MacArthur's invasion of the island of Leyte in October triggered the Battle of Leyte Gulf, the greatest naval engagement in history that practically destroyed what remained of the Imperial Japanese fleet. One ominous development during the battle was the appearance of a new enemy weapon: the *kamikaze* or suicide pilots. The campaign to liberate the main island, Luzon, where Japanese forces numbered 275,000, began in January 1945 and continued for months. The house-to-house fighting in Manilla, which left some 100,000 Filipino civilians dead, untold numbers of them victims of the retreating Japanese troops, was the tragic highlight of the struggle.

While the seaward circle drew tighter around Japan, the Allies pressed the war from another direction, the China-Burma-India theater (CBI). American forces there were under the command of General Joseph Stilwell until October 1944, when General Albert Wedemeyer replaced him. The CBI's main contribution to the war was to keep hundreds of thousands of Japanese troops occupied, primarily in China. American military activities began in China with the formation in 1941 of the American Volunteer Group (AVG) by then Colonel Claire Chennault. When Chennault had retired from the army in 1937, the government of Chiang Kai-Shek had recruited him to train Chinese fighter pilots. The AVG, known subsequently as the Flying Tigers, actively engaged in the air war against the Japanese before Pearl Harbor and, after Chennault's recall to active duty in 1942, it was absorbed into the Fourteenth Air Force under his command. Strategic bombing efforts from bases in

China against Japan began in June 1944, but proved ineffective and ended in December of that year. American army pilots also established an air ferrying service to get supplies to the Chinese, taking off from bases in India to make the dangerous flight over the Himalayas — the so-called "Hump." American army personnel, furthermore, helped train, equip, and lead Chinese troops in a ground campaign in Burma designed to reopen the Burma Road, which had been closed by the Japanese, and to open a new land supply route to China, the Ledo Road.

The decisive push toward Japan came from the Pacific. The seizure of the Marianas in mid-1944 had placed the enemy homeland within range of the new strategic bomber, the B-29, which began operations from Saipan in November. The bloody victories on Iwo Jima and Okinawa in the first half of 1945 brought American forces to the edge of the Japanese home perimeter — and weighed heavily on the minds of planners in Washington as they contemplated an invasion of the enemy's homeland. Intercepted Japanese communications confirmed that the high command in Tokyo was preparing feverishly for suicidal resistance on a national scale. But the success of the Manhattan Project made the final invasion unnecessary as the shock of Hiroshima and Nagasaki brought Japan's surrender.

The dropping of the atomic bombs was the most controversial act by the United States during the war. Predominant historical and military opinion today is that they were not necessary for military victory — and, as critics emphasize, they resulted in the deaths of great numbers of Japanese civilians. But many more Japanese civilian lives had already been lost to conventional bombs. The fire-bombing raid on Tokyo on the night of March 9, 1945, had caused more deaths and destroyed more square miles of urban property that did the A-bomb attack on Hiroshima. By putting an earlier end to the Pacific war than anticipated, the atomic bombs probably saved hundreds of thousands of Japanese lives, which would have been sacrificed to further conventional bombing, to starvation and disease in the event of prolonged naval blockading, and certainly to American firepower had an invasion of the home islands become necessary. Those two bombs, furthermore, prevented additional loss of life in China, where Japanese troops were killing massive numbers of people every month. But those for whom the morality of the atomic bomb is questionable might well consult the people perhaps best qualified to judge its convenience: the American soldiers, sailors, and marines awaiting orders to risk their lives and futures by boarding ships and planes bound for holocaust on the Japanese mainland. From that perspective, the real meaning of Hiroshima and Nagasaki is that tens of thousands of young American men would live to go home. They would live to love and to marry and to raise families, live to study, open businesses, teach school, practice law and medicine, work in offices and department stores, drive a bus or a taxi, and farm the land. They would live to enrich American life with their efforts — and they would live to remember.

Raymond Rockhold

Raymond Rockhold recalls, prior to joining the Marine Corps, "thirteen of us bought an airplane and learned to fly." Rockhold's flying lessons on the jointly-owned lightweight Piper Cub allowed him to earn a pilot's license and taught him skills that would later prove valuable for his work arming fighter planes in the Pacific during World War II.

Rockhold: I was thirty years old my first day in the Marine Corps. When I came out of boot camp, I took a test for what I wanted to go into it. I wanted to go in and fly. So I passed that and went into flying.

My younger brother, one of the twins — his other twin got killed — he quit LSU and went into the Marine Corps. He joined the Raiders. I found out about it and gave him hell. I told him, I said, "Lloyd, we don't know how long this war is going to last; we don't know how bad it's going to get; and, being in the marines, we'll be damn sure lucky if we come out alive." I said, "Here you go and join the Raiders; you ain't got one damn good chance of coming out alive." The Raiders would go up at nighttime, penetrate the enemy, capture them from camps and bring them back for questioning. We were told that if we even went on a trip with any of them, the Raiders, we'd be court-martialed. They told us in no uncertain terms that we were not expendable. They told us, "We don't want to catch you picking up a gun unless the condition is black." That's when they are attacking you in force. "You're here to keep those planes flying." And, believe me, that's what we had to do.

I got my brother out [of the Raiders], incidentally. I got to be good friends with a sergeant-major when I got North Island—that's where they shipped us to from boot camp, to North Island, which is across the bay from San Diego. I got thirty days of K.P., and I got to know the master sergeant there. He and I got to be pretty good friends. He told me one day, he said, "I sure would like to have some shrimp from Louisiana." He said, "I passed by there one year, and they're good. I sure would like some." I said, "Well, Sergeant, just consider it done." I got on the telephone, called Mama and told her to send me some shrimp. I made some points. He said, "Anything I can do for you?" I said, "Sergeant, I got a brother that joined the Raiders." I said, "Can we get him out?" He said, "Tell him to put in for a transfer." So I called him up, told him, I said, "Put in for transfer." He put in for transfer. The day the transfer came through, he was waiting on the shore, with his sea bags, waiting to go in the boat. My master sergeant got in his truck and went down there to pick him up.

After thirty days [on North Island], we got sent to Jacksonville, Florida, for school. We got all the [training for] fighting during our boot camp days, but this was to learn about all the airplanes: the colors, the numbers, different things. Maybe [for] five or six months, we had to learn all things about airplanes.

Foster: So were you classified as a mechanic?

Rockhold: Well, I kept the guns for it, honey. I was armaments. Each would have an airplane, and when they'd come in, we'd have to reload them, check them over, and be sure they fired again. We'd get some of those ninety day wonders over there, those pilots [who only lasted] ninety days. They'd get up there, and the Jap might be two miles away, and they'd be liable to open up on them. By the time the Jap got close enough, [the pilot] was out of ammunition. So we lost quite a few fellows before they finally learned how. They took an extra potato up with them. They'd shoot some bursts out of that and then throw that container overboard. Then, [they still had ammunition when] the Jap would close in.

    We had a lot of dog fights up above us. We'd sit up there sometimes, outside, and watch the dog fights in the nighttime. It was very beautiful watching a dog fight in the skies there.

Foster: Where did you see the dog fight?

Rockhold: On Guadalcanal. We had skipped Guadalcanal and gone up to Russell Islands, which is not quite a day from Guadalcanal. Guadalcanal was pretty well under control, but Guadalcanal had gotten hit pretty bad [and the planes severely damaged].

    They got a bunch of us up and put [us] in the boat for one of them. We went from Russell Islands to Guadalcanal, and we were there several months, working night and day to get those planes all flying again. We were there all night, working. The only time we'd quit would be if we'd get an alert that the Japs were coming in close to us or something like that, overhead.

    I contracted dad-gummed yellow, not yellow fever, malaria fever.

I went up to where we worked on the airplanes, and I told the sergeant up there, I said, "Sergeant, I'm burning up with fever." He said, "Go back, lay down in your bed." Well, the sergeant-major, checking everybody out, came up there. He looked over, and he said, "What's the matter, Rock?" I said, "Sergeant, I'm pretty hot with the fever here." He came over and felt me, went down and got on his telephone to the captain of the sick bay and said, "Come get Rockhold and put him in the sick bay." So they came and got me, took me down to the sick bay. I looked down there and there were two men just playing cards. I'm laying there, just burning up. They ain't said [anything] but just, "Put him to bed" when I walked in. I went and lay down in the bed and sat there for a few minutes. I looked over and I said, "Look, you bastards, I didn't come down here to die." I had to go through two doses of medicine before I got that fever, malaria fever, out of me. I had fever of a hundred and six two days straight. You could have higher fever back there in the islands like that. But I had a hundred and six two days straight. It took two doses to get that out. I've never been bothered since with it. Nighttime, when we'd have an air alarm, somebody would help me down to the cave, down there. We had caves to go into.

Foster: How long were you at Guadalcanal?

Rockhold: Honey, I guess, probably about seven months all together. We went to the Russell Islands, and then some of us got sent back to Guadalcanal. The day we left Guadalcanal, the Japs pulled the biggest raid they'd ever pulled. The biggest raid at that time. They were trying to take the canal back. And there was really some fighting. They lost more airplanes in that one day, I think, than any other day. We were sitting out there in a small boat, in the bay out there, and they wouldn't let us go up above. They wanted us to stay in the cabin because if the Japs saw it was a boat with men in it, they'd want to try and get it. Of course, we could watch it a little bit, peeking out of windows and things. We could watch the dog fights going on.

Louie Reinberg

Soon after the bombing of Pearl Harbor, Reinberg became Adjutant and G-1 of the Marine Force's Fourteenth Naval Division. He held that position until he returned to the states and joined the Twelfth Defense Battalion. At Cape Gloucester, New Britain, Reinberg took command of the Fourth Battalion of the Eleventh Marine Division before moving into Papua.

Reinberg: In 1942, we went down to Townsville, Australia, unloaded our ships and back-loaded the navy L.S.T.s [landing ship tanks]. We found out that we were going up to what they call Woodlark Island. We left Townsville, Australia, which was no paradise at all. It looked like a United States town about the turn of the century; there wasn't anything in it, no merchandise or anything. Australia had been in the war a long time. We went to Woodlark Island [part of] the Trobriand Island group. It was in the vicinity of Guadalcanal, but above it. An army regiment was with us, too, but we never saw those people. They kept to themselves. We were the defense battalion defending with anti-aircraft machine guns and sea coast artillery.

We didn't have any [Japanese] opposition at all. I think one airplane came by once or twice. So we had it pretty nice. Everything was going along all right until about the end of November or December. We pulled up stakes and moved over to a bay, which is off the coast of New Guinea, and prepared to go up to Cape Gloucester, where we were supposed to provide anti-aircraft fire and sea coast artillery. We went over to Cape Gloucester [and] stayed there until the following June. That was uneventful too. There was some fighting. It was eventful as far as the infantry was concerned, but not as far as we were concerned.

Hebert: What were conditions like there?

Reinberg: It was a rain forest that we landed in. It was horrible. It was wet. Everything was wet, and it stayed wet. We couldn't get dry until we got out in the sunlight. We finally moved out from the beach and got up close to where the airstrip was. We had some sunlight, so we did all right. Our people cleared out and got squared away. We stayed there until June.

About the same time we left Cape Gloucester, we heard by radio of landings in Europe. But that was far away. It didn't bother us. We [went] down to the Russell Islands, and I was transferred from my original outfit, [the] Twelfth Defense, to the First Marine Division. I was given the Fourth Battalion, Eleventh Marines, and I told them, "Get ready," [because] we were going up to another operation pretty soon. I had to learn a whole new bunch of people. I knew what it was all about, but I didn't know the people or anything. But they were very cooperative, and we worked very well together.

We went up to Peleliu and landed up there on the fifteenth of September. I was not on the first wave, but I was in the first group. I was on the second or third wave.

I had an artillery battalion at that time, and I had to make a reconnaissance of where the battalion was going to be located. I had a lot of experienced people there, too. It wasn't too much knowing what to do or how to do it; it was when to do it. So five or six of us in the command group came ashore, [to look for the place] where we were going to locate this outfit, and we finally picked out a place after having a little bit of scrimmage to try to get into it. There were some Japanese there, but we took care of that. We brought a battalion in and had them in firing position by the evening — registered and ready for supporting fires, which we were very fortunate for. We did all right for ourselves.

When we got there to Peleliu and uncovered it, why it was a

mess, I mean, as far as terrain was concerned. If you ever know what a coral outcropping is, it's just a bunch of coral rocks, and it's high, rugged, and sharp. It's not sloping or anything; it's just a hump, there.

We went in on boats there. I was in a tractor. That's how I got ashore. My battalion was in what we call "ducks" in those days.

Hebert: Were the Japanese on high ground?

Reinberg: No, they were on the beach of Peleliu. There wasn't any high ground except up in the upper end, and we went up there later on. But this was down on the beach. The Japanese had built a landing field there, and it was flat. Just to the north of the landing field, that's where this little outcropping was, and it was really rugged in there. We had a lot of fighting there. My battalion was general support, and I'd say we fired thousands of rounds of ammunition. We fired all over the place: the heights; in the hole; everywhere. Indirect fire, direct fire, and everything else. We finally secured the airstrip and the greater part of the island, and then the Japanese were holed up in the hills.

I was up there, and they wanted [to] get an artillery piece up there and to snipe these positions. So we brought a couple of batteries up there, and we were firing in there. Then I got another piece, and we were trying to shoot that one. We built a trestle on the bed of a truck so we could get some elevation. I was trying to shoot [at the Japanese], and I'd just gotten down out of the thing when a mortar shell landed and hit me and my operations officer and laid us out. So from there on out, I was in the evacuation troop coming home.

Hebert: How did the war in the Pacific, the war that you fought, differ from the war in Europe?

Reinberg: We were just going from island to island, with nothing on them but natives, no improvements or anything else. Whereas in Europe, there was quite a civilization and cities and towns and everything else. We were in one jungle after another, that was the major thing.

Hebert: Did you meet up with the Japanese often?

Reinberg: No. At Cape Gloucester in the First Division [we did], but I didn't have any personal contact there. I was in sea coast artillery. Then I was executive officer of a defense battalion, and I was number two commander. It wasn't any close combat as far as I'm concerned.

  [The natives] were fuzzy wuzzies as far as we were concerned, and we never had any dealings with them. The Australians were the people who looked after them. We never saw them. They brought some of them in to build temporary shelters out of palm trees and coconut logs and stuff like that, and they [would go] back to wherever they [slept] at night. We never had any reason to have any close contact with them.

Hebert: What about diseases in those places — malaria?

Reinberg: When we were out there, they started giving us Atabrine. You've heard of Atabrine? I think when I got home I was two shades of yellow [because] I took Atabrine. In fact, I was almost forced into taking it every day, and as far as I know we didn't have any great problems with Atabrine as they did at Guadalcanal in the early part of the war.

Hebert: You mentioned how large the mosquitoes were. Please describe them.

Reinberg: Well, they seemed to be the size of mountains. There were just normal mosquitoes, but there were [also] malaria-bearing mosquitoes. In those days, the military would spray DDT and all kinds of sprays over the area, and I guess that was very effective. I don't remember ever having any bouts with mosquitoes or anything — no swarms or anything like that.

John A. Cox

Major John Cox's Thirty-seventh Infantry Division fought the Japanese throughout the South Pacific, including battles on the islands of New Georgia, Bougainville, and Luzon. Cox still has shrapnel in a lung from a Japanese 140 millimeter mortar shell, the injury that forced him to give up military service.

Fiser: John, tell me a little bit more about your first brush with combat.

Cox: In 1942, we went from San Francisco to Auckland, New Zealand, for a few months. Then we went to the Fiji Islands to train. At that time, the Japanese had fishing camps all around the Fiji Islands. Viti Levu was the main island, and [the Japanese] were ready to take that place over any time. The New Zealanders were defending [Viti Levu], but they didn't have the resources to really defend it. [The decision was made] to train the natives and the New Zealanders and to call them "commandos." Their purpose was to carry on guerilla warfare [so that] when the Japanese took [Viti Levu] over, they would make it real uncomfortable for them.

They asked for volunteers to go train with the Fijians and New Zealanders, and I volunteered. That was some really satisfying life I had there. If I knew I was going to get home alive, I could have just lived there, because we had a great life.

The Fiji Islands provided a good training area for the Thirty-seventh Infantry Division, which was originally from the Ohio National Guard. I learned a lot of woodcraft from the Fijians, and we taught them demolitions, explosives, and weaponry.

The Fijians didn't really go into battle as a unit. What happened was we were supposed to fight behind the lines on Guadalcanal. Our navy, as you remember, just got crippled up, and we couldn't get there. I was going to go with one of these units if my outfit would let me, but they sent us back, gave me a rifle company, and took the New Zealanders and the Fijians to what we call the Southern Independent Commandos. They served as scouts for our division commander and other commanding generals that were in the Pacific. They were very valuable people during that war.

Fiser: Yes, [many of them were coast watchers and] were brave men that probably never got the attention they deserved or the decoration. They sat out on some of those lonely islands there, just one or two of them together with a radio, hiding out from the Japanese and sending in reports. The Japanese were just about at their zenith when you and I entered the war, and they never got that high again. They went back from there. Your first full-scale battle was where? Which island?

Cox: Our first big action was on New Georgia. It was [an] airport on New Georgia, and that was a really tough battle. We did it differently from Guadalcanal. We went in from the rear and took the high ground first. But it was not easy. We were cut off for about six weeks. That's the first time in my life I hadn't shaved in six weeks. When we took the airport, we didn't have but about sixty or eighty men left in the rifle company, out of one hundred and ninety-seven. We looked pretty bad, I guess. When we took New Georgia, I remember, "Here I am with about thirty men left out of a rifle company." We had these old, dirty jungle suits on, these old Marine suits really.

[On New Georgia,] we were going toward the beach, and an old man came out of a bunker. He had a white cloth tied around his head, and he had on shoes. But he had a whole handful of grenades. So I asked the men to move back. I put my pistol in my pocket and tried to get him to surrender. I kept waving at him, and he looked at us, pulled the pin out of the grenade, threw it on the ground. Put his foot on it and stood on it. Let it go. It didn't kill him; it just blew his leg off. He was defying us, but he didn't even have anybody to watch him but us. That's the way it went at that point in history.

We did take New Georgia, and then we went to Vella Lavella and established a perimeter defense and built a fighter strip. These were all islands in the Solomons, and Vella Lavella was up north, the closest to Bougainville. I got my first [decoration] in New Georgia, but I got the Distinguished Service Cross on Bougainville.

We'd been on Bougainville for a long, long time. We went there in November [1943], and then in March [1944], the Japanese decided they were going to knock us off the island. We were opposing the Sixth Route Army of the Japanese. That's the outfit that was credited with the raping of Nanking. They were pretty vicious. They had artillery; they had everything. But we had air superiority. They breached our lines, and they almost got in [to Bougainville]. But we held them off. We killed about 6,500 Japanese in that outfit, and we had no way to bury them. We had to take bulldozers, dig big trenches and bury them like that, because you had to. You couldn't let them lay out on top of the ground. Nobody had the time or energy . . . we were exhausted, too. Then, of course, we had to chase [the Japanese] back across the island, [those that were] left. That was a vicious fight.

You know we had these latrines right behind the main line. [The Japanese] thought that was our headquarters because they would see these people going into the latrines which were covered with olive drab mosquito netting. They'd see them going in there every morning. So the first thing they blew up with their artillery was our latrines [laughs]. But they came in and just stayed, all night long. They came in at three o'clock in the morning in the rain, and they took some of our positions.

[During the battle at Bougainville,] I was in the hole and looking up to my left, up the hill. We were not on the crest of the hill; we were down below. You could see three or four soldiers that had been killed, and they were just in a kneeling position. They couldn't get them out because they were under fire. Then, off to the right, I saw these two Japanese heads sticking up. I knew they were Japanese because they had camouflage on them. I didn't have anything but a pistol. I was the S-3 then, the plans and training officer for the battalion, and I asked these boys, I said, "Give me a BAR," Browning Automatic Rifle. They said, "Get back down here! You're going to get us all killed!" But I got the gun, and I fired one blast at those two heads, then the second blast kicked me over right, because those things kick up a storm. They said, "I told you you were going to get us all killed, now where're you hit?" and I said, "Give me an M-1 rifle!" So I looked up, and there was another head still showing, so I fired at him. Then, I asked them to cover me with fire.

I had a flame thrower set up to come over and to go up that hill. I was going to go with him. We were going to end that fighting that day one way or other. There was a sergeant with a light machine gun, and he said, "I'll cover you." So I took off, and by the time I got over there, the flame thrower had already got there. He shot that flame thrower up right in the air, and I didn't know whether he'd been effective or not. But, I stood there until the smoked cleared. I ran up onto the hill and, boy, there were so many dead Japs in about a hundred and fifty foot square, you couldn't even walk.

There was a guy trying to kill himself, a Japanese soldier laying flat on his back. He was badly wounded, and he was trying to stick a bayonet in his stomach. So I shot him in the stomach [and] in the chest with his own gun because I didn't even have mine out. He started slinging that thing at me, and he cut me right across the little finger. After I went to the aid station, they wanted to know what caused that.

230 Japan

I told them, "Barbed wire." I wasn't going to tell anybody I got wounded with a bayonet in my little finger. Anyway, that's about the way the fighting looked at that point in history. But we'd been there for a long time, about two weeks.

Fiser: We touched on the legend of [your gun] Bloody Mary in our earlier taping. Apparently you were a pretty good pistol shot right from the start. You didn't need much training in that, did you?

Cox: No. I had made expert with a pistol. But [Bloody Mary] was a special gun. I still have that gun. It doesn't have any paint on it, but it will shoot. [Bloody Mary] was given to me when I went in the Army in 1941, by a guy named Stapp, and he had had it in World War I. He gave it to me with the statement that, "I hereby give John A. Cox this Colt .45 Army Automatic Gun." He gave the serial number, and he said, "May it serve him well." And it did. I finally just took it around in my hip pocket, or jungle suit pocket, with no holster at all. It ended up being a good luck charm, really.

When we took Manila [in 1945], we were getting ready to pursue the enemy up north, and I had a Lieutenant Robert Reck, who was extremely nervous for some reason. Normally, he was not nervous. So I asked him [about it]. He said he just couldn't explain it. So I said, "I'll tell you what I'll do. I'll give you old Bloody Mary. You take that gun, and I guarantee you nothing is going to happen to you." He did, and I got a brand new gun, a .45, and the first thing that happened to me, I walked up on a Japanese soldier that was asleep, his machine gun in place but [he was] on top of it. I leveled down on him and pulled the trigger, and the thing misfired. So he jumped down in his hole and fired with this machine gun. We got him out with grenades. But my gun, Bloody Mary, went with Robert Reck, and he came through the war unscathed.

[Once the war was over], in Los Angeles, California, [Reck] and another couple of guys that were in the army with us, shipped [Bloody Mary] back to me in three packages. You know, in order to conform with the postal service regulations. And I still have that gun, and the museum wants it down at the U.S.S. Kidd, but we don't think we need to put it down there. We might need it (laughs).

I don't know why he called it Bloody Mary, but that's the name that it got. It has eleven notches on it. In the capacity of company commander you always had a "striker" they called him. The last one [I had] by the name of Garcia, from Sacramento, California, always put a notch in my gun. I don't know why anybody would want to put notches in a good gun like that.

Fiser: You didn't go in at Leyte with MacArthur when he returned, but you did take part in the fighting for the island of Luzon. Tell me about that. You went in the Iron Gulf, right where the Japanese had invaded.

Cox: That's true. We went into northern Luzon the same way [the Japanese] did. We fought our way down through Clark Field to Manila. There was some tough fighting in there. MacArthur came in right behind us. We didn't have too much trouble with civilians except when we hit that road from northern Luzon down to Manila, when we were marching along and took some villages. The thing that impressed [me] was that the school kids were out on the street singing, "You Are My Sunshine" and "God Bless America." You know we had a lot of school teachers in the Philippines before the war, and they did a very good job with students and the education system.

Right before we got to Manila — we were under the Army then — we were criticized because we captured a brewery. They accused our men of spending a lot of time filling up the canteens with beer. But that was some pretty tough fighting all the way down to Manila. Then the fighting within Manila was bad. But we got in there in time to free some of the prisoners [the Japanese had] taken. One of the bargains for letting the Japanese Army out [of Manila] was that we would let them go free if they wouldn't kill any prisoners. So that's what happened. Those were [the same Japanese] that eventually caused my demise later on when we were chasing them up to northern Luzon.

[Once we got to Manila,] we took the post office building. We had a detail that was supposed to put the flag up. I was with them, and they couldn't get into [the post office building] to do it. [There was] a big siren up on the top of that building, and they had a Japanese flag up there. So I climbed out and stuck [the American flag] up on top, and we still had a hundred and fifteen Japanese in the basement. [The post office] is a building similar to the [Louisiana] state capitol building, backed up against the river. I almost got relieved because the regimental commander had reported the building secure, and we were still getting casualties. Anyway, we got [the Japanese] out later on by drilling a hole in the floor and putting a couple of flame throwers in there. They came out.

Fiser: I guess they were surrendering more readily than they had before that?

Cox: They weren't surrendering. They were just getting out of that building. But, the people that stayed in Manila, their mission was to kill as many Americans as they could and make us destroy everything.

There were some real touching things that happened during the battle to capture what they call the Walled City, built by the Spaniards years ago. [The Walled City] was really razed when we got there. We took the post office building and all the government buildings, but the Japanese defended the churches. In one church, [the Japanese] had about eighteen hundred civilians. We couldn't fire on it, but they were firing on us. So we waited until about five o'clock in the afternoon, [when] they let all the civilians out. We didn't blow the church up, but we got them out. If you can picture it, [the Japanese] came out with white flags, and then the civilians [followed]. As they would march along, if one of our soldiers would show himself, the Japanese would fire on him from that church. When they would fire, the civilians would throw everything down and run for cover. There was an old lady, right in front of me, that did that. She threw all of her belongings right in the middle of the street and ran over and got behind a building. So I saw her, and I waited just a few seconds until I knew the Japanese weren't watching, and nobody was moving. I ran out and scooped up her clothes, and I took it over and gave it to her. I remember writing my wife a letter about that. That old lady was so gratified. She started kissing my boots. She said they were so glad we had come. I didn't have time to converse with her, but I wanted to tell her this wasn't exactly the time to socialize. But anyway, they all were so happy to see us there. I don't know how long they had been in that building.

When this happened at Saint Augustine church in the Walled City, Santa Tamas had already been relieved. But this was kind of a mop up exercise. Well, a lot of things happened over there. I had the honor of hanging an American flag on the post office building.

That wasn't the end [of the war for me]. MacArthur made my battalion his personal MP's, which is something. We never did like the MP's.

Fiser: There was no honor in it?

Cox: No. Anyway, we were the MP's, and we made a lot of battlefield appointments for sergeants and second lieutenants. So we made them train, and the rest of them rested. And this is the first civilization this outfit has seen in about thirty-three months. So they had a good time. We trained the officers and then we had a lot of training exercises, but not like we would have otherwise. We didn't think we were going to have to do too much, but actually, it was a pursuit situation with the Japs. Japanese were going up in the northern part of the island. The first mission [in Luzon] was to secure the Wa-Wa Dam, that was an auxiliary water supply for the Philippines, and that's where I got my ticket.

Before we could even get going good, we fought several days, and I ended up getting hit with a Japanese 140 millimeter mortar shell fragment. They thought I wasn't good for any more duty then. As a matter of fact, they had put me in the wrong stack of casualties, you know the ones you can't do anything for. I had a sergeant from Illinois. He made them take me out. He waked up the chief surgeon, who was just taking his nap that night, around two o'clock in the morning. I heard him saying that they put me over there. And they probed around a while and they couldn't find it, so they sewed me up. For six weeks, I had up to 104 fever. They were just running blood through me. I had a lot of internal bleeding, and they'd take the blood out, first. They took 750 ccs out and from then on it was less, but they put penicillin in there. You know that penicillin really saved my life.

Robert Barrow

As a boy, Robert Barrow says he was not merely interested in nature, "I was a part of it." He spent a great deal of time alone, roaming the woods around his childhood home in West Feliciana Parish. During World War II, Barrow again found himself roaming the countryside. This time, however, Barrow was far from Louisiana, organizing and arming Chinese guerilla forces, allowing them to defend their country against the Japanese.

Barrow: In the early spring of 1944, I went to Washington and was interviewed by a Navy officer, a lieutenant commander, who began by saying something which I thought was amusing. He said to me, sternly, eyes fixed on me, "Do you want to go to China, live in a cave, and eat fish heads and rice?" I was such an enthusiastic young lieutenant, I came to my feet and said, "Yes, sir. I want to go to China, live in a cave, and eat fish heads and rice." The truth is, I didn't live in a cave. I once was evacuated into a cave [because of a] Japanese bombing. I ate some fish heads, I guess, but it wasn't my only diet. I learned later that he had never been to China; he was just using some words on me [laughs].

Robert Barrow with village children in China

Historically, the navy had been the premier service in China. I hastily add navy and Marine Corps, and they wanted to keep that relationship, even in wartime. The first and most important requirement for people like myself being there related to Navy's need for better weather forecasting for the operations in the western Pacific, the weather flowing from west to east. [The navy] wanted to put weather stations in China for that purpose. When they went to the Chinese with that proposition, the Chinese said, "You can put weather stations just about anywhere you want, including some places that are loosely occupied by the Japanese, but we want some things in return." That's typical. One of the things they wanted in return were people to train and equip — more equip than train — some of their irregular forces, nationalist-recognized guerrillas who were working in and near the Japanese occupied parts of China. Well, the marines, the navy, immediately said, "Well, we'll keep this in the family. That's something the marines can do." So that's why there were some marines recruited, as I was.

The [usual] way you went [into China] was by boat to India, and then you flew the famous Hump [i.e., over the Himalayas]. In my case, I went to Norfolk, Virginia, and got aboard the *A.E. Anderson*, which was one of the great big transports, about five thousand people would be on the *Anderson*. There were three marine officers, two others beside myself, a few navy officers going to China, and a small marine detachment on that ship, but all of the other officers were army. Also, there were some Red Cross girls and some WACs on there, and they were going to the China-Burma-India theater. A lot of [the men] were Army Air Corps-affiliated engineers, etcetera, building air bases and roads. There weren't many people going to China because there wasn't much one could do. The nationalist government had retreated to Chungking, and the rest of it was kind of a no man's land or occupied by the Japanese. The Fourteenth Air Force were in forward air bases as near as they could be to the Japanese occupied parts of China, but they were very austere bases with [only] the bare necessities that a base should have.

The *A.E. Anderson* left Norfolk, went through Panama Canal, and swung way south to avoid Japanese submarines. I remember we went south of Tahiti, to Pitcairn Island, [and] we went between the North and South Island, New Zealand; that's taking you way down. We stopped briefly at Melbourne, Australia, to refuel and then went way out into the Tasman and around through the Indian Ocean to Bombay

[India], forty-five days.

We arrived in Bombay, and I had a week-long train ride across the breadth of India, in wooden cars, British-style; they opened to the outside, not to the vestibule. And the train took so long because it went slowly and stopped for refueling and watering and cattle on the tracks, sacred cows that you had to be very careful about moving. I spent almost six weeks in the outskirts of Calcutta, which gave me some interesting insights into India and British control of India. I think this is, perhaps, well known, but my impression then, and I believe the correct one, is the British, wherever they had colonies or control, led lives apart from the people that made up the bulk of the population. You found these little oases, these little cells of British life right in the heart of India, all around them. [The British] made an enormous change to India, from agriculture to transportation to education; you name it. They did it not only their way, but they did it with minimum integration with the local people. My impression was that they might be integrated at work during the day, but when they went home, and on the weekends, they lived like British gentlemen.

After six weeks [in Calcutta], I went up closer to the Himalayas for a couple of days and flew the Hump in a Dakota or a C-117 or a DC-3, or whatever you want to call it. The pilot was an Australian, [and an] American [was] co-pilot. They flew at eighteen thousand feet altitude, which was the height of what that plane was capable of, and they went in and through mountain passes because where they flew the Himalayas [the mountain peaks] ranged up to twenty-eight thousand feet. They had to fly there because to fly farther east and south, the Japanese Zeros would come up and have at them. It was awesome to fly in a two-engine airplane at its maximum altitude and look out the window and see mountaintops way up above you. [Once] I landed [I found] you went so far in a jeep, and then you started walking.

There were a number of different camps in China, some of which were devoted to a mission exclusive to that camp, some of which were very active, and some of which were not, depending upon their Chinese counterparts — what they were willing to do and what they were interested in doing. My first tour was what was called Camp Tu. I found myself out in the field from Camp Tu, which was simply a place where some forty Americans operated out of for some given period of time and would come back to get a rest, to have inoculations brought up to date, to sort of check their health, etcetera. Well, I went out with that group, which put us on a peripheral adjacent to the Japanese occupation, and went on a couple of operations against the Japanese.

After the Camp Tu experience, I found myself right in the heart of China. I was moved down to the French Indo-China border, down into Nanning, which is not too far from Canton. We had to stop in Guilin, and this was done by air. When I got to Guilin, I was in such bad shape physically, I had to go to the hospital and was diagnosed as having dengue fever, sometimes called "bone-break fever," a mosquito- borne disease. I was there for about a week, and that's when every night a Japanese nuisance raid took place near the so-called ambulatory, which is where I was. We'd go into the caves at Guilin for a few hours and then come back. We went down to Nanning, where I recuperated. Didn't do any operating there, did the work of quote "training" these folks, many of whom were Annimites, from down in Indo-China. I lived on a diet of bananas for about six weeks and got healthy, and about that time, I was ordered back to Camp Tu.

[I was ordered back to what] became the most interesting assignment that I had over there. I was put in charge of a four-man, five counting myself, team to go across the corridor into Japanese-occupied central China and work with a guerilla group that was well identified, well established. Now, a little background.

In 1944, our submarines and the Fourteenth Air Force, which were the bombers in China itself, were so effective in interdicting

Japanese shipping in the East China Sea that [the Japanese] sought alternate ways of re-supplying their troops in French Indo-China, Thailand, even shuttle supplies over to Indonesia, wherever they were that hadn't been rolled back yet. So while they had these enclaves in China — mostly coastal, but some as far inland as Hankow, which is on the Yangtze River well west of Shanghai — they opened up a land, water, and rail corridor that had transportation from Hankow down to Canton, which took care of going through much of China. All of it had a railroad, [so] you could go by land, and parts of it, you could go by river. I mention that because if they lost out on one, they could switch you over and move things on the other until that one was repaired, which would be the railroad. So we were ordered to go behind all of that, inside what was called "Japanese occupied territory," and operate against the railroad line that went from Hankow to Canton.

This was a most interesting experience for a young marine lieutenant. I had two chief petty officers in the navy, much older than I, who had been made chief petty officer from civilian life. They were not career navy men. They were demolition experts, one from Texas, one from Chicago. I guess one blew up buildings and the other one did oil wells. I had a radio operator whose father was a carpenter, and he was a carpenter, from Missouri, [but] we had no radio. He had all of the technical skills that one would like to have in a situation like that. He could fix anything, and he became the armorer and anything else that needed fixing. I had a school teacher named Barney Rebert from Pennsylvania, who was a corpsman, much older than I. He was the most valuable member of this team. He was well trained, he was smart, and he had a very, very fine supply of medicine. Everything transported by man pack.

Going in across this corridor into Japanese occupied China, we had "coolie trains" as they would be called. Peasants [were] recruited for a day's work, and then [at] the next stop [new peasants] were recruited for the next day. They always turned back and walked back home after they had done their job. Going in [to the corridor] and after we got there — when we had to move as we did, out of necessity or because we wanted to — we're talking about upwards of two hundred coolies, peasants.

They would have a yo-yo pole, which is a stick that is sort of flat as it sits on their shoulders, and it points a little bit like, almost like a bow and arrow. On each end of [the yo-yo pole], they tied whatever they want to tie to be transported. In our case, we had bamboo woven baskets that would be cubed, that is equal in dimensions about thirty inches: thirty inches wide, thirty inches deep, thirty inches in all directions. One basket would fit over the other so the lid went all the way down to touch the bottom of the bottom. So it was a very secure arrangement, and it could be made water-proof with treated paper on the inside. One of those would hang from each end of a yo-yo pole. If you were carrying ammunition, you didn't fill the basket; it would be much too much for any individual to carry, but it was nevertheless in the basket. [We also transported] medical supplies, demolitions, and a little bit of food stuff — not our food; we ate totally with the Chinese. A typical load would be up to a hundred pounds, fifty pounds in each basket. These coolies grew up using a yo-yo pole. You see them cut to the size of a five year old, carrying water or something in the rice patties. So it's as natural for them as walking is for anyone else. They assume a kind of fast walk; it's almost like a little pace that they do. It's in the neighborhood of four or five miles an hour that they're clipping off. They are moving at a pace that causes the yo-yo pole to flex up and down, the center point always in contact but not constant contact. It seems to go up a little bit. The point is that it's not a constant drag weight. A military pack, if you have it on your shoulders, has a constant drag. You get no relief. I don't know very much about physics, and I don't know all of the explanations about this, but I do believe that they find some relief in that pole doing that. I've tried [to use a yo-yo pole] many times. Of course, [it is] great entertainment for one of them to see you trying it. They would get in to this trot, pace, whatever it was, and we had to move at the same [pace] to keep up with them, and I would be unencumbered. I didn't carry any pack or anything else, just my weapon and myself and a couple of canteens. Well, [it was not unusual for us to go] thirty miles with a couple of rest stops. Some of these people would be recruited early in the morning and take a load like that all day long and be fed on the other end. Usually [the peasants had] wooden buckets of rice, with a little flavoring in it, like some vegetable or Chinese cabbage or something, maybe a little piece of meat would cast its shadow with a little flavor. [They would] eat several bowls, turn around and go home with their own yo-yo pole. We only provided the things to be carried, not the pole; that's a very personalized item.

My five men, with the Chinese that were with us, lived in Chinese farmhouses. Once in a while [we stayed] in a school [or] maybe some other kind of public building. [But] we never had a large contingent of Chinese guerrillas with us. They were scattered. It would be like, scattered over [an area] almost like the state of Louisiana. We would have three hundred in the vicinity of Lake Charles, another two hundred in Lafayette, four hundred in the vicinity of Baton Rouge, one hundred up around St. Francisville, another fifty in Gonzales with some organizational cohesiveness. Somebody in that general area was in control, but they were detachments from the main body, if you want to call it that. All of these were scattered over a large area easily the size of this state. We moved frequently from one [group] to the other to bring some re-supplies, give some medical attention, and primarily to stimulate doing something to accomplish our mission, which was to [disrupt the lines of communication that the Japanese had established in 1944. I might add, in doing that, the Japanese had to put into effect a pretty good military operation to create that corridor. People don't realize it. Whereas they landed in China in 1937, and much was secured not too long after that, here we are near the end of World War II, and they launch an offensive down through the heart of China for this purpose of having the lines of communication.

That last eight months we were inside occupied China, the guerilla formations [were] scattered around and so were the Japanese occupiers. It wasn't every acre or square mile with some Japanese presence. You could move in and out and around and about. We had good intelligence as to where they were, and, from time to time, when they knew where we were, they would come looking for us because we represented a problem to them. But it was not something we worried too much about because we would be tipped off in time to get up in the middle of the night and move. So we had good intelligence.

The Japanese were engaged in food drives. That was another thing that they did in Hunan Province, which is the "rice bowl of China." They always produced a surplus. The Japanese weren't content with taking the surplus. They went out to the countryside and swept up rice from the farmers that was needed to sustain them for the next year. [The Japanese] created a lot of bad feelings. If you would take a man's food away from him, he's really got bad feelings about you. So we had those kind of folks [the farmers] in support of us. That was our source for coolie transportation and that was our source of intelligence.

Our intelligence, our information, was all local, within a small radius of miles. I had no radio, as I indicated earlier, and neither did my Chinese counterpart. Our opened-ended mission: "Go into this area and do the most you can to interdict this line of communication," and implied in that is: "When the war ends, your job is over," which is exactly what it turned out to be. With no radio communication, I had no follow-on instructions and no way to report what it was we were doing.

If ever there was a chance for independent action, for one's own initiative being put forth, it was there. It was a very important part of my background as a marine officer in subsequent years. To be a lieutenant and put in a place, an alien environment in every sense of the word, in close contact with the enemy, and [to have] a fairly clear mission, it was open-ended as to how you [followed] the very general mission orders. "Do this, period." Not how to do it, not when to do it, not where to do it, except in broad terms. It wasn't until after the war that I learned there had been something called Iwo Jima and Okinawa and all the things that happened in Europe that brought us to the surrender and so forth. I didn't know of any of that.

I acquired a lot of knowledge about the Chinese. I must tell you that among the various things that have shaped my life, coming from a very rural environment and a loving family, I was very much a nature person and all of that. Some of my experiences are shaped by the sudden contact with lots of people, diverse people at LSU, then my Marine Corps experience. But nothing has shaped my life more, I would reckon, than living as we did with the Chinese. We were totally dependent. Unlike the OSS, which came later into China and air dropped themselves in and were re-supplied with food. They lived apart from the Chinese. They had magazines and whatever else is mailed. We were completely dependent on [the Chinese] for not only information and transportation, walking, carrying our stuff, but food. We ate two meals a day, mostly rice. And to a Louisiana boy that's like Brer Rabbit in the brier patch, you know, serving me rice twice a day. I'd been lucky enough to have had it once a day. I found the Chinese, who were peasants for the most part, in whose houses we stayed had never seen anyone other than perhaps an occasional missionary. We were curiosities wherever we went. We stayed in their houses; we ate their food. And I have never received such hospitality and acquired such good feelings about people as I did with my Chinese friends.

Wiltz Segura

Wiltz Segura's lifelong love of flying was not diminished during World War II, despite the fact that he was almost killed, twice, when the Japanese shot down his plane over China. Although Segura was not a civilian volunteer, after Pearl Harbor he became a member of General Claire Chennault's famous American Volunteer Group, which became more widely known as the "Flying Tigers" because of the unusual nose art on their planes: a row of tiger shark's teeth. During the war Segura shot down six enemy airplanes and damaged three more. He also is credited with sinking a one hundred foot gun boat.

Segura: I got a set of orders, and I didn't know where I was going. I got aboard an airplane, at Miami International, and first thing I know I'm in India. We flew across South America, the Ascension Islands, across Africa, Saudi Arabia, to Karachi, India [now Pakistan].

Now, General Chennault had been fighting the war in China since 1937 as an advisor to the Chinese. He was a pioneer in fighter aviation and had run the fighter training school for the Army Air Corps before [retiring] in 1937. He retired mostly because they wouldn't listen to him, and in a way they were glad to get rid of him because he had strong ideas about how fighter aviation should be used and the kind of airplanes we ought to develop. The army was not having any part of it.

Before Chennault retired, he put together an acrobatic team, the forerunner of the Blue Angels and the Thunderbirds. They would take three airplanes and tie their wings to each other with ribbons three feet apart. They called them the three men on the flying trapeze. They would go around putting on air shows. This came to the attention of the Chinese, who were desperate for someone to help them develop their air force. The Japanese started fighting the Chinese at Shanghai and that was the beginning of all out war against China. That is when they hired Chennault to go to China to help develop and train their air force. But China had an obsolete and antiquated air force. It did not take long for the Japanese to decimate completely the Chinese air force. During this time, Chennault was observing the tactics of the Japanese.

Finally, it became evident that the Japanese were going to take

China if someone did not step in to help them. The Japanese were indiscriminately bombing at will, whatever city they wanted. They used the Chinese cities for target practice.

The Chinese and some American sympathizers convinced President Roosevelt that it would be a bad thing if China lost to the Japanese. China was not an important factor in the war at that time. Europe and the Pacific were the first priority during the war, but they realized that it was important to keep China free or the Japanese would soon occupy it. It would have been very hard to get them out of China after we had cleaned them out of the Pacific.

China was allowed to buy one hundred P-40 fighter planes and to recruit two hundred and fifty men from the U.S. Armed Forces. They did not have time to train them, so they allowed General Chennault to recruit them already trained from the armed forces. President Roosevelt, against the advice of the chief of staff of the U.S. Air Force, agreed to go ahead with the forming of this volunteer group. He wrote an executive order and authorized Chennault to recruit within the armed forces. They went around hiring active duty pilots for six hundred dollars a month and five hundred dollars for every plane shot down. The [military recruits] of course had to resign from the U.S. service.

Hebert:　　　　Was this prior to World War II?

Segura:　　　　This was prior to Pearl Harbor, and so a lot of these guys took their offer. They had been in the service for a while and did not really think we were going to war. Chennault put together a hundred pilots and airplanes, and a hundred and fifty ground personnel. They shipped everything to China.

The Japanese Zero was superior to the P-40 in combat, as far as maneuvering was concerned. The P-40 was a sturdier airplane, stronger, and had more armor plate in it. The guns were better and it had self sealing gas tanks which would not explode when hit. The Japanese didn't have all of that which made their airplanes very light. They could out maneuver us in the air. So the thing was not to dogfight with them if you didn't have the advantage. Chennault stressed that.

The name of the game was survival. Chennault used to say, "I can replace you, but I can't replace the airplane." So he would say not to take a chance. "I don't want dead heros. If you don't have the advantage, get the hell out of there, come back and fight again tomorrow." That worked just fine.

Hebert: Did you work closely with Chennault?

Segura: When I got there [after the bombing of Pearl Harbor], there were only three squadrons in China. There were a hundred pilots, you see. Then later on we got three more squadrons and then started building up. By the time I left there, we had a pretty big air force. But [Chennault] controlled everything. He had trained these Flying Tiger guys. About a handful of them stayed in the service and became the commanders of these squadrons when we military guys arrived. We were being led by [men] who had already gone through the fights within the Flying Tigers.

During that time, I flew eighty-six missions and didn't get a scratch. I thought I was invincible. You begin to be too complacent, and you start taking too many chances. I was shot down twice in five weeks by ground fire. The second time I went down was on my birthday, August 6, 1944. I had to bail out both times.

Hebert: What did you do after you bailed out?

Segura: [The first time] when I jumped out, the airplane was on fire. Usually, when you jump out of an airplane, the wind at two hundred miles an hour pushes you back, and you got to be careful not to hit the tail. So the idea is to dive for the wing, pull your legs up, and hope that you're not going to hit the tail. Well, if you can slow the airplane down to a hundred miles an hour, then you'll normally drop between the wing and the tail. But I didn't have time. I just had to get out of there. The plane was on fire, and the cockpit was full of smoke. Fortunately, I jumped head first, like they taught me, and I hit the tail with my legs. You can live without your legs, but you can't live without your head. I had a big leg cast, but I was fortunate. It didn't break my leg, but it cut me pretty bad.

I landed in a rice paddy, and I had a high wind in that rice paddy. [The parachute] just dragged me down that rice paddy, like a plow, [while I was] trying to collapse that chute. You know what they fertilize their rice paddies with in China? They don't lose anything down there.

I finally collapsed the chute, and then I realized my legs were hurting, and I couldn't walk. So I crawled off to the edge of the rice paddy, and I sat down there. I said to myself, "What in the hell is a country boy like me from South Louisiana doing on the other side of the earth flying these monstrous things?" I says, "I could have stayed home on the farm, been a 4-F." Then I said, "If I ever get out of this mess, I'm never going to get back in an airplane." I made myself a promise sitting right there. You're dirty; you're hungry. It was only my second mission that day, and I had had two donuts and a cup of coffee. It's two o'clock in the afternoon. Well, the Chinese came out the hills and found me, picked me up, carried me out to a little village that they had, and cleaned me up. They didn't have any beds. They had two saw horses and a door, and they put a blanket on it. [They] put me on top of that. Then they took my clothes and went out and washed them.

I was hungry. By this time, it was about five o'clock in the afternoon. Well, I'm trying to communicate. You got to be careful in the interior of what you eat because the sanitation conditions down there are not the same [as in the U. S.]. We had been trained in that. You don't drink anything except boiled water. So we drank hot tea and rice. They had a lot of rice. You boiled the rice so that you know that's sanitary. You could have a boiled egg; not much you can do to a boiled egg to pollute it. So I ate a hell of a lot of boiled eggs and rice.

[The Chinese] took good care of me, but I had a hard time telling them what I wanted. Every one of these little villages has a leader and a little school or something like that, and I noticed all their surroundings. One old guy was in charge. Well, believe me, they had never seen a white man in their lives. This is in a valley, remote from everything else. This airplane came out of the sky and crashed, and there's this guy in this big white parachute. It's an honor to save you, you know. Whoever the village chief is that recovers you and brings you back . . . well, Chang Kai-shek had them brainwashed pretty well about these American flyers out here to save your country, "take care of them," and "do whatever you have to do." So I mean, they really did. They exposed themselves to lots.

They would send these runners out to find out where the Japanese were, and then, they would walk you out at night. Sometimes you would have to lay low for a few days in a village, and sometimes, you would be right around the Japanese, but they wouldn't know it because [the Chinese] hid you. It would be very hard for the authorities to find out if the whole population was on your side. If you had a couple of turncoats, well then, they would tell on you. But, the Chinese were very good about that because if you don't obey down there in China, well, life is very cheap. If you cross the authorities, they don't have any qualms about getting rid of you. The Chinese know this, and they want to survive. So they embraced us.

The next morning, they put me in a sedan chair. I couldn't move. By that time my legs were as big as my head. I couldn't walk. So they picked me up like a baby and put me in a sedan chair, [held up with] two big bamboo poles. Two guys picked me up, and they looked like they're about seventy or eighty years old. I'm seventy now, but they looked real old to me. One guy had varicose veins on him as big as my finger.

We had to go over a three thousand foot mountain about thirty miles away before we could get to somewhere they could get to me with some military aid, and an airplane could come in and pick me up. I said, "We'll never make it." Things looked pretty dim about that time, and I was afraid that the Japanese would close in. There were four guys: one guy was the leader; one guy carried my parachute; and two guys carried the sedan chair. About every hour or two hours, the guy carrying the parachute would take one of the other guy's place. They would rotate. They went all day long, right up that mountain and never stopped except twice. I made them stop because I saw a spring in the mountain and figured, well, that water was safe to drink. So I stopped them and got them to rest, but they wouldn't stop [otherwise]. They're like mules; they can go all day long.

When I got to where they had a little civilization, there were some vendors on the side of the road with peanut stands and stuff. I had some money, escape money, so I wanted to buy them some food. Oh no. They wouldn't take anything. So I had this money, and I wanted to give it to them; they wouldn't take it. There were oranges and stuff like that, which I bought and ate. They wouldn't take anything from me. [They] brought me out to where they had sent word ahead to my unit, and they sent a covert unit to run a jeep into there. They picked me up and brought me to a little airstrip. An airplane picked me up and brought me home.

That was my first experience, but wouldn't you know it, five weeks later, about three missions later — I was in the hospital for about three weeks — I get hit again . . . Bam! . . . a rifle shot came through and cut an oil line. This time, I was able to get away from the scene. I was about twenty-five feet off the ground, when they hit me. I nursed that airplane. I could see my oil pressure going down. This was a common occurrence to a lot of us. The guy said, "You're smoking," so I looked down at my gauges and the oil pressure was going down. I knew I didn't have too many minutes left, and I was on the deck. You got to get up high enough to bail out, and you got to get away from the scene of the battle because if you get caught there, and you've been strafing them, then you know what's going to happen to you. They'll gut you right quick because they have no compassion. Therefore, we were told, "Get away from the scene of the action, if you want to survive."

Capdevielle: You were flying P-40s then?

Segura: Yes, P-40s. Anyway, I managed to climb up to three thousand feet, and seven minutes after I got hit, the engine froze up. But, I had a lot of time to think about how I was going to get out, and of course, I had seven other airplanes with me. So they're circling, and I'm going very slow, climbing and trying to get as much as I can get out of that engine. Finally, the oil pressure goes to zero, and it wasn't a minute later, the thing froze. So I'm all ready to go, and, I said to myself — you know, when you're twenty-one years old, all sorts of imaginative ideas come into your head — "I've seen these guys in the movies get out and walk on the wings," you know. I said, "Well, if I got to go, why don't I try it?" So when that engine quit, I pulled that airplane up a hundred and ten miles an hour, rolled the canopy back, stood up in the cockpit, and put my foot on the wing. You have no idea how strong a hundred and ten mile [per hour] wind is. It pinned me back against the cockpit. Now, I got a foot out on the wing and one in the cockpit, and I'm stuck. I'm sitting on the parachute of the seat pack, it kind of dangles, and I couldn't get up high enough over the side of the canopy. The parachute is holding me halfway in and halfway out. All of a sudden, I realized that I was getting pushed back stronger and stronger. What happened, sticking halfway out of the airplane made the airplane turn and start diving. So I looked down at the air speed, and I was doing a hundred and fifty in about a thirty degree dive, picking up air speed, see. So I said, I got to get back in that cockpit. I couldn't get out so I went back in the cockpit, grabbed hold of the stick, pulled that airplane up. When [the airplane] hit a hundred and ten miles an hour, I did what the book said, I dove for the wing, pulled my feet back, and then the thing went just as advertised. [The] parachute opened. This time I had gotten away from the enemy.

The Chinese in the field saw me, and they came over, got me, and walked me out. They kept me two weeks behind the lines and got me out okay. This time I could walk. You have to walk everywhere; there's no transportation. The Chinese did a fantastic job. Of every six [pilots] that went down, four would get back.

My father was the first [of the Spanish Seguras] to marry a French lady. But that was an asset to me, being in the military and traveling all over the world, to be able to speak a foreign language. French was the international language. Any educated person in a foreign country usually spoke French.

Many of the Chinese, especially their railroad engineers, had been sent to France. One time, when I crash landed about a hundred miles from my base, the Chinese recovered me and put me on a train and headed me back to friendly territory. If you ever seen the movies, or these documentaries on Chinese trains, they 're really packed full. They put me in a compartment, and they had a guy there that looked like he was an educated guy. He and I tried to communicate, but Chinese is very difficult; he couldn't speak English. We must have ridden for about three hours until something was said in French. A word came up, and I said, "Parlez-vous français?" "Ah, mais oui!" He spent twelve years in Paris, and he could speak [French] perfectly. That was like a breath of sunshine, you know, to find someone in the middle of China, surrounded by maybe a thousand Chinese on that train, that could talk your language.

Otherwise, we would have a little walkie-talkie book [with words] written on one side of the book in Chinese and written on the other side in English. It was divided by different subjects, like food, enemy, you know, and different things. We would point to it, they would read it, and then, they would point to an answer, yes or no. That's how we communicated.

Segura, far left, with his plane and crew in China, 1944. Note the ivory-handled pistol under his left arm.

Hebert: You had "Flash" written on your plane. Why was that?

Segura: Well, everybody was given a nickname. It was a code name that we used in the air. I guess we were thinking we were fooling the Japanese in not knowing who we were, you know. But I guess they knew. They had spies, and I'm sure they knew who we were, where we came from, and everything else. One guy was Buckshot; the other one was something else. We always gave each other a name, and they would normally give you that name. I don't know why they called me Flash — because I was always a very conservative, humble individual. [laughs]

I really enjoyed my tour, you know. I was the type of guy that had a shoulder holster, and I had an ivory handled gun. I had the boots and everything to go with it. I liked to play the part. But I think that was part of the psychology of putting up with a dangerous occupation. Now, it's not as dangerous as it seems. It's not half as dangerous as hitting those beachheads. But in a fighter, or in a military airplane, if you're trained well and you pay attention to the rules, you'll make it.

Both times I got shot down, I could have avoided it, I'm almost sure. But the first thing you know, you're taking too many chances. You're getting closer and closer to the target. I think in my career later on, it helped me to have had gone through that kind of thing because I became the guy that had to train the other fellows. The air force then became more sophisticated and more advanced, and we realized that it was too much of an expenditure to send a man to combat unless he was very well prepared. So we started preparing our fighter pilots in combat readiness before we brought them into combat, like in Korea, Vietnam, and so forth.

Capedvielle: Lou [Louie Reinberg] has been telling me, that there's a vast difference between the World War II he fought in the Pacific and the World War II that I participated in in Europe.

Segura: That's right. China was entirely different. We're talking about a primitive theater war, limited by the resources that they allocated to us. It was probably not as critical, as far as the immediate situation, as the Pacific or Europe. But, it was critical enough to preserve. It was called the holding action. We had meager supplies out there we had to live off of. The Chinese fed us, housed us, and did everything for us except fly and maintain the airplanes. All the supplies had to come over the Hump. After [the Japanese] occupied Burma, you had to fly everything from India. You could bring [supplies] to India by boats, and then from India, it had to be flown over the Himalayan mountains, which was a very treacherous route, and we're talking about the C-47 airplanes that carry five to six thousand pounds at the maximum. A lot of times, it would take as much fuel as what you were bringing in.

Hebert: Did you take part in freeing the Burma Road?

Segura: I didn't, because by that time, there was an air force out of India that would look after Burma. That thing got kind of bogged down into jungle warfare, and there wasn't too much action going on there except to keep the Japanese from coming too far north. Most of the action was in the Southeast.

Hebert: One of the positive things about being in the military is that you get the chance to travel all over the world. Did you enjoy that aspect of the service?

Segura: I had an inquisitive mind, and I wanted to see the world, or see as much as I could. So my service gave me an opportunity to travel. To give you an idea, everybody when they got their orders to come home from the war couldn't wait until they got home. I took three months to get home. I was in China, on the other side of the Earth, and everywhere I would stop, I would get off the airplane and give somebody else my seat. I would stay a week or two. Calcutta, I stayed five weeks. Karachi, I stayed four weeks. Cairo, Egypt, I stayed two weeks.

Casablanca, I stayed four weeks. I knew I would never see those places again because in those days travel was so primitive. I had no idea that you would ever [be able to] get on a supersonic airplane and go to Paris and be back that night. You couldn't visualize something like that because it took me two weeks, by airplane, to get to India from Miami.

So I wanted to see those things, and I wasn't married — though I was engaged and I knew I was going to get married when I got home. But I wanted to see those places because I had no idea I was going to stay in the service, or what was going to happen. I thought I would go back to this rural community. I took advantage of seeing as much of the world as I could. Even when I landed in New York City, I didn't go straight home. I stayed there for two or three days because New York City was a fabulous place [to] someone from New Iberia, which had eight thousand people.

Carlos Spaht

In the fall of 1942, Spaht was a lieutenant colonel and the executive officer of Jackson Barracks in New Orleans. He decided to join the infantry and was sent to Command and General Staff School at Fort Leavenworth, Kansas. Soon after, he went to a desert training center in California and later to China where he received his promotion to full colonel.

Spaht: General [Joe] Stilwell convinced the War Department that if the Chinese troops were trained and equipped that they could drive the Japs out of China without the necessity of American forces. They approved that plan, and then Stilwell asked for officers and men in order to form teams that would go out with the Chinese units to train them, help them get equipment, and then, accompany them into combat. So I was selected to be in one of those teams, and I went with the Eighth Chinese Army.

It so happened that the liaison team that was made up to go out into the field with the Eighth Army was ambushed, and the full colonel who commanded that team was rather seriously wounded. That left me as the senior officer, so I became the commanding officer of this liaison team and commanded it during my whole stay in China. I got to be promoted to full colonel after about six or eight months.

Hebert: What was working with the Chinese troops like?

Spaht: Well, they were very cooperative. My team and I got along fine. Some of the Americans didn't, but they [the Chinese] were very cooperative. They were eager to be taught. Their training was very poor, and their equipment was very poor. The Eighth Army got along very well [with them].

Hebert: Did the Americans bring the equipment and supplies in with them?

Spaht: At that time, the only way that anything could get to China was to be shipped to India and then flown by plane over the Hump, which was a very treacherous, difficult flight to China, so we had a very limited amount of equipment for them for a long time. We were able to get ammunition and some supplies that they needed very badly.

Hebert: Tell me about your involvement in the campaign to open the Burma Road.

Spaht: The Burma Road was the only road that led from India to China and China to India. The first mission of our Chinese troops under our guidance was to reopen the Burma Road. The Japanese had held everything up to the Salween River. Our Eighth Chinese Army [had] to dislodge the Japanese units that held the mountain that overlooked the crossing of the Salween River, and that was where our fighting took place. Within about two or three months, we did get that Burma Road reopened. That was then a new way supplies could get to China, and we did almost immediately begin to get additional supplies and equipment.

The Salween River, which is a mountainous stream, is down in a valley, and just as you crossed it, the road went right up to a mountain. It was about nine thousand feet to the top of that mountain. The Japanese could hold that and, from there, could direct artillery fire down to the bridge crossing the Salween. So it gave them a very strategic position, and dislodging them was a very important task. We had heavy casualties.

Hebert: Were air strikes employed in freeing the road?

Spaht: We had artillery support from across the river, but we did not have any air strikes. It would have been nice to have had them, but the problem was they had these pill boxes on the mountain. We would drop artillery rounds on them, and they'd go down in the ground. As soon as the artillery would stop, they'd come back, and the mountain was so precipitous that it was difficult for our troops to move very fast up that difficult terrain. So they'd be able to come back out and open up their machine guns on us before we could move up. Finally, in order to get to the top of the mountain, we burrowed under it about a hundred yards and planted a lot of TNT. We literally blew off the top of the mountain and were able to take it and hold it. That's actually what happened. The Chinese didn't have the expertise for that sort of thing. My engineers handled the operations and planted the TNT and so on.

I don't know as I can claim complete credit for it, but we were discussing [it] and I said to the Chinese general at dinner one night, I said, "You know, maybe we could burrow up under that mountain and blow

258 Japan

the whole top off." "Well," he said, "I think we could do that." Sure enough, he talked to his people, and it took about a week. We were terribly afraid the Japanese would find out about it. It was supposed to be ultra secretive; nobody would talk about this thing that we were doing. The Chinese didn't keep it quiet, and when we scheduled it for a certain time, we had visitors from everywhere to watch us. But the Japs never did catch on.

The only Japs we captured were those that were blown up and covered up with dirt and not killed. The rest of them fought until they died.

Hebert: Who was the Chinese general, do you remember his name?

Spaht: Yes, General Limi.

Hebert: Was this burrowing done at night?

Spaht: It went on twenty-four hours a day. And, particularly in the daytime we tried to be very careful [that] nothing could be seen. Most of it was done at night.

Hebert: How long did it take to open up the road?

Spaht: I guess that campaign started in about June of 1944. We had a lot of fighting at Myitkyina, and I think it probably was over by early October, 1944, about four or five months.

When that fighting was over, Burma was ours. Then the Japs were pretty much cleared out. We made plans to drive them out of the cities they held, particularly along the Chinese coast. All of the units that had participated in the Burma Road opening then were re-equipped, and we had to get new recruits because we had heavy casualties. [They were] trained, and we were ready to attack the Japanese that were holding posts along the coast.

Hebert: The war ended right about that time.

Spaht: About that time they dropped the atomic bomb. As a matter of fact, I was pulled out of the Eighth Chinese Army and was given the task of taking a team over to the Chinese coast to sort of supervise the taking of the Port of Foochow. We even had our planes loaded with our equipment and everything to go over there and had made full preparation when the first atomic bomb was dropped. They said to hold up everything, and then, two or three days later the second atomic bomb was dropped, and the war was over.

Hebert: Did you ever meet Claire Chennault?

Spaht: Oh, yes I did. Chennault was, of course, the commanding general of the Fourteenth Air Force, and when we were going to the Foochow area to make this survey, he flew us over there with his planes. We got a lot of intelligence information from him. We had this briefing with him. But, he was always very attentive to anybody from Louisiana. I'd been to one or two parties where he was. He would find out that you were from Louisiana and would always come and visit with you and speak to you. So I got to know him mostly at parties and at this briefing. At the briefing, he called me aside afterwards and said, "What do you hear from Louisiana?" you know, something like that.

Hebert: When did you come back to the United States?

Spaht: When the war was over. The chief of staff from the

Chinese combat command at Tongking was a General Boltner. General Boltner was from New Orleans. He was always very nice to me, and he called me in. Since [our] mission was over, I didn't have a job. [Boltner] called me and told me, he said, "You know you're out of work right now." He said, "I'll send you to wherever you want to go to take Japanese surrender." We had to send Americans to every place where the Japs surrendered, and at that time, they had a plan in the service that you got points for overseas duty. I had a lot of points because I had been over there over two years. I told him, "Well, General Boltner, I appreciate that, but I believe, if it's all right with you, I'll just go on home." He said, "Well, you shouldn't do that. You can get a chance now to have some fun." He said, "I'll send you wherever you want to go." Well, I'd been away over two years and had a daughter born while I was away. So I said, "Well, I appreciate that really, but I think I better go on home." Within about two weeks I was on my way home, and in September of 1945, I was back home.

1. John W. Dower, *War Without Mercy: Race & Power in the Pacific War* (New York, 1986), p. 42. For candid acknowledgments of participation in atrocities by former Japanese military personnel, see Hanuko and Theodore F. Cook, *Japan at War: An Oral History* (New York, 1992), *passim*.

Chapter Seven

The End

Anthony Palumbo

May eighth, oh golly, V-E Day, May eighth. We were one happy group of individuals May eighth. I got home in July, I think. I happened to be home when V-J Day hit. I couldn't believe the war was over. I went walking downtown with the rest of the family. My brothers that were home and all of us got together. There were still two or three out somewhere in the U.S. Pacific waiting an invasion of Japan when they dropped the nuclear weapon. Of course, I was very happy to see that, because if it hadn't a been for that nuclear weapon, we would have still been in over there. It certainly saved lives as far as I was concerned. Although it did cost the Japanese two cities, and probably three or four hundred thousand people, but it's either them or us in a case like that. That's what war is, war is hell, they tell me.